1934

The Chatham Coloured All-Stars'
Barrier-Breaking Year

Royalties from the sale of this book will go towards supporting the excellent educational work done by the Chatham-Kent Black Historical Society.

1934

THE CHATHAM COLOURED
ALL-STARS'
BARRIER-BREAKING YEAR
HEIDI LM JACOBS

Biblioasis
Windsor, Ontario

FIRST EDITION
10 9 8 7 6 5 4 3 2 1

Library and Archives Canada Cataloguing in Publication
Title: 1934 : the Chatham Coloured All-Stars' barrier-breaking year / Heidi LM Jacobs.
Other titles: Nineteen thirty-four | Chatham Coloured All-Stars' barrier-breaking year
Names: Jacobs, Heidi LM, author.
Description: Includes bibliographical references and index.
Identifiers: Canadiana (print) 20220464332 | Canadiana (ebook) 20220464375 | ISBN 9781771964777 (softcover) | ISBN 9781771964784 (EPUB)
Subjects: LCSH: Chatham Coloured All-Stars (Baseball team) | LCSH: Baseball players, Black—Ontario—Chatham—History—20th century. | LCSH: Baseball teams—Ontario—Chatham—History—20th century. | LCSH: Baseball—Ontario—Chatham—History—20th century. | LCSH: Chatham (Ont.)—Race relations.
Classification: LCC GV875.C43 J33 2023 | DDC 796.357/640971333—dc23

Edited by Daniel Wells
Copyedited by Rachel Ironstone
Designed and typeset by Michel Vrana
Indexed by Allana Amlin

Cover image: King Terrell, Stanton Robbins, Earl "Flat" Chase, nd. Courtesy of the Chase Family.

Published with the generous assistance of the Canada Council for the Arts, which last year invested $153 million to bring the arts to Canadians throughout the country, and the financial support of the Government of Canada. Biblioasis also acknowledges the support of the Ontario Arts Council (OAC), an agency of the Government of Ontario, which last year funded 1,709 individual artists and 1,078 organizations in 204 communities across Ontario, for a total of $52.1 million, and the contribution of the Government of Ontario through the Ontario Book Publishing Tax Credit and Ontario Creates.

PRINTED AND BOUND IN CANADA

"Someone, I tell you, will remember us, even in another time"
— Sappho

For all those who kept this story alive,
but especially for Pat Harding.

CONTENTS

PREFACE

DAYS AWAY FROM THE EIGHTY-EIGHTH ANNIVERSARY
of the Chatham Coloured All-Stars becoming the first Black team
to win the Ontario Baseball Amateur Association Championship, I
found myself in downtown Toronto on a warm fall night. Leaving
the gala reception for the All-Stars' induction into Canada's Sports
Hall of Fame, I made my way in uncomfortable shoes to my seat in
an auditorium packed with well-dressed Canadian sports legends. I
was in a row close to the stage with a University of Windsor colleague and representatives of the Chatham Sports Hall of Fame and
the Chatham-Kent Black Historical Museum. In spite of seeing
posters and displays with the All-Stars' photograph under a heading
that said "Order of Sport: Class of 2022" for weeks, the reality of
what was happening hadn't really sunk in until the lights dimmed
and the team photograph, which has sat on my desk since 2015, filled
the screen on stage. I looked at each of the faces on the 1934 team
photo and named them: Coach Louis Pryor, Gouy Ladd, Sagasta
Harding, Wilfred "Boomer" Harding, Coach Percy Parker, Hyle
Robbins, Earl "Flat" Chase, Kingsley Terrell, Donise Washington,
Don Tabron, Ross Talbot, Cliff Olbey, Stanton Robbins, batboy Jack
Robinson, and Len Harding.

I looked around me and saw other faces with a distinct resem-
blance to the men on the screen. Ferguson Jenkins Jr, whose father
was also an All-Star, was in the row in front of us, twelve members
of Earl Chase Sr's family behind us, and Donald Tabron Jr, with his
mother, wife, and young sons, sat beside them. Blake Harding stood
at the base of the stage steps, wearing the Canadian Sports Hall of
Fame's Order of Sport scarf on behalf of the All-Stars families. He
was watching, rapt, like all of us in those rows were, as the evening's
host Tara Slone spoke these words: "This year Canada's Sports Hall
of Fame established a new category that reflects teams that blazed a
path for those that came after them. One could say," she continued,

that the time to recognize the trailblazers in sports history could absolutely not be more critical. Only playing as a team for seven years, they made a lasting impression during a difficult and hostile time for Black Canadians. They forged ahead, in spite of barriers, leaving baseball immeasurably enriched by all they had overcome. Representing the newly minted Trailblazer category in the sport of baseball: the Chatham Coloured All-Stars.

The lights then dimmed and a video washed over the screen. David Amber's voice filled the auditorium with the All-Stars story:

More than a decade before Jackie Robinson broke the Major League Baseball colour barrier, the Chatham Coloured All-Stars were making a statement of their own in Southwestern Ontario. Formed in 1932 by a group of neighbourhood friends in a town that was once a stop on the Underground Railroad, they spent two years playing exhibition games before being invited to join the local City League. The All-Stars immediately attracted attention both from fans and newspaper reporters alike ... and then went on to become the first Black team to capture a provincial title in Ontario. Of course, it wasn't easy. They faced overt racism, whether in the form of taunts from the fans and opposing players or even direct threats of violence. There were deliberate attempts to injure, and some umpires, well, they seem to have had their own agendas. When the team went on the road the players were confronted by hotels where they couldn't stay and restaurants where they couldn't eat. Jim Crow was not limited to the American South ... In 2002, the Toronto Blue Jays honoured the team and its history by donning replica All-Stars uniforms and celebrating its last two surviving members with Sagasta Harding and Don Tabron throwing out a ceremonial first pitch. It was a potent reminder that the Chatham Coloured All-Stars opened doors for generations of skilled athletes who were previously denied opportunities to play baseball because of the colour of their skin.

As the video faded and the lights raised, Tara Slone said, "We have more than a few family members in the audience, but representing the Chatham Coloured All-Stars please welcome to the stage, son of Boomer Harding, Blake Harding." Applause filled the auditorium as Blake climbed the stairs and walked to centre stage. After posing with the award, Blake moved to the podium and began his speech:

> My name is Blake Harding. I have the privilege of being the spokesperson and family representative for the Chatham Coloured All-Stars. I was going to stick to the script, but I've noticed people going over their two minutes, and the guy with a big hook said he wouldn't come and get me.
>
> This induction continues the story of the All-Stars legacy. I heard "legacy" mentioned earlier today. And that to me is the key of why we're here. A legacy that was only talked about by members of the community and family members until September of 2000, when the Chatham Sports Hall of Fame inducted the 1934 Chatham Coloured All-Stars and brought the stories of the team back to life in our community. This legacy I speak of is one that was earned through dedication, hard work, and passion for the game. It opened up many doors that had previously been closed due to racism and bigotry in the Chatham area. A few jobs became available to the team members through the community exposure. Young minority children in the community looked at the All-Stars as role models; for example, Fergie Jenkins Jr looked to his father. Fergie Sr played on the team, and Fergie went on to be inducted into the Baseball Hall of Fame in Cooperstown.
>
> The story of the team grows more after a collection of articles and documents, passed on from my grandmother to my mother. And after she passed away, to my wife, Pat, who

put these articles together with line scores and everything else she could accumulate into three large volumes. She then passed them to the University of Windsor to Dr Heidi Jacobs and Dr Miriam Wright. And they published a well-documented website, and if any of you have not had the opportunity, Google it. It's a fantastic website, and it's viewed all over the world. Russia, Korea, wherever. It gives a very good account of the Coloured All-Stars. They also interviewed family members. They brought up archives, they brought up audio tapes. I heard an audio tape of my father, and he's been passed away thirty-some years ago. They were instrumental in putting it out in the front.

Along with the University of Windsor, I have to give some credit to the Black Mecca or the Chatham Black Historical Society in Chatham-Kent, who have a standing display in their museum of the All-Stars.

I believe the members of the team would be overwhelmed to be standing here today in the presence of all these fantastic athletes from now and from the past. It's such a great honour.

I'm going to deviate a little bit from my script when thanking the Canada Sports Hall of Fame. I said it this morning when we were talking to the young people at our press release and media scrum. In 1934, these athletes, superb athletes, just wanted to be seen as men and recognized. Canada's Sports Hall of Fame has not only seen them, they've recognized them, and they are known from east coast to west coast now. And I have to thank them for that honour and that privilege of having the opportunity to stand up here and thank them. It's done so much for our community. That legacy lives on, and it shaped a lot of the older young men that are sitting here in their seventies and their eighties today from that community. So, again, on behalf of the families and the team, I want to thank the Canada Sports Hall of Fame.

★ ★ ★

These videos, speeches, and, indeed, this whole event, make the All-Stars receiving the Order of Sport, Canada's highest sporting honour, seem not only logical, but expected. This plush gala event was less than three hundred kilometres from the rough red soil of Stirling Park's baseball diamond in Chatham's East End, where the All-Stars first came together as a team. But the All-Stars' journey has been long and arduous, and their recognition, both as men and as trailblazing athletes, was never as certain as it may have appeared to be this evening on Front Street, in downtown Toronto.

INTRODUCTION

AS A BASEBALL FAN AND SOMEONE WHO SOUGHT OUT
local Black history, the story of Boomer Harding and the 1934
Chatham Coloured All-Stars was nevertheless a revelation for me.
This was a story that was well-known in parts of Chatham, but in
Windsor, just ninety kilometres west on Highway 401, no one I knew
had ever heard about it.

My own journey with the Chatham Coloured All-Stars began
when Pat and Blake Harding brought three scrapbooks filled with
brittle documents, cloudy black-and-white photographs of men in
baseball uniforms, and box scores printed from microfilmed 1930s
newspapers into Leddy Library in the summer of 2015. Pat had met
my colleague Miriam Wright from the University of Windsor's
History Department at an event a few weeks earlier and, having
heard of some of the work the university was doing with local history, asked her if the University of Windsor could build a website
to share Boomer Harding's story. Knowing my role with Leddy
Library's Centre for Digital Scholarship, Miriam contacted me. She
and I suggested to the Hardings we might be able to pull something
together by fall. None of us could have imagined where these conversations would take us.

I'd passed by Stirling Park, the Chatham Coloured All-Stars'
home field, hundreds of times while riding the VIA train through
Chatham, never once noticing it through the thin stand of trees
that lined the tracks. It wasn't until a June afternoon in 2016 when
my University of Windsor colleagues and I gathered with the
Harding family and the Chatham Sports Hall of Fame at Stirling
Park to launch our joint *Breaking the Colour Barrier: Wilfred "Boomer"
Harding & the Chatham Coloured All-Stars* project that I realized how
often I'd passed by the diamond without ever knowing it was there.

That June day I got to the ballpark early and stood alone in the
field with my feet on home plate, conjuring players I'd read about in

Front row (L to R): Stanton Robbins, batboy Jack Robinson, Len Harding. Second row: Hyle Robbins, Earl "Flat" Chase, King Terrell, Don Washington, Don Tabron, Ross Talbot, Cliff Olbey. Back row left: Louis Pryor, Gouy Ladd, Sagasta Harding, Wilfred "Boomer" Harding, Percy Parker. Not pictured: Happy Parker.

the scrapbooks. I imagined the hush of the crowd as the ball left Earl "Flat" Chase's hand, the crack of the opposing team's bat, the scuffling of feet in the sandy basepaths, the rich, leathery snap of a ball trapped in Kingsley Terrell's glove at third base. Don Washington, the catcher, probably stood to watch the precise arc of Terrell's throw to first, where Boomer Harding stretched to meet the ball before the runner's foot hit the base, the cheers of the neighbourhood filling the summer night. I was jarred from my reveries by the sound of a train passing no more than twenty metres behind me. With the All-Stars now in Canada's Sports Hall of Fame, their story and their role as trailblazers has become much more visible. For decades, though, the story of the Chatham Coloured All-Stars was, for most Canadians, not unlike the view of Stirling Park from the train, hidden in plain view.

For those from the East End of Chatham, however, Stirling Park has been anything but invisible. Stirling Park was the heart of the community, and no one in this neighbourhood has ever forgotten the

Chatham Coloured All-Stars. People still talk about how Chase hit home runs so hard that people are still looking for those balls, and how left-handed Terrell dazzled fans with improbable—near impossible—plays from third.

To be sure, this is a book about baseball and a trailblazing baseball team. But it is also the story of a community and a neighbourhood. This is a book about stories and the act of finding, preserving, and telling them in ways that help us see and hear what is in front of us in new ways. This is a book that asks us to rethink what we think we know and to listen to voices overlooked by history. But perhaps most importantly, this is a story about a group of men and the families, friends, and neighbours who loved them and who lived different lives because of them.

It is fitting that it would be Blake Harding, the only child of Boomer and Joy Harding, who would accept the Order of Sport on behalf of the Chatham Coloured All-Stars in 2022. Not only did all four Harding brothers play baseball—three at least for the All-Stars in the period between 1933 and 1939—the Harding women, as Blake mentioned, played a key role in preserving, documenting, and sharing the story of the All-Stars from its earliest days. The story of the All-Stars would not have been so fulsomely preserved had it not been for Sarah Holmes Harding's saving the first newspaper clippings about her children, Beulah Harding Cuzzens and Wanda Harding Milburn interviewing Black Chathamites for a significant oral history project, and Pat Harding assembling the above material alongside her own meticulous and rigorous original research into those three large scrapbooks.

Andrew and Sarah Harding had eight children: Florence, who died as a child, Georgina, Beulah, Carl, Len, Boomer, Andy, and Wanda. The family lived on property that was, as Blake Harding recalls, "an old grant from the federal government for direct relatives of slaves, as was North Buxton. And that part of town, were land grabs. It's almost as east as you can go on Wellington Street." It is believed Andrew Harding Sr was from Kentucky and made his way to Chatham via Amherstburg and Buxton. He had family connections with Black communities across Kent County, whereas Sarah Holmes was a white woman, also with family in the area. According to Wanda Harding Milburn, her parents met while Sarah was living with relatives at a farm where Andrew was working. In this era, interracial marriages were not as uncommon as we might imagine. Regional historian Irene Moore Davis reflects that "while there was a high degree of acceptance of these marriages within communities of African descent, reactions within other communities were not so accepting." Family stories confirm what Moore Davis describes. Blake recalls that the Holmeses "had a doctor in the family, and Chatham's not that small. And they would actually cross the street if they saw my grandparents walking down the street. That's the way it was. They disowned her when she married my grandfather." Despite having an interracial background, Beulah said the Hardings saw themselves as a Black family: "We became Black children, not half-white, not half-Black, we became Black. And we were raised in the community to always take pride in our Black family."

The 1921 census gives us a snapshot of the East End in which the All-Stars players grew up and the occupations of their parents. The vast majority of the men in the East End were listed as labourers, but there were also occupations such as carpenter, butcher, teamster, or plasterer. Married women tended not to be employed outside of the home, but single or widowed women frequently worked as domestics, maids, or washerwomen. In this way, Andrew and Sarah Harding were quite typical: he worked as general labourer while she undertook the domestic work required to keep a household and large family running. Blake reflects that his grandfather Andrew "was the one that gave them their work ethic, I believe, because he worked really hard twelve months a year." Using a horse and wagon, Andrew transported ice or coal shipments from Lake Erie to Chatham. He sometimes took his sons with him on his trips to the lake, and Blake says "my dad recalls stories of going out there in the wintertime and how cold it was. And Erieau's not that far by car, but it's a long way by horse and wagon."

Blake also explains that Sarah had high expectations for her children and encouraged them all to get an education: "The boys were all encouraged, the girls were all encouraged for education and to

Andrew Harding and Sarah Holmes Harding, nd. Courtesy of the Harding family.

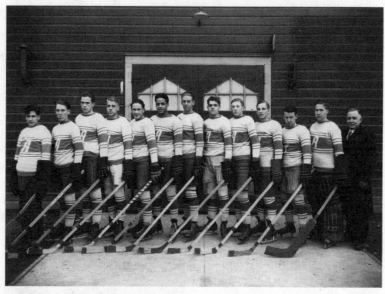

Boomer Harding on all-white hockey team 1931–1932. Courtesy of the Milburn family.

Boomer Harding in postal attire, nd.
Courtesy of the Harding family.

Boomer Harding and Joy Handsor
Harding. Courtesy of the Harding
family.

Portrait of Len Harding. Written on
the back "James Leonard Harding,
'The Very Best,' Born Nov 23, 1912.
Died February 23, 1942." Courtesy of
the Milburn family.

Portrait of Carl Harding. Courtesy of
the Milburn family.

Carl Harding and Len Harding on the Central School Baseball Team in the Chatham Public School League, 1924–1925. Courtesy of the Milburn family.

Wanda Harding, member of the Senior Track Team, at the Kent Field Meet, 1940. Courtesy of the Milburn family.

Gloria Robinson-Powell, Marianne VanDusen-Morgan, and Wanda Harding (left to right). Courtesy of Chatham-Kent Black Historical Society.

MAY BE 'FIRST' IN PRO HOCKEY

"THE BOOMER"—That's the nickname Wilfred Harding, above, earned during his hockey playing days around Chatham, Ont., where he spent his childhood and learned the rough game of hockey. Now "Boomer" is bidding for a position on the Auto Club hockey squad, one of the Detroit Red Wings' subsidiaries. Harding is a forward, and according to those who have seen him in action, is an excellent one.

"Negro to Play on Local Rink. May be 'First' in Pro Hockey." *Michigan Gazette*, *16 November 1946. Courtesy of the University of Windsor, Archives and Special Collections.*

get through at least high school." Blake recalls, "the girls all went to either college or university" and "it was very much the mother that was behind them." Beulah went to the Normal School in London, Ontario, and became a teacher in Windsor, Wanda worked in the hospital system, and Georgina worked as a legal secretary. Of the Harding sons, Carl worked in and managed gas stations in the St. Thomas area, Len, who played with the All-Stars, died unexpectedly from complications after a routine surgery at age twenty-nine, and Andy became the first Black police officer in Chatham. After three years in the military, Boomer became a civil servant with the post office and was Chatham's first Black postman. Reflecting on his grandfather and grandmother, Blake believes that "he taught them what work was about, and she pushed the education and the sports aspect." The pride Sarah Harding felt in her children and their accomplishments is evident in the newspaper clippings she collected about each child's accomplishments in school and sports.

Sports were a large part of the Harding children's lives and most, if not all, appear to have participated in sports at some level, often excelling. The *Chatham Daily News* has frequent mentions of the Harding brothers' victories in baseball, hockey, basketball, and track and field throughout the 1930s and into the 1940s. While we rarely see the girls' names in the paper in terms of sports, interviews with the Harding daughters suggest that sports played an important role in their lives too. We know that Beulah, for example, played softball with the Bloomer Day Girls. Excelling at sports, as the Harding children did, opened up doors for them, but it also showed them precisely where the colour and class lines lay. Wanda recalls,

> When I went to high school in the '30s there definitely was a lot of prejudice. We were accepted in some lights, but yet there was a class distinction, if not just in colour there was financially. There were the rich and there were us poor, and we didn't have anything in common. But being in sports lots of times I found that I had a little bit of companionship with some of the kids. And I was on the basketball team, and then I went to school with my coloured friends and we played

basketball together, and then we just came home and forgot about it.

Excellence in sports offered the Hardings opportunities for racial and economic mixing that did not happen in other aspects of their lives. A photograph from the Central School Baseball Team Champions of the Chatham Public School League from the 1924–1925 school year shows Carl and Len Harding, who would have been around thirteen or fourteen, as the only two players of colour on the team of ten. Similarly, a photograph of Boomer as the only Black player on the Bevan Trophy–winning hockey team is evidence that there was room for racial integration when stellar players of colour were available. In these cases, sports were the rare instances in which the Hardings and other children of colour could participate on what appeared to be, at least on the surface, a level playing field with white children.

As the interviews with the Harding siblings and their children reveal, the Hardings' drive and ability to excel at sports offered opportunities and experiences that had lifelong consequences. This was especially true for Wilfred "Boomer" Harding, who excelled in hockey, baseball, track and field, and any other sport he tried. Although I focus on Boomer's years with the Chatham Coloured All-Stars, a book could—and should—be written about Boomer Harding's life and all the barriers he helped break.

Wilfred Harding was known throughout his life as Boomer. Most people assume the nickname relates to his athleticism, but Harding family lore says he was given the name as a small child, and that it came from a comic strip character. Blake said many of Boomer's lifelong friends didn't know his father's name was actually Wilfred until his funeral. In the early 1930s, his name appears variously as Boomer and Wilfred throughout the sports pages documenting his many victories and successes in high school track and field, basketball, and hockey.

The box scores and game recaps of the All-Stars' 1933 season has Boomer, aged seventeen, playing both for and against the All-Stars, alternating between catching for what appears to be a mostly white team, the Chatham Juniors, and playing a range of fielding positions for the All-Stars. Coverage of the July 11, 1933, matchup between the Juniors and the Stars notes that this was Boomer's first time on the Juniors' roster, and the box score shows him playing against his brother Len and several others who would play with him on the 1934 team. By August 1933, as the All-Stars looked towards the City League playoffs, Boomer appears to be playing almost exclusively for the All-Stars. Though one of the youngest players on the team, Boomer was athletically equal to his older teammates and a tough, disciplined competitor.

Boomer was also a very skilled hockey player and these skills served him well after joining the Canadian Armed Forces and serving overseas from 1943 to 1946. During his time with the army he competed in athletic events such as pole vaulting and was part of a travelling hockey team that entertained Canadian soldiers. Boomer continued to play baseball upon his return from the war, but he also spent considerable time playing hockey and trying to break into that system. In 1946, he earned a spot in the International Hockey League on the Windsor Staffords, the farm team for the Detroit Red Wings. Notably, he was the first Black player in that league and was the first Black player to skate at the Red Wings' arena, the Olympia, at a time when only a few Black players were in advanced hockey. In an interview from 1980, Boomer recalls how as a child he hadn't been allowed to skate in that arena: "They claimed on public skating night that the sign didn't mean that as far as colour was concerned. But I went back after the war and they accepted me as a hockey player." There's more than a little sense of vindication in Boomer's recounting of this event as he describes what it meant to finally skate at the Detroit Olympia.

The colour barrier in hockey was different from that in baseball. For one thing, hockey did not have the strong traditions in the Black communities in Southwestern Ontario, nor in the rest of Canada and the US, that baseball did. On baseball teams, Blake reflects, Boomer was "one of several and they were like brothers, a band of brothers, more or less, and their victories were all of theirs; their defeats were all of theirs." But on hockey teams, Blake says, Boomer was

very much alone. He was an individual. He was marked
and he always told me, he says—and this was again before
helmets, or anything like that—he said: "It's hard to hide a
Black man on white ice." He knew that going into his own
dressing room there was a hostility. Before he could earn
the respect of teams he was playing against, he had to earn
the respect of the guys he was playing with, and he had to
narrow that down to the guys on the same line as him.

Boomer's high level of athletic skill and unstoppable work ethic made
white Chatham notice him. Once noticed, Boomer insisted that
attention come with respect. One of the ways Boomer commanded
respect on the playing field was through hard work, perseverance, and
competitive excellence. Blake comments that his father "found that
he could gain respect through just going out every day and playing
the hardest he could," and that eventually respect "went through the
dressing room. And then he gained it with other teams."

Respect was vital for Boomer. As Blake recalls: "It was always
important for him to be respected. He passed that on to me, and he
just demanded respect." Boomer's insistence on respect was not limited to sports. He demanded it off the field as well. Blake tells an
anecdote from his father's time as a postal worker: Once someone said
to him, "Well, how are you doing today, Sunshine?" Blake recalls his
father replied, "You can call me Boomer, you can call me Mr Harding,
you can call me sir. But if you call me Sunshine again, you're going to
the post office to pick up your mail." Blake remembers that his father
"just wouldn't accept" disrespect in any form. It is difficult to say precisely how much Boomer's sports successes facilitated his demand for
respect off the playing field, but there were definite connections.

For Boomer, Blake reflects, sports were much more than just a
pastime or a hobby. Boomer not only had a gift for sports, he had
a passion for them. Sports also offered a way for Boomer to put
himself out there and to be the best. In this way, sports shaped how
he existed in the world and offered him occasions to demand and
gain respect. As Blake recalls in an interview, "He was very quiet,
but when he spoke, you listened to him. But on the field, there

was a totally different person . . . When he went on the field, he didn't have to be subservient to anybody, and he wouldn't be. And I think that, that shaped all of their lives, as much as it could. So, I think it was a passion, more than anything. It was a chance to be equal or better."

Blake Harding's comments about his father's demands for respect point to the larger impact sports had on the daily lives of East End residents. Later in this interview, Blake mentions Jackie Robinson and makes connections between Robinson and his father and uncles. Robinson, Blake says, "was picked not because of his total ability, because there was a lot better players in the Negro League . . . But they didn't have the mental toughness and the mental discretion" that Robinson did. Similarly, Blake says, "Dad, Uncle Ken [Milburn], and Uncle Andy were picked because it wasn't so much a gamble by putting them into public positions. They knew they would do the work, they knew they would not get in trouble, and they opened the doors." In this way, as Blake highlights below, sports had a direct impact on the lives of players, opening up employment not only for themselves but for the larger Black community in Chatham.

If you talked to any of the real community leaders from the Black community, they would admit that the Harding boys had a lot to do with opening things up in this community. Again, there are still things. A friend of mine, a good ball player, he's about two years older than I am, applied for Union Gas. He got a standard form letter back saying, "You are totally qualified for the position, but we gave it to somebody else." He jumped right on it and said, "Why didn't I get the job? How many people of colour do you have in the head office at Union Gas?" He ended up getting a job, but there is a recourse now. And there is a recourse because my dad and my uncles, once they got their foot in there, and they were doing their job, and they were earning their respect on the ice or on the basketball court or on the ball diamond, they demanded that you treat them with respect. They wouldn't accept anything else.

But Boomer was just one of the Harding children, and his insistence upon respect is also seen in the interviews with his sisters as they talked about their own lives and experiences. While we do not have interviews with Len Harding, it is clear from his letters and statements published in the *Chatham Daily News* on the All-Stars' controversies in 1939 that respect on and off the field was also nonnegotiable for him.

The story of one other Harding brother, Carl, who also played hockey and baseball, similarly reveals the complications of race and sport in this region and era. Although I have not found evidence that Carl played for the Chatham Coloured All-Stars, his name is listed on the Duns roster playing against Len, Boomer, and the rest of the All-Stars in the 1933 City League playoffs. By 1934, Carl appears to have relocated to St. Thomas; in June of that year, *Chatham Daily News'* sportswriter Jack Calder reports that the *St. Thomas Times-Journal* had this to say about Carl Harding:

> Next winter, if all goes well the Wolverines will be strengthened by Carl Harding, who helped Glencoe beat St. Thomas. As there are plenty of wings, his addition should just about make St. Thomas "tops" in the group race. Here's hoping!
>
> Carl Harding is wearing a Tom Cat uniform this summer and although he hasn't created a sensation he has been ready at all times to do his best and he is likely to pitch a few victories before long. In fact, some critics say that he has more stuff on the ball than Gordie Weeks used to have, but he lacks control. If Carl steadies down he will be a great asset to Manager Leo Doan's mound staff.

Like his younger brothers, Carl was also a gifted multi-sport athlete. Blake Harding recalls, "My Uncle Carl, he was an excellent ball player, and played around here, and eventually played up in the St. Thomas, London area. And his name is fairly well-known around that area, even today." In many ways, Carl Harding's story parallels that of his athletic siblings, but his life diverges from that of his brothers and his sisters in significant ways. Although they all grew up in the same house in the East End, Jennifer Miss, his daughter, explains that

> my father was a white mulatto. He was the only one in the family who was red-headed, a freckle-faced little white boy. He had many complications from his birth, primarily he felt like he didn't fit, and I think he probably had problems with relationships in the neighbourhood because of that. His family was all slightly darker skinned. He was very talented as a boy. He would catch and he would pitch.

Boomer Harding recalled that Carl "was a very good hockey player. He was allowed to play with—having a white skin—the [Chatham] Maroons," a team that never accepted Boomer in spite of his obvious talents.

Carl's complexion offered him athletic avenues and economic opportunities not available to the other Harding brothers, but it also presented challenges to negotiate that were unique in the family. While acknowledging that Carl had access to the opportunities offered by white privilege, his sister told an interviewer he did not try to "pass" as white or deny who he was. Wanda recalls that Carl would "ride with my dad and there was all the difference in the world because my dad was very dark. And yet everybody still knew—we were a small town—and everybody still knew that he was a Harding." Although not resentful, the siblings all spoke about the way Carl's lighter skin gave him access to jobs and opportunities denied to them and to other Black people in the community. Beulah remembered Carl could get into the "white" section of the movie theatre with his white friends unless an usher found him and made him move. She recalled her sister Georgina, whom she called a "fighter," encouraging him to defy the usher and remain in his seat. Their sister Wanda also recalled that Carl could get better jobs, like working at a garage, while his brothers had to work at hotels.

While Carl's lighter complexion opened some doors, it did not mean life was necessarily easier for him. Jennifer Miss recalls, "I think he missed opportunities, and I think that he felt he missed a lot of opportunities because of his colour, and because of his family. I don't think he was accepted as a Black kid in the neighbourhood, and he didn't really get to play the sports that he wanted to play in Chatham-Kent and he had to grow up and leave." In Jennifer's reflections about her father, there is a recurrent sense of a lack of belonging and discrimination:

> Because of the colour differences, I feel that he was definitely ostracized, and he encouraged his brothers to be more involved, and he left home. I think he felt that the only way to play the sports that he wanted was if he left the Chatham-Kent area. Which is what he did when he moved to St. Thomas, and what he did when he was sent up to Kirkland Lake to play ball.

Jennifer's comments regarding her father's life and the way the Harding siblings spoke about their oldest brother's experiences offer insights into the ways that these unspoken yet very pronounced racial lines worked in the community.

For these reasons, Jennifer believes Carl's story is a vital part of the larger narrative of the Chatham Coloured All-Stars and the Harding family: "I think it is important that people know that Carl was a part of the family. Even though he wasn't in the Chatham-Windsor area, he spent time there, he grew up there. He encouraged his family, and he had wanted to be more involved in sports." Jennifer Miss also believes many of her father's difficult memories and experiences were kept from her: "There were challenges . . . he didn't talk about it much. It was pretty hard to elaborate on things he didn't talk about. He talked about it a little bit when I was growing up, but when you are a kid you don't press." As we will see in almost all the other interviews with players' families, many of the memories from the 1930s were ones the players and their wives kept from their children.

MAY
1934

LAST MAY, I WALKED AROUND THE EAST END OF
Chatham, down Wellington Street, across Princess Street, along Park
Street, towards Scane Street. Even with directions to Scane Street,
it's easy to miss the wooden sign for Stirling Park in the small playground with a thin stand of trees. If you do see the sign, and you walk
through the trees, you'll find yourself on a fairly ordinary looking ball
diamond: rough green grass, a chain-link backstop and fences, and a
red clay infield. On this day, I was alone there. The silence of the park
was punctuated only by the sounds of crows and redwing blackbirds
and a distant train whistle. But on the evening of May 17, 1934, most
of the neighbourhood, easily a few hundred people, would have been
filing into Stirling Park, milling about, catching up with neighbours,
grateful for the lengthening days and the still-new green of the trees.
Tonight's home game was opening day—and the first in what would
be the Chatham Coloured All-Stars' barrier-breaking season.

It isn't hard to imagine what the East End looked like in May
1934. The trees were undoubtedly smaller, but Sterling's Variety is still

on the corner of Park and St. George Streets. Some of the one- and two-story houses that line the East End streets have newer aluminum siding and small additions built on. Others have fresh coats of paint on the clapboard, but they look like the houses captured in snapshots in the players' family photo albums. Most of the houses have stoops or porches, and it's easy to imagine families sitting there on May 17, 1934, shouting out to neighbours walking down the sidewalk, sharing laughs and maybe some chatter about the upcoming baseball season. Some might have predicted that the Stars would beat the R.G. Duns that night. Others might have even predicted the Stars would have a stellar season, but few could have predicted how far the All-Stars would go that year. Most people on their way to the park that night were probably excited and relieved that it was opening day, baseball's annual reminder that winter has passed. Within weeks, a cool spring would melt into a warm summer.

If you walk around the East End today, it's not difficult to imagine the crowds walking these streets to the ballgame that night. Fergie Jenkins Jr said of the three hundred or so people who would come to a game in Stirling Park, at least a third were friends and family from the East End, proud to see their sons, friends, brothers, and fathers play baseball. In fact, you can still retrace the steps families would have taken to Stirling Park that night. The Hardings, living at 265 Wellington Street East, likely passed Lou and Blanche Pryor's house at 225 Wellington and then went on to Princess Street, where they might have entered the park to watch Len and Boomer. The Olbeys, living just up from the Canadian National rail line, at 44 Scane Street, would have walked half a short block to watch Clifford. If you were walking on Wellington Street at the edge of yet another rail line, you might have run into the Ladd family going to watch Gouy. If he wasn't already at the ballpark, Earl "Flat" Chase, who lived for a time with the Hardings, might have joined you on the walk, as might Ross and Ben Talbot's family, who lived at 151 Wellington. Kingsley Terrell might have just got off work at the William Pitt, at 6th and King, the hotel where he and a number of players worked as bellmen. Coach Joseph "Happy" Parker might have met up with Terrell after leaving his barbershop at 55 King Street West.

While the streets look about the same as they might have in 1934 and you can still find many of the players' houses, Stirling Park has undergone significant changes. Today it looks little like it did in 1934. In addition to a baseball diamond, there was also a wading pool and a swimming pool, separated by a walkway, on the south end of the park alongside the train tracks, where the ball diamond is now. Images from the 1920s show this park as lively, the pools packed with both Black and white children. Just beside the pools, towards Park Street, there were bleachers facing the ball diamond and dugouts on the east and west sides of the park. A scoreboard, long gone now, was parallel to Park Street, and a playground with swings and teeter-totters sat beside the grandstand.

Given the proximity of the ballpark, residents of houses along Park Street likely found many baseballs in their yards and gardens in summer months, or, as happened to one family, in their kitchens. A clipping from the *Chatham Daily News* recounts: "Leo Belanger's back yard is adjacent to Stirling Park. Last evening while Leo and his family were eating supper, some of the Duns were practising in the Park. A ball came in through an open window of the Belanger domicile, landed in a dish of corn on the table, bounded into the sink and broke some dishes." When I stood at home plate surveying the barely green grass, it wasn't hard to believe that a ball flew into a kitchen or to imagine the chatter of adults, the joyous splashing of children in the pool, the crack of a bat, on that Thursday evening in May 1934, when the All-Stars took on the R.G. Duns.

The 1934 Shepherd's city directory for Chatham shows that most of the players lived and worked in the East End, a stone's throw away from the Stirling Park baseball field where they first came together as a team. On opening day, the core of the 1934 roster had been playing organized ball together for a little over a year. The All-Stars and the Duns were part of the four-team Chatham City League, along with Kent Bridge and C.C. Braggs Insurance. The All-Stars had entered the City League in 1933 with the assistance of local baseball fan, businessman, and future mayor of Chatham Archie Stirling, who owned Sterling Variety a few blocks away on the corner of Park and George Streets. Stirling Park is situated on the site of what was

Earl "Flat" Chase at Stirling Park, nd. Courtesy of Chase family.

Archie Stirling. Courtesy of the Chatham Sports Hall of Fame.

Stirling Park today.

White and Black skaters at Stirling Park, c 1920s. (Chatham-Kent Museum 1982.1.25.1)

Children at Stirling Park Pool, c 1920s. (Chatham-Kent Museum, 1982.1.24.7)

the Stirling family farm. As Archie's lifelong friend Bob Widdis recalls, it was the Stirling family who first built the "swings, teeters, traveling rings, may pole, and sand boxes. Later we installed tennis courts, pee-wee golf course, skating and hockey rinks and a baseball diamond. We built the backstop and dugouts in sections of [the Stirlings'] basement. This backstop was built so that we lost very few balls. The bleachers were seven steps high behind the screen and seated six hundred people." It was at this park and on this baseball diamond where Archie Stirling watched the East End men and boys competing in neighbourhood and regional pickup games.

Seeing their talent, Stirling helped this neighbourhood team with the paperwork and backing necessary to get into the OBAA. They were first registered as the Chatham All-Stars as Stirling told *Chatham Daily News* columnist Doug Scurr in 1946:

> The fellows didn't know whether or not to tackle the OBAA
> games and they worried that they may not be accepted
> because of their colour . . . But we got around that. We just
> signed the certificates and mentioned nothing about the
> Coloured All-Stars. They were entered as the Chatham
> All-Stars, but as soon as they played a couple of games and
> OBA heads found what drawing powers they had, they
> were sent all over the [nearby] country.

It's not clear if the All-Stars ever *officially* changed their name to the Chatham Coloured All-Stars but we see out-of-town newspapers using this name in their write-ups and game advertisements. Racializing this exciting team in this fashion had as much to do with marketing as it did with anything else, as Chatham sportswriter Art Cartier remarked in 1966: "They drew terrific crowds and some from north of London frankly admitted they went to the games because they had never seen a coloured team before." Stirling's omission of the team's race in the OBAA application paperwork not only suggests he feared that the All-Stars' race could complicate their acceptance into the league but that his support for the team was primarily rooted in their talent and level of play, not as any kind of marketing ploy.

In addition to this crucial early support, Stirling was also fondly remembered for giving a brick of ice cream to players who hit home runs—a generous and welcomed offering in the Depression. In 1933 the All-Stars finished their first regular season with four wins, eleven losses, and four ties. In spite of their less than stellar regular season, the Stars won the City League's Wanless Trophy with five straight wins. Their post-season success coincided with the arrival of Flat Chase from Windsor.

★ ★ ★

The origins of the Chatham Coloured All-Stars are summarized well by Blake Harding in a 2022 interview. They were "a group of friends who basically got together to stay out of mischief in the community of Chatham. They were from a poorer part of the community, and by getting together and playing some exhibition games in the early thirties, the late twenties, it kept them out of trouble. They began that as just an experience. The camaraderie between the players grew and lasted a lifetime, and till the last one passed away, they were lifelong friends." In a 1980 interview, Kingsley Terrell offers a similar overview, recounting that this core group of original players came together from existing teams:

> From what I can remember it was in 1933. A bunch of us got together . . . Boomer and Flat and myself played for different teams in the county like Tilbury, Dresden. We played for Wallaceburg, we played for teams in Blenheim and Tilbury—the three of us. It seemed like when they asked one, they always asked the three of us . . . And that's the beginning of the All-Stars as far as I can remember. But we had a lot of fun.

Among the crowd on opening night was nineteen-year-old *Chatham Daily News* sports columnist Jack Calder who'd published a column that morning saying, "This evening at Stirling Park the City Baseball League is to have its official opening. The game naturally demands and deserves your attendance." As one of the main sportswriters for the *Chatham Daily News*, Calder's detailed coverage of the 1934 season is one of the main sources of information we have about this team.

Under a headline that reads "Stars Win Opening Game of City Baseball League: 1934 Inaugural Indicated Real Battle for Honours," Calder's narrative resembles that of the first chapter of a novel. He establishes the opening scene by describing the setting, providing the names of those who will be important in the coming weeks and months, and posits the major question of the All-Stars' 1934 season: After a strong showing in 1933, how far can this team go this year? As he will do throughout the season, Calder describes the evening's events in such vivid detail that we can almost imagine that we, too, are at Stirling Park:

> The All-Stars, '33 champions of the city baseball league, got away to a flying start in the '34 campaign by taking the R.G. Duns into camp in the season's inaugural at Stirling Park last evening by the score of 9 to 3.
>
> The game got away about six o'clock after the opening ceremonies. City Manager A. L. Thompson as master of ceremonies addressed the members of the teams lined up along the first and third base lines, complimenting them on the fine brand of entertainment provided last season . . .
>
> Shaw started on the mound for the Duns and got by until the big fourth. Although he had difficulty with his control, his free passes to first did not do any damage as far as run-making was concerned. His two wild tosses to first in the fourth were costly. Thompson succeeded him with two men down in the fourth and three runs in. He remained the only man to face him in the frame via the strike out route. His slants did not bother the Stars to any extent the remainder of the game as indicated by the seven bingles collected off him.
>
> Ross Talbot hurled four innings for the Stars and was nicked for 6 hits, the same number yielded by Shaw. Chase went to the mound the last three frames and effectively

checked any intentions the Duns might have had to fatten
their batting averages by allowing only one hit.

Through Calder's 1934 columns, we're able to see the strengths of
each player, how each evolves through the season, and how the team
comes together to become a formidable force. He not only captures
players' actions on the field but also gives us a sense of who the
players are, what skills they bring to the team, and how each of them
contributed to the team and its legacy.

As the above column from opening day reveals, Calder's writing
conveys the small details about baseball in the East End in 1934
that escape most sports coverage of that era. On May 23, he writes,
"If you haven't been to Stirling Park yet this season you've missed
something for few of the accoutrements of a modern stadium are
missing. The diamond is in dandy shape and the outfield is equally
good. Facilities for the fans are tributes to the work of league officials and if you haven't heard about the new dugouts, you don't talk
baseball." To date, I've been unable to find clear photographs of the
Stirling Park baseball field in the 1930s, but Calder helps to capture
in print those ephemeral details that would otherwise be lost.

The box scores for the first week of games in 1934 provide us with
a roster of players that remains fairly consistent throughout the season. Most of these players are the ones shown in the championship
team photo taken in October 1934: Len Harding, King Terrell, Ross
Talbot, Flat Chase, Ben Talbot, Boomer Harding, Clifford Olbey,
Donise Washington, Gouy Ladd, and a player at shortstop whose
name goes from Tappon to Tupper to Taborn to Tadburn until it is
finally correctly spelled in the first week of June. This continual misspelling of Don Tabron's name suggests two things: one, he is a new
player and two, he is not a local player whose name would be known.
The newness suggested in this misspelling confirms what our interviewees told us, that Washington and Tabron came to play with the
All-Stars in time for games around the Victoria Day long weekend
and that they then stayed. The only players in the 1934 championship team photo not in this list are Sagasta Harding, Hyle Robbins,
and Stan Robbins. Though the All-Stars had players come and go

between 1933 and 1939, Boomer and Len Harding, Flat Chase, Gouy Ladd, and King Terrell formed a core who played together for most, if not all, of the seven seasons the team existed.

★ ★ ★

There are few other places in North America where this particular team could have formed. In order to understand this team and its accomplishments, we first need to understand the history of a geographic triangle of under a thousand square kilometres in Southwestern Ontario. What is now called Chatham is located on what the area's Indigenous people call the Eskunisippi River and what white colonizers later renamed the Thames. This was and remains the traditional land of the Three Fires Confederacy, which is made up of the Odawa, Potawatami, and Ojibwe, but is now called Kent County. Walpole Island, roughly forty kilometres north and west of Chatham, is unceded territory inhabited by the Ojibwe, Potawatomi, and Odawa peoples of the Walpole Island First Nation. In later chapters, we will see baseball teams from Walpole Island whose impact on the game warrants a much deeper investigation than this book can offer.

Given its proximity to rivers and the Great Lakes, Chatham was viewed by the British as a strategic military centre and was thus established as a naval dockyard in the 1790s. As railroads developed, Chatham became a rail hub and a commercial centre for Kent County, and steamers connected Chatham with Amherstburg, Windsor, and Detroit. Throughout the twentieth century and into the twenty-first, Chatham has been home to industry and is surrounded by rich, verdant farmlands that extend as far as the eye can see.

The story of the Chatham Coloured All-Stars is also the story of Black diaspora, with its connections to the Middle Passage, enslavement, the Underground Railroad, emancipation, and the Great Migration in the early twentieth century. In this way, the geographic triangle in this book is not merely a setting or a backdrop to this baseball story but an integral force that shaped the players, the community, and the legacy of this team. Moreover, by understanding these baseball stories, we are also better able to see and understand

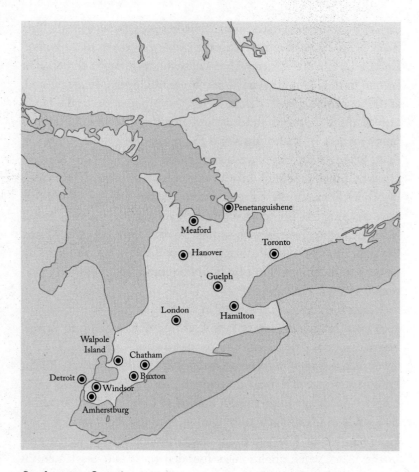

Southwestern Ontario

the history of this region and the various forces that shaped and defined it.

It is not entirely certain when people of African descent first arrived in what is now Kent County, but records reveal a Black man was living in Chatham in 1791 and there were seven Black families living there in 1832. As Chatham historian Carmen Poole has shown, "the Fugitive Slave Law of 1850 is often credited for the increase in the number of blacks who settled in Ontario. Unfortunately, the city's historiography often failed to acknowledge the fact that a number of blacks, free and former slave, had made their way to Kent County earlier than the post-1850 influx." Further records suggest the first Black people may have arrived in the early 1790s when Black United Empire Loyalists—African Americans who had fought on behalf of Britain in the Revolutionary War—came to Upper Canada "armed," as Irene Moore Davis writes, "with the promise of land." Upon arrival, these Loyalists did not find freedom but instead "a community where white Loyalists and European-stock settlers, many of them belonging to the slave-owning class, held the reins of power. The only other people of African descent were enslaved." Research by Afua Cooper, professor of Black Canadian Studies, shows that slave-keeping was prevalent in the early colonial days of the Detroit River area among the French settlers. In 1701, Antoine de la Mothe Cadillac brought several dozen slaves of Indigenous and African descent from Montreal to help build the fort at Detroit which functioned as a fur trade outpost.

After the abolition of slavery in the British Empire in 1833, refugees from American slavery as well as free Blacks fled into British North America. In the early 1830s, destinations along the Detroit River such as Sandwich were a "particularly appealing destination for Detroit residents of African descent who needed to seek safety." This Upper Canada area (alternately known as Canada West) attracted thousands in places such as Anderdon, Dresden, Shrewsbury, Puce, Gesto, and New Canaan. Some larger groups arrived in the area in the 1840s, when abolitionists founded the Elgin Settlement at Buxton and the Dawn Settlement near Dresden. As some of these communities' names suggest, these settlements represented opportunities for freedom, hope, and new beginnings.

After the passing of the Fugitive Slave Act of 1850, there was a marked increase of activity on what was referred to as the Underground Railroad. With this Act, US Congress granted slaveholders and their agents the right to apprehend escaped enslaved people anywhere in the United States and charge anyone aiding their escape. Crossing the border into Canada, where slavery had been abolished via the Slavery Abolition Act, which took effect in 1834, meant that, in theory at least, those laws did not apply to those who reached Canadian soil. Slave catchers, however, also crossed the border and attempted, often successfully, to take freedom seekers back into the United States. Even though, legally, formerly enslaved people were protected in Canada, Black communities close to the border understood that laws and practices were not always the same thing. Black residents were always on alert for reports of slave catchers in the area and had procedures in place to protect the vulnerable.

The dominant narratives surrounding the history of the Underground Railroad have long focused on the role of white abolitionists—the helpful and benevolent white "conductors" who helped enslaved people find their way to freedom—and not on the individuals who sought their emancipation. But, as scholars have argued, the vast majority of those seeking freedom "found their way to the borders of British North America without any assistance at all" and "the courage, ingenuity, and initiative of people of African descent continue to be either omitted entirely or marginalized in the much-mythologized portrayals of African American/Canadian abolitionism in the media, school curricula, and public discourse." Although records are understandably and intentionally vague, it has been estimated that by 1863 approximately thirty thousand freedom seekers made it to Canada, which does not even touch on the number of enslaved people who, as Moore Davis writes, were "dissuaded from making the journey to Canada, or disrupted in their journeys and returned to slavery."

Even though laws might have suggested that there were significant differences between Canada and the United States in terms of slavery, emancipation, and citizenship, racism and racist practices knew no borders. American historian Tiya Miles has written, "prior to the nineteenth century, Upper Canada was as much slave territory as the United States." Contrary the popular mythology of Canada as the land of freedom, there are examples of enslaved people crossing the Detroit River from Canada to Michigan to find their freedom after the passing of the Northwest Ordinance of 1787. As scholars of Black history Karolyn Smardz Frost and Veta Smith Tucker suggest, "Although Canada may have been a haven for refugees from American slavery, it was no heaven." In his 1855 *Autobiography of a Fugitive Negro: His Anti-slavery Labours in the United States, Canada, & England*, the self-emancipated Reverend Samuel Ringgold Ward writes, "the grand difference betwixt Yankee and Canadian Negro-hate—the former is sanctioned by the laws and the courts, the latter is not."

Those who arrived in Canada in search of freedom found themselves in what Smardz Frost and Smith Tucker describe as "a deeply racist and discriminatory environment, despite the supposedly color-blind laws under which the colonies were governed." Black citizens in Upper Canada often found their children excluded from schools and themselves denied entrance to hotels and churches, shut out of employment opportunities, and actively or passively denied opportunities to which they were entitled as Canadian citizens. Indeed, after the Civil War ended, many of those who had sought their freedom in Canada returned to the United States. Undoubtedly, many sought to reconnect with lost family members, but the return to the US also reveals something about the realities of life in Canada for newly emancipated people of colour.

In the nineteenth century, amidst this emigration from the US, Black settlements were established in at least six areas in Ontario, or, as it was then called, Canada West. Of particular interest to this story are the Detroit River settlements of Windsor, Sandwich, and Amherstburg, which were destinations for freedom seekers in the nineteenth century, and the all-Black settlements around the Chatham area, including Dawn and Elgin (which later became Buxton). Eighty kilometres west and north of Chatham lie Windsor and neighbouring Sandwich, which are across the river from Detroit, Michigan, where several other All-Stars came from. One hundred kilometres west and south of Chatham lies Amherstburg. Fifteen kilometres south of Chatham, Buxton is a community established by and for those who sought freedom from slavery in Canada; several of the All-Stars were from Buxton. Although the official paper trail is thin and inconclusive, almost all the players on the 1934 roster can claim some sort of connection to those early settlers, as well as to those who entered the country through the Underground Railroad.

Many of those who sought freedom in Canada returned to the US after the Civil War to reconnect with family and their former communities. As was the case with many communities in Southern

Ontario, the Black population of Chatham shrunk steadily each decade from a high of 28.4 percent at the outbreak of the Civil War in 1861 to 4.9 percent in 1911 and in 1931 to 1.48 percent. Still, with just over two hundred residents, there was a sense of a strong Black community within Chatham.

★ ★ ★

The Hardings were one of the families who had stayed, their roots in the region going back several generations. Boomer and Len played with the All-Stars and other Chatham teams throughout the 1930s, 1940s, and 1950s. Their younger brother Andy, who became Chatham's first Black police officer, also played on local baseball teams, including the All-Stars. Clifford Olbey, born in 1912, grew up a few houses away from Stirling Park. In the 1934 team photograph, his pose reveals a bit of a confident swagger, suggesting something of his dynamic personality on and off the field. While playing with the All-Stars, he worked at the William Pitt Hotel with several other players and then later moved to Windsor where he worked for the Prince William Hotel. In that same photograph, Ross Talbot, born in 1910, has his ball cap tilted stylishly. He was an infielder and pitcher for the All-Stars and would go on to become a successful poultry farmer in Kent County and be remembered as a beloved uncle to his niece and nephews.

King Terrell, born in 1909, whose name is pronounced to rhyme with "turtle," gained fame for being that rare baseball entity, the left-handed third baseman. A skilled pitcher, Terrell played baseball in Chatham throughout his life and worked at the William Pitt Hotel for forty years. He would be an important mentor and role model for many younger East End residents, and his detailed interviews with researchers in the 1980s have made valuable contributions to our understanding of the All-Stars team and the challenges it confronted. Also a lifetime Chathamite, Gouy Ladd, born in 1909, was involved with baseball throughout his life, both as a player with the All-Stars, the Taylor ACs, and other local teams, and as a coach.

As the All-Stars grew more competitive, they recruited players from nearby towns, as other City League teams had done earlier. The

All-Stars drew from other Black communities in the region, including Buxton, Windsor, Detroit, and, in 1935, from the First Nations community of Walpole Island. Earl "Flat" Chase, born in 1913, lived his early life in Buxton before moving to Windsor in the 1920s. Chase's family lived on Mercer Street in what is called the McDougall Street Corridor, a neighbourhood very similar to Chatham's East End. Chase developed his soon-to-be-legendary hitting and pitching playing baseball at Wigle Park, just off Mercer Street, and in Detroit church leagues. Chase came to Chatham in 1933 to play with the All-Stars and spent his remaining years playing on teams around the region, including the Intercounty League's London Majors. Through Chase's Detroit connections, the All-Stars learned of Don Tabron and Donise Washington, who would join the team in May 1934.

Other players had Buxton connections. Born there in 1908, Sagasta Harding was a left-handed batter and a good runner. His teammates called him a "frog-handed batter" because, as Terrell explains, "he didn't hold a bat like an ordinary person. When you're a left-handed batter, your right hand is at the bottom of the bat and your left hand is at the top. But he always changed it around and put the right hand at the top and the left hand at the bottom. And that's why they called him Frog Hand." He was a good ball player, a good runner, and an allegedly fierce piano player. He moved to Detroit in 1928 but returned to the Chatham area to play for the All-Stars before returning to the Detroit area for the rest of his life. Sagasta Harding, no relation to the other Hardings on the team, was, along with Don Tabron, one of the two remaining players from 1934 who were honoured as part of Major League Baseball's 2002 Negro Leagues celebrations when the Toronto Blue Jays recognized the contributions of the All-Stars. The Robbins brothers were also from Buxton. Hyle Robbins, born in 1910, was a "good, fast runner" who played some games in the outfield for the All-Stars. Hyle's younger brother Stanton, born in 1915, was a left-handed pitcher, described as "a classy southpaw" with "an arm about as strong as any one of the ball players on the team" who "got his share of hits too." Hyle moved to Detroit in 1935 and Stanton spent the rest of his life in Buxton.

The coaches seen in the 1934 team photo lived in Chatham for most, if not all, of their lives and had connections with baseball before the All-Stars. Percy Parker, born in 1898, a third-base coach for the All-Stars who became famous for his humorous antics and memorable catchphrases on the field, appears to have played for earlier teams in Chatham in the 1920s. Joseph "Happy" Parker was a neighbourhood barber as well as the team's manager and fierce advocate. Born around 1893, Parker played with the Chatham Giants in the 1920s, and it was Happy Parker who advocated for better employment opportunities for the All-Stars players in 1934.

Someone named Jenkins appears in some of the 1934 box scores, and it is believed to be Ferguson Jenkins Sr, who joined the All-Stars with more regularity in 1935 and was a strong hitter and outfielder. Born in Windsor in 1909, he worked as a cook on Great Lakes freighters, at the William Pitt Hotel, and later as a chef and chauffeur to a local family. Jenkins appears to have played several games for the All-Stars over the summer of 1934, but it is thought he was unable to find work in Chatham and had to return to Windsor. He is perhaps best known for being the father of pitcher Ferguson Jenkins Jr, Canada's first inductee into the National Baseball Hall of Fame and still the winningest Black pitcher in MLB history.

The lives of the players and the documentation about the baseball games they played show the connections between towns and cities in this geographic triangle. During the Emancipation Day weekend events of 1933, for example, the All-Stars played both the Walpole Island team and Taylor's Stars of Detroit. The sports pages of the early 1930s helps us understand the physical and social geographies of these regions and to see how these multiple histories contribute to the broader scope of this story about a Black baseball team from 1934.

★ ★ ★

Particularly significant to the story of Chatham's East End and the Chatham Coloured All-Stars is proximity to the Detroit River, which divides Canada and the United States. Prior to 1863, the Detroit River had been more than a geographic feature or demarcation between two nations. Smardz Frost and Smith Tucker describe the Detroit River as a "conflicted borderland": it was both a passage-way and a "tangible, concrete border." In the early twentieth century, citizens, Black and white, Canadian and American, routinely crossed the river freely for work, family, church, and various social activities. This fluid frontier was vital for the Black communities in the Windsor-Essex and Chatham-Kent areas. As Smardz Frost and Smith Tucker note, "Isolated from their white neighbours because of prejudice and racial discrimination, the Black communities on each side of the border developed their own cultural, political, and social identities in ways that often meant they had more in common with their counterparts across the river than they had with their own countrymen." By 1934, we can see by the movement of players and teams between Windsor, Chatham, and Detroit, that this river was a highly permeable crossing, a blurred boundary between nations.

It is also important to keep in mind that there were no laws in Canada formally or legally barring Black players from playing on or against white teams, which is a significant departure from the history of Negro leagues teams in the US. In Archie Stirling's "Brief History of Baseball," written around 1960, he tells a story that embodies racial practices on each side of the Detroit River:

> The Detroit Tigers had a great team winning the American League, then the World Championship. At this time [1934 to 1935] my oldest son Archie Jr. was going to Assumption College [in Windsor], and many of the Detroit players would come over to the College and coach the boys, one of these players being Bill Rogell ... [Rogell assembled a team of] professional players from Cleveland, Chicago, Washington, St. Louis, and Detroit, we would pick the best of the players around this district and play benefit games for the hospitals, minor ball etc. . . . These games drew large crowds to Chatham. During one game, I had Flat Chase and Don Washington of the Chatham Stars come out in uniform, knowing I would have to obtain permission to play them, as it was the rule that neither the National or

the American League players could play with coloured
players. I went to Rogell and told him that the crowd
would like to see them play. Mr. Rogell said, "I am sorry;
but we are allowed to play against Indians." So I told him
they were Indians. A few minutes later I was talking to
Denny [Galehouse], the pitcher, and he said to me, "Those
fellows are the darkest Indians I ever saw." But they played.

Black teams in Southwestern Ontario did play against each other,
but unlike Black teams in the US, they routinely played against
white teams in predominantly white leagues. Not only are there early
examples of Black players who played for white teams in Ontario,
we also see white men on the rosters for the All-Stars. Dutchy Scott
was one among others who occasionally played for All-Stars and the
All-Stars also had a white coach, Leslie Hyatt, in 1935.

The fact that Black and white teams played each other in Ontario
did not mean that there were not deeply entrenched cultural and
social practices that upheld a kind of de facto segregation. Nor did it
mean that Black teams like the All-Stars were always treated equit-
ably or respectfully on and off the playing field. Racist practices, as
Reverend Samuel Ringgold Ward wrote in 1855, were not just sanctioned by the laws and the court but also by cultural attitudes and
social practices.

★ ★ ★

Most of the Chatham Coloured All-Stars resided in the East End, a
predominantly but not exclusively Black working-class neighbourhood. Some families had always lived there, and newcomers gravi-
tated to the neighbourhood. If you walk around Chatham's East
End today, you'll notice that it is still very much the working-class
neighbourhood it was in 1934. If you are new to the area and attempt
to drive to an address in the East End, you'll be continually stymied
by the railway tracks that border the neighbourhood on three sides.
Carmen Poole's research into the Black community in Chatham
provides a detailed analysis of the history of this community and
she argues, "the lives of blacks in Chatham remained constrained

and shaped by systemic racism. Race determined where an individual could work . . . and it would also determine in large part where
an individual could live." In the mid-nineteenth century, the East
End was Chatham's commercial and industrial core, but by the early
twentieth century it became, as Poole writes, "an area of the city
sown in and shaped by the classist and racist policies of the city and
its white inhabitants" and "locally characterized as 'the wrong side
of the tracks,' due largely to the values assigned to real and imagined
racial and socio-economic differences." These train tracks are a key
social and geographic demarcation as they put boundaries around
this community, setting it off as a separate but also self-contained
area of the city.

Compounding this long-standing racial marginalization and discrimination, the lives of the East End residents were further affected
by the political and economic forces felt around the globe in the 1930s.
Headlines on the front page of the late edition of the *Chatham Daily
News* a few days before the All-Stars' 1934 opening day game show
some of what might have been on the minds of those heading to the
ballpark: "Jobless Problem Solution Seen in Back to Land Movement,"
"Arms Parley at its Last Gasp: Armaments Race is Predicted by British
Official," "Germany Reported as Teaching the Beauties of War in the
Schools," "Rural Urban Relief Plan Put Forward," "Long Trek Back
to North and Work Camps Started by Local Unemployed Men,"
"Winter Took a Heavy Toll of Fall Crops," and "US Government
Moves to Aid Mid-West Farmers." Between 1929 and 1933, Canada's
GNP fell by 29 percent and the national income halved. Canada was
hard hit, as was Southwestern Ontario.

In 1933, the year the All-Stars entered the City League, 30 percent of Canada's population were out of work and 15 percent were
receiving government relief. Working-class Canadians were hit
harder than white collar workers, and Canadians of colour were particularly disadvantaged. In the early 1930s, Chatham was, like the
rest of Canada and other parts of the globe, weathering the economic and social consequences of the Great Depression. Financial
precarities compounded by racial inequities are an ever-present if
often unstated aspect of this story. Sometimes these precarities are

not unlike those that would also affect white amateur teams and players, such as players needing to work rather than play baseball. Other times, as we will see later, conflicts with the league or other teams about fair and equitable financial arrangements most certainly had racialized undertones.

Given the economic climate of the time, it is no wonder that so many Chatham residents found refuge and escape through watching and playing sports. When we look at the sports pages of regional newspapers from the 1930s, the depth and detail of the local sports coverage is almost incomprehensible to modern readers. In a year when the Detroit Tigers, the closest MLB team to Chatham, would go to the World Series, about half of the sports pages in the summer of 1934 were dedicated to local amateur sports. Stories about an evening church league softball game frequently took up as much space as coverage of a Tigers game. High school track and field results got the same coverage as the MLB standings, and the City League's batting averages were posted up there with those of Gehringer and Gehrig.

Local sports in Chatham had a few advantages over professional teams. Few people had radios, and travelling to professional sports was not an easy or affordable option for many Chathamites. Local sports, on the other hand, offered live entertainment in the neighbourhood for free or for a nominal entry fee. Watching and playing baseball was, as Boomer Harding reflects, something to fill idle hours: "There was no TV in those days," he recalled. "Few people had radios and hardly anybody who grew up in the east end around Stirling Park had a car. If a young fella didn't get himself into baseball he generally got himself into jail. The game was a kind of release from it all, for most of us." Don Tabron echoes Harding, recalling long days at the ballparks in Detroit and Chatham: "We either played baseball or did nothing at all. If we didn't play ball there was just the street corner." Ross Talbot, speaking to a newspaper reporter in 1984, perhaps summarizes things best when he says, "There was no place else to go but Stirling Park. During the Depression, jobs were scarce and most of [us] fellows had nothing to do. We always went to Stirling Park and played ball all day." Stirling Park was not just at the geographic centre of this neighbourhood, it was also at the centre of community life.

Baseball was a key element in defining and sustaining that community. In a 2022 interview, Dorothy Wright Wallace describes Stirling Park as "our community centre." "It was," she says, "the centerpoint of our lives because that's all we had." Orville Wright, who was record-keeper for the All-Stars, recalls, "We had fun in those days. You could pick up three teams at Stirling Park to play any place, any night of the week. There was always baseball at Stirling Park . . . everything in town seemed to centre on Stirling Park in those days." Beulah Harding Cuzzens echoes Wright: "Every night of the week we were on Stirling Park to see a ball game. Baseball was really our breakfast, dinner, and supper. We ate, drank, slept, and played baseball." Her brother Boomer recalled of those days: "We used to practice past dark and we lived at the ball park." For younger boys, watching the older boys and men play ball at the park was a part of growing up. John Olbey, younger brother of All-Stars player Cliff, remembers the swimming pool, and playing pickup games of baseball: "You'd choose up sides and play ball."

Throughout the twentieth century, baseball seemed to flourish in neighbourhoods like the East End in ways that other sports, with the relatively recent exception of basketball, have not. Some of the reasons are undoubtedly economic. Like others, John Olbey recalled part of the attraction to baseball was that it was something they could do without any money. He remembered everyone sharing "raggedy gloves," saying, "when you come in from the field the glove went down on the ground" and the fielder from the other team picked it up and used it. He added, recalling the tough times growing up: "It was good because there wasn't much money floating around and it got the guys together." In a May 17, 1934, column, Calder obliquely articulates why baseball might have taken such a stronghold in communities like the East End: "The greatest ball players seldom come from well-to-do families where the cost of a baseball glove or a regulation ball is regarded as practically nothing. Your average prospective ball player has all he can do to collect a dime a week from the family provider. That's why softball has made such strides here:

the youngsters need only a bat and ball and a vacant lot." Unlike a sport like hockey that requires access to a specific space and lots of equipment, baseball has always been a sport that can be played almost anywhere with a minimal amount of equipment, all of which is comparatively inexpensive and shareable.

Thus, it's not a coincidence that baseball took root so deeply within this community at this particular time. As was the case with many other communities across North America, sports offered this Chatham neighbourhood an escape from daily realities and something to cheer for and get behind. In the East End, baseball was an inexpensive way to bring people together, entertain them, and build a sense of community and identity. Advertisements for the OBAA games in Chatham in 1934 list admission prices as five and ten cents and exhibition games at ten cents, which is equivalent to roughly one and two dollars in today's currency. A tournament featuring the All-Stars and other teams playing for a cash prize was twenty-five cents, the equivalent of just over five dollars, but ladies entered for free. Sometimes games were free, and often a hat was passed to help pay for expenses.

Baseball offered the men of colour who played on the All-Stars the rare opportunity to exist on the same literal and metaphoric playing field as white men in a space where the rules were the same for both races. In many cases, baseball was an arena to best their white neighbours in front of their friends, family, and community in socially sanctioned ways. It provided occasion and opportunity to demand and gain respect both on and off the field. As Blake Harding recalled, on the baseball field, unlike in daily life, "when it got nasty," the All-Stars "were just as nasty and aggressive and tough as anybody else out there. And if you wanted to play to hurt one of them . . . they gave what they got." For the All-Stars, baseball was the only place where they could play on the same field under the same rules as white men. The significance of beating these teams and garnering respect as worthy competitors cannot be overstated, for both the players and their fans.

★ ★ ★

The All-Stars came together at a key point in the history of Chatham baseball, when, as Blake Harding told filmmaker LeSean Harris, baseball culture "was almost dead in Chatham."

> They hadn't won any Ontario Baseball Association championships. The league, the City League was basically dying. And in '34, when the Coloured All-Stars or the All-Stars got into the league, it brought excitement back to the city. But more so, what it did for the community was that it brought them together, gave them something to cheer about. They'd just gone through the First World War, the Depression and all of that. And it gave people hope. They could come out and see people that looked like them doing well.

The story of the 1934 Chatham Coloured All-Stars remains, as we shall see, a source of pride to the East End community, and one that many of its citizens have long held onto and fought to preserve and share. It was a year the men talked about for the rest of their lives and that their siblings, children, grandchildren, nieces, and nephews continue to talk about today. Many of these descendants—in particular, Blake Harding, Earl Chase Jr, Horace Chase, Douglas Talbot, and Donald Tabron Jr—have been active in sharing their memories and preserving this story beyond their immediate family and friends, hoping it would be better known outside of Chatham.

The extant records from the *Chatham Daily News* suggest the All-Stars were undefeated in seven games in May 1934: five against the other three teams in the Chatham City League (with scores of 9–3, 3–2, 10–3, 12–2, and 9–3) and two exhibition games against Walpole Island, one at home and one away (a 9–5 victory and another victory with an unknown score). The available scores reveal the All-Stars were not only undefeated in the month of May, but that they scored fifty-two runs and allowed only eighteen. Clearly this was a team to be reckoned with both offensively and defensively. The *Chatham*

Daily News column below from a game on May 21, 1934, when the All-Stars squeaked out a 3–2 win in the final inning, is an example of the kind of baseball fans were coming out to see:

> Going into the last of the seventh, with the score knotted, the Stars were determined to start something. With two men down, Belanger got the count three and two on Talbot. The next pitch curved over the corner inches wide, according to the umps and Talbot walked. It was one of those ones which the ump's the only person in a position to judge. Washington then came to the rescue of his mates with a two-bagger, scoring Ross [Talbot] and the game was over.

Similarly, an exhibition game between the All-Stars and the Walpole Island team on May 31 reveals that the All-Stars were a solid team with diverse skills rather than just a few good star players upon which the rest of the team relied. Calder writes, "Every member of the winning team secured at least one safe knock and King Terrell led the parade with three hits, while Chase secured a home run and a single and Ben and Ross Talbot, Washington, Ladd and Olbey all obtained two hits." These newspaper accounts show us the action on the field and the skills of individual All-Stars players:

> Chase began proceedings in the second when he slapped the first ball pitched far over the fence in centre field for a home run. Washington grounded out, pitcher to first, but Ross Talbot singled to resume the rally. After Tabron had fanned, Olbey singled and when [Braves] shortstop Soney threw wildly to first Talbot scored. Olbey pulling up at second. Terrell doubled, scoring Olbey and Boomer Harding walked. Terrell was caught going into third base to end the inning.

In the same game, Ross Talbot is shown "working on the mound for the Stars and allowed eleven hits. Five of these were bunched in the fifth for the visitors' big splurge, but otherwise Talbot kept the safeties well distributed, allowing no more than one to an inning." By the end of May, Calder shows us strong players and a promising team getting into its rhythms. The upcoming months seem to be promising fans some exciting baseball.

★ ★ ★

In the snapshots preserved in the Chase and Harding family scrapbooks, we see how often Harding, Chase, Terrell, and Ladd were together not only on the field but also off of it. Many of the photographs capture the fun and joy of playing baseball as well as the deep friendships that existed between the players. In their interviews for the *Breaking the Colour Barrier* project, John Olbey, Blake Harding, Earl Chase Jr, Horace Chase, Douglas Talbot, and Donald Tabron Jr all circle back to that 1934 baseball team and what it meant to their fathers, uncles, or brothers as well as their families, the community, and the future.

Talbot's comment that "there was no place else to go but Stirling Park," is a reminder of the importance of this space to the Black residents of the East End and the centrality of it in their community and their identities. Having to navigate through many urban spaces that excluded them passively and actively, Stirling Park, in the heart of the neighbourhood, was a place where residents could go, feel welcome, and feel at home. Although born after the 1934 season, Horace Chase grew up watching his dad, Flat, play baseball at Stirling Park and remembers what it was like when he was a child. He captures what was so important about baseball and Stirling Park: "They used to crowd Stirling Park, sometimes get as many as 400 people coming out to watch the game. And sometimes, mostly on Sundays, they would crowd [the park]. So, they had a good following here when they played ball, I'll say that much. They liked them and, like I say, you knew the guys, you grew up with them, worked with them, ate with them, you know you socialize with them. So, to me it's also like one great big family."

In 2016, Clifford Olbey's younger brother John "Usher" Olbey reflected on the team's importance to the community. Describing what it meant for the men of Chatham's East End to be part of this baseball team at that moment in history, Usher says the team was important because

> they could do something together. They could get together and do something because they were unwanted on the other teams in Chatham. There's lots of ball teams that flourished around here but there was no coloured team and when it was formed, it became a unit that was well known. And I know they all had pride in their accomplishments. I think it left a legacy that lasted for quite a while anyway, until the boys were gone.

In the Multicultural History Society of Ontario (MHSO) and the *Breaking the Colour Barrier* interviews, players, family, and community members return time and time again to 1934 as a turning point. Partially it was because of the team's eventual victory, but more predominantly it was because of the pride in what the team had achieved—both with and for the community—through baseball. Winning the provincial championship as the first and only Black team in the OBAA showed both white and Black Chatham that this team could not only play as equals to white men but they could also be victorious. As Blake Harding reflects, the 1934 Chatham Coloured All-Stars changed the hearts and minds not only of the East End, but also of the broader Chatham community. These changes were limited, of course, but hearts and minds were nonetheless changed.

As we head into June and the remainder of the 1934 season, Calder writes of the All-Stars with critical admiration for the team and solid respect for their abilities, skill, and their prowess on the field. In his coverage, he is an enthusiastic supporter of the team but also a measured celebrant. He conveys unwavering respect for the team but never falls into uncritical boosterism or local jingoism. He doesn't look the other way when they lose games due to errors or missed opportunities, and he isn't afraid to call out individual players when they make careless errors or sloppy plays nor take the team to task when they play bad games. Calder holds the players and team accountable, demanding that they live up to their potential. In this way, Calder's columns can be read as part of the larger and recurrent discussions of respect within the history of the Chatham Coloured All-Stars.

The All-Stars' last game in May sets the tone for much of the rest of the season. Fans coming to the ballpark on May 30, 1934, would have seen a five-and-a-half inning 9–3 blowout of the Braggs. As the winning pitcher, Chase struck out five players and held the Braggs to four hits. In his three at bats, he got a triple and two doubles. Teammates Washington and Tabron each stole a base. The All-Stars' passion and skill on the field drew the attention of white Chatham and likely made them view these Black men in new ways. As we shall see throughout the season, their prowess, success, and the increased attention that resulted from it made them targets for some hostilities. But these also opened doors for new opportunities.

JUNE

1934

SPRING IS JUST TURNING TO SUMMER IN THE FIRST week of June 1934. The days are getting warmer, and the longer summer nights mean baseball can stretch into the evening hours. The Chatham Coloured All-Stars remain unbeaten in early June, and five of the top ten batters in the City League are All-Stars: Len Harding (.545), Don Washington (.473), Ben Talbot (.470), Earl Chase (.389), and Clifford Olbey (.357). Batting averages are always askew at the beginning of any season due to the small sample size, but these early statistics hint at a trend that will continue throughout the season, as does the team's winning record coming out of May.

Throughout June, the play between teams becomes a little rougher. Some of this roughness appears to be rooted in fairly standard intraleague competitiveness, but there are a few occurrences, developments that continue throughout the season and beyond, that indicate something else is going on. One game in early June suggests that the All-Stars are the team to beat for reasons other than their place in the standings. Before proceeding with the events of June 4, it is important to look at the history of Black baseball in the larger region of Windsor-Essex and Chatham-Kent for the context it provides for understanding the 1934 season more fully.

★ ★ ★

At first glance, the 1934 Chatham Coloured All-Stars appear to come out of nowhere. But if we look more closely at the local and regional newspapers, we will see that the seeds for this championship season had been planted over the generations. The most significant precursor to the All-Stars were the all-Black Chatham Giants. Their roster is printed in the June 15, 1915, *Chatham Daily Planet* and includes several familiar names: Talbot, Terrell, Harding, and Robbins. In August 1915, another article in the *Chatham Daily Planet* lists a J. Parker at first base and a P. Parker at shortstop. These two players are Happy Parker and Percy Parker, who both played for the Chatham Giants and then went on to coach and manage the 1934 All-Stars. In-depth genealogical research would likely reveal that many of the 1934 players were related to the men on these early rosters. In this way, we can trace the beginnings of the Chatham Coloured All-Stars to at least 1915, but their origins run even deeper than that.

As many of the region's Black freedom-seekers were arriving, baseball was becoming firmly established in Southwestern Ontario. Many scholars have convincingly argued that the first documented baseball game was not in Elihu Phinney's cow pasture in Cooperstown, New York, in 1839 as Abner Doubleday claimed, but rather in Beachville, Ontario, in 1838. Robert Douglas Day's research into sports in Chatham from 1790 through 1895 suggests that the first print record of baseball in Chatham is when the Royal Oak Club of Chatham played the Detroit Unexpected Base Ball Club in June 1871, though baseball was almost certainly played in the city earlier than this. What is most interesting about this discovery is Day's suggestion that one or both of the teams may have had Black players because some of the names on the roster, such as Washington, Shadd, and Sparks, are names closely associated with the Buxton community. Day's research has also brought to light the existence in 1887 of a Black team called the Jubilee Base Ball Club as well as that of a Black junior squad in 1888. The possible presence of Black players on white teams or Black teams playing against white teams offers another distinction between Canadian and US baseball history. While never formalized or codified, the era of segregated baseball in the US began around 1867, supported by gentleman's agreements and perpetuated by practice until Jackie Robinson and Larry Doby broke the MLB colour barrier in 1947.

Black baseball in this region was not limited to Chatham teams, as the regional newspapers from the early twentieth century reveal. Although inconsistent and incomplete, local newspapers' sports sections and the community notices sections, the latter of which more commonly covered Black teams, remain our best source of information about early baseball and early Black baseball in this area. A survey of these predominantly white regional newspapers reveals a number of stable Black teams at this time, particularly within historically Black settlements such as New Canaan, Harrow, Buxton, Gesto, and Colchester. There are recurring references to teams like the New Canaan Cyclones, the Harrow Earthquakes, the Buxton Invincibles, and an unnamed team from Colchester. For both Black and white teams, baseball games mentioned in the community notices sections are frequently part of homecomings, holiday weekends, or church-related events. In the "New Canaan" section of the *Essex Free Press*, for example, a story in the May 17, 1912, edition describes a baseball game that is almost certainly part of Victoria Day celebrations: "The New Canaan AME Sunday School will have a grand time, May 24th. There will be a baseball game in the afternoon and refreshments served, also a concert at night. No admission." Often these stories are brief, cursory, and factual, with little description or editorial commentary, but regularly the race of the team is included. A June 9, 1905, community notice in the *Amherstburg Echo* notes, "On June 28, a team of coloured ball players who are touring the country will visit Leamington. It is a fast team and a good game is assured"; and a July 30, 1909, notice in the *Essex Free Press* recounts, "The

coloured ball team from here defeated Colchester South last week."
Little else is known about this travelling team or who the coloured
team was, but notices like these, which overtly mention the teams'
race, help document not only the presence of Black baseball in the
region but the fact that they played white teams.

Baseball featured prominently in the region's only Black newspaper of the time, *The Dawn of Tomorrow*, out of London. The
front page of the August 11, 1923, issue, for example, features a
grainy photograph of the "Conquerors of the Fast Arkona Giants:
Coloured Star Baseball Team of London" just below the byline and
a very interesting story about Harry Coursey (1905–1976). Coursey
was a highly successful Black athlete in his own time, but to date
very little research has been done on him.

Newspapers in the first part of the twentieth century not only
document the existence of Black teams in the region, they also reveal
some of the ways white spectators approached Black baseball. As
mentioned above, newspapers frequently racialized Black teams, even
in the shortest of notices. In the *Amherstburg Echo*, it is not a "team
of ball players" touring the country, but a "team of coloured ball players." In the *Essex Free Press*, it is not the "ball team from here" who
defeated Colchester South last week but the "coloured ball team from
here." Whether or not the mention of race is a form of marketing,
as it was with the All-Stars, is unclear. These racial designations do,
however, suggest that the Black teams were seen by white spectators
as different or unusual. In the June 15, 1915, *Chatham Daily Planet*, for
example, the commentary and word choice in a story titled "Reach
Ball Was Maltreated. Local Colored Giants and Buxton Boys Were
Responsible" reveal how some white spectators saw Black baseball:

> A poor little inoffensive bit of leather, rubber, yarn and
> cork, commonly known as a Reach baseball, was horribly
> maltreated yesterday afternoon on Tecumseh Park, when
> it survived nine innings of about the weirdest baseball
> seen here in many years. Fished out of the creek, at least a
> dozen times, small with great gusto against different right
> field trees on other occasions, fouled up against the brick

wall of the armoury too often to mention, and twisted
out of its ordinary shape by the agonizing deliveries of
the respective pitchers, it ended up a mere shadow of the
glistening sphere that was tossed onto the diamond at the
commencement of play.

To get down to plain English the local coloured Giants
and the North Buxton Invincibles, another aggregation
of the same colour, were responsible for the treatment
accorded to the sphere. Starting play about two-thirty in
the afternoon, the Buxton outfit managed to acquire a 13–12
verdict just after the market clock pealed seven bells. The
game was weird from start to finish and baseball such as
was never seen in the major leagues nor even dreamed of by
a Cobb or Daubert, was provided for the several hundreds
who witnessed the affair. From the players' standpoint, the
game was all right, the Buxton gladiators leaving the city in
high spirits and the local hopes not a bit downhearted over
the trimming handed them. From the spectators' point of
view, the affair—well—it was a bit different.

The inclusion of this game within the predominantly white newspaper reveals a degree of acceptance of these two Black teams. This
acceptance, however, is complicated by the author's use of words
like "weirdest" and "a bit different" to describe the game. It is not
entirely clear what is meant in their comparison to Ty Cobb and
Jake Daubert, players known at the time for their fierce style of play,
but the phrase "baseball such as was never seen in the major leagues
nor even dreamed of by a Cobb or Daubert" does suggest that the
author sees something very different about Black baseball. Indeed,
they conclude their article by drawing a distinction between the
Black players' perceptions of the game and those of the presumably
white spectators. For the players "the game was all right," but "from
the spectators' point of view, the affair—well—it was a bit different."

This early article articulates a thread that runs throughout the
press coverage of Black baseball in the region and one we will see
resurfacing in discussions of the All-Stars well into the 1930s: Black

baseball is not like white baseball. For some writers and spectators, this difference is welcome as it means the baseball will be fast, exciting, and entertaining. To other spectators, that difference implies there is something suspect about these teams and about Black baseball.

Race is something that surfaces often in discussions of Sunday baseball. While opposition to Sunday baseball is not exclusive to Black teams who played on Sunday, race—as well as class—appears to have added fuel to some of the opposition. The Lord's Day Act in Ontario, mandating that Sundays should be days of rest, was enacted in 1906 and was upheld until 1985, when the Supreme Court of Canada ruled it impinged upon religious freedom. The Lord's Day Act had a particular impact on the working-classes and on sports. Some interpreted "a day of rest" as a day to do whatever one pleased with this one guaranteed day off. While intended to facilitate days of rest that involved attending church, historian Allan Downey argues these laws had "the effect of securing a day of leisure for working-class Canadians to attend athletic events." Disallowing Sunday sporting events had a particular impact on working classes whose leisure and recreational time was limited to that one day off. Given that the Black teams were predominantly working class at this time, these laws had more of an impact on these teams and the communities who came out to see them.

There was a distinction between law and practice, though, as can be seen in the number of Sunday games listed in the newspapers. While legislation technically prohibited Sunday baseball, games were still played and many were well attended. What's interesting, for our purposes here is how often stories about Sunday baseball mention Black teams. For example, in September 1931, a wire story from Sarnia was printed in the *Windsor Star* under the headline "Stop Game." The story begins, "Taking their stand against Sunday baseball in Sombra Township, provincial police and Constable R.J. Whiting Sunday broke up a ball game between Port Lambton and a coloured team from Detroit. The police were forced to disperse a crowd of over 300 disappointed fans." A letter to the editor of the *Leamington Post* in 1933 also takes issue with a Sunday baseball game, again involving a Black team:

It seems a pity that baseball fans have no respect for the Sabbath as evidenced by the games that are being played all over the county on that day. The latest exhibition of this form of Sabbath desecration was witnessed at Albuna last Sunday where it is said 1,000 people witnessed a game between the Cottam team and a negro team from Windsor.

In addition to conveying that there was some resistance to baseball games on the Sabbath, the 1931 article and 1933 letter reveal that the three hundred and one thousand people attending, respectively, appear not to have taken issue with baseball on Sundays. Nevertheless, these two news items reveal the ways race and class intersected in this region in the early 1930s. In addition to confronting racialized spaces, the All-Stars navigated many of the same issues as were working-class citizens in the region.

★ ★ ★

On June 5, 1934, a headline in the sports section of the *Chatham Daily News* reads "Kent Bridge and Stars to Replay Game: Stars on Long End of the Score, but Game is Protested." The recap of the June 4 game begins with what sounds like a fairly straight-forward baseball narrative: "King Terrell was the hero of last night's city baseball league game between the Stars and Kent Bridge, when, with two strikes on him and two out in the last frame, he got hold of one of Bus Reed's good ones for a home run over the centre field fence, with two of his mates aboard. The blow put the Stars on the top end of a 6–4 count." "However," Calder writes,

the boys might just as well have remained at home, as far as the league records are concerned. At a meeting of the league executive held immediately after the game, . . . Kent Bridge lodged a protest. The executive after some discussion on the play questioned voted to throw the game out and ordered it replayed. The controversial play emerged in the 5th inning, when the All-Stars scored three runs to tie the

game at 3–3: Washington opened the Stars' half of the fifth
with a single, stole second, and scored on Olbey's single,
after Tabron had fanned. Ladd singled through short,
Olbey rounded the keystone sack and headed for third.
Stevens threw to third to flag the runner but the ball went
through Millen's legs and rolled to the fence. Olbey shoved
Millen, toppling him over and scored, while Ladd pulled
up at third. Then Ladd evened the count on Len Harding's
single. The next two men went out in order.

The controversy was whether or not Olbey's play at third—which
allowed him to score and for Ladd to move to third and subse-
quently score and tie the game—was what we would now call inter-
ference. By allowing Olbey's run and enabling Ladd to advance to
third, the on-field officials signalled it was fair play. The final score
was 6–4 for Chatham.

It is important—but certainly not surprising— to note that the
challenged game of June 4 was close. As Calder writes, "It was a
tough game for the Kent Bridge lads to lose. They outhit and out-
fielded the Stars, while Bus Reed on the mound, turned in another
well-pitched game." The closeness of the game might have fuelled
the vociferousness of the challenge issued by Kent Bridge to the
league officials after the game.

Since records for the Chatham City League are no longer extant,
it is not certain how typical it was for a complete seven-inning game
to be challenged, stricken from the records, and then replayed at a
later date. Moreover, I have not been able to find official rule books
from this time that would elucidate when, how, and why games
would be replayed. The events related to the June 4 game, while perhaps unusual, were not uncommon. In the June 28, 1934, *Chatham
Daily News*, for example, there is a report of the Kitchener-Waterloo
Panthers protesting a Stratford win from the previous week: "The
two umpires who officiated in the protested game have been asked to
appear to give their version of the incident which forms the basis for
the protest." This story suggests that the kind of protest Kent Bridge
lodged against the Stars was not unique, even if there's no telling at

this distance how common they may have been. It's uncertain if or when this rematch occurred, but the next time the teams played, the All-Stars convincingly defeated Kent Bridge by an 11–5 tally. King Terrell was once again highlighted as the hero of the game, who "was on the mound for the Stars and ... in addition to limiting the Kent Bridge fellows to six hits, helped his own cause along by getting three hits out of four trips to the plate, one of them being a three-bagger."

We will likely never know what actually transpired on the field during this game, but William Scurr, *Chatham Daily News* sports editor, comments in his "Sport in Short" column that "the action of the City Baseball League executive regarding the deportment of players while on the field, will be appreciated by the fans," suggesting that the All-Stars were playing too rough and the League's actions were appropriate. There is not sufficient evidence to confirm or deny that race played a part in the nullification of the June 4 game. But racial tensions were undeniably present at the All-Stars' next game, which took place on June 7, 1934, at Stirling Park.

The game on June 7 was the All-Stars' first loss of the season. The next day, the *Chatham Daily News* not only documents that the loss was due to pitching and fielding errors but also describes an argument that almost came to blows. Under a headline that reads "Duns Hand Stars First Defeat of Present Campaign. Leaders of City Baseball League Lose Last Evening. Score was 5–2—Considerable Excitement After the Game but No Damage Was Occasioned—Stirling Turned in Good Game," the story recounts that there was

considerable excitement just after the game ended and it looked for a few moments as though there would be a near riot. It started on one of the bleachers when two fans, each an ardent supporter of the respective teams, got into an altercation which resulted in one of them being shoved off the stand. Several of the other fans showed a willingness to "mix" but there was no damage. As the players were walking off the diamond, some of them got into an argument and it looked as though there would be a general melee but peace was restored with no damage occasioned.

The writer does not mention the races of the two fans, but it would be logical to assume, given that Stars fans were predominantly Black and Duns fans predominantly white, these tensions formed along racial lines. The near "general melee" between the players would also have split down racial lines. Whatever the cause of this tension, it was significant enough that the columnist gave almost as much space to it as to the game recap: twenty lines of the story were devoted to events on the field and seventeen to the "considerable excitement" off of it.

As we proceed with the rest of the All-Stars' 1934 and subsequent seasons, the games of June 4 and 7 force us to acknowledge the limitations of the print record in reconstructing the ways race played out on the field. While many of the oral histories from the players and family members describe racial tensions and hostilities in the stands and on the field, Calder's seeming silence on the matters of race might appear to be at odds with this history. But sportswriters then, like sportswriters today, were writing for audiences with an assumed and shared knowledge that is difficult to access from our position. Additionally, Calder—or perhaps his editor, given Calder's young age—would have been very aware of the readership of this paper and what they might consider acceptable. In his interview with then–University of Waterloo graduate student Dan Kelly in 1977, Boomer suggested that Calder "had to be careful of what he said, or it might cost him his job." William Scurr was also cautiously pointed in his observations, printed only a few inches away from the description of the near-melee: "A lot of people who attend the city baseball league games at Stirling Park take their favorite seriously. Some of them took it a little too seriously last evening." This incident will be worth keeping in mind in a subsequent chapter about a remarkably similar incident in June 1935.

★ ★ ★

It's difficult from our current perspective to fully understand the role local sports played in the 1930s. On the day the *Chatham Daily News* printed the recap of the Kent Bridge versus All-Stars game, the stories, standings, and recaps printed in the *Windsor Star*'s sports section gives a sense of the scale and scope of amateur baseball in Southwestern Ontario. There is a mention of the Essex County Baseball League with teams from Leamington, Amherstburg, Harrow, Walkersides, Chatham, and Sandwich, a senior league with teams from Niagara Falls, Chatham (the Merchants), St. Catharines, Merritton, Brantford, Kitchener, Guelph, Stratford, London, St. Thomas, Peterborough, Belleville, Port Colborne, Dundas, Moodie, Hamilton, Galt, and Tillsonburg. An intermediate league has teams from Aylmer, Bayham, Waterloo, Galt, Welland, Port Colborne, Wainfleet, Fonthill, Woodstock, Ayr, Southampton, and Paisley. A junior league is mentioned with teams from Galt, Stratford, Port Colborne, Welland-Crowland, Port Robinson, Brantford, and Kitchener. Towns and cities of all sizes had teams, often multiple teams, that played in the region. In a city with a population of around 99,000, Windsor had the Border Cities Independent League (with four local teams and a Detroit team) and a number of softball leagues, including the seven-team City League softball league, a nine-team Industrial League, a three-team girls' league, plus intermediate and junior church leagues. One of the Industrial League softball teams, the BME Rangers, was almost certainly a Black team. The mention of this team is both an indication of the trove of Black sports history still yet to be discovered and a reminder that the All-Stars were part of a much broader story.

Examining the *Windsor Star* sports pages, with its primarily factual coverage, alongside the sports coverage in the *Chatham Daily News* highlights that Calder's coverage is rare and remarkable and serves as a reminder of how easily much of the All-Stars story could have disappeared had it not been for his columns. At the beginning of this season, Calder was nineteen years old. His columns reveal an extensive knowledge of and a deep passion for baseball, likely by-products of growing up in a baseball-besotted town. In his "A Brief History of Baseball in Chatham," Archie Stirling reminds readers that "baseball was played here long before Chatham became a city." Stirling recounts how the Chatham City League was organized in 1919 and games were played in Tecumseh Park: "These games drew large crowds with good baseball." They were only allowed to take a collection from fans, resulting in around eighty-or-so dollars per game. In order to enter the OBAA, Chatham had to build a regulation diamond. After fundraising activities, what is now Rotary Park and Fergie Jenkins Field was built, allowing them to enter the OBAA in 1920. That year, when Calder was five years old, Chatham won the Kent County League and went to the OBAA playdowns, where they lost to St. Thomas. The following year, the Kent County teams began importing players to strengthen their teams. Stirling notes that Chatham raised $3,800 to import four players but still lost. Stirling captures the financial precarity of baseball when he says, "that year Chatham spent 8,000 on baseball and finished in the red." In 2022 dollars, this is approximately $193,000 that was spent on amateur sports in Chatham, a sum that reveals a great deal about the importance of local sports in pre–Depression era Chatham.

During Calder's childhood, Stirling Park was made into a regulation OBAA park and three more ballparks were built in Chatham. In 1928, when Calder was thirteen, Chatham had three teams in the OBAA—senior, intermediate, and junior—and a professional coach from Detroit was brought in to coach the intermediate and junior teams. In 1929, some of the players on the senior team formed another team that went deeply into debt. In attempting to get out of debt, they were suspended from the OBAA for three years. According to Stirling, this suspension "ruined baseball for the Kent League." In 1931, baseball returned with the formation of the City League, with the R.G. Duns, Braggs Insurance, Ontario Steel, Kent Bridge, the Chatham Merchants, the Chatham All-Stars, and the Chatham Youth Organization (CYO).

Growing up alongside this baseball culture in Chatham appears to have left an indelible mark on Calder. In many of his columns, there are discernable threads of a wistful nostalgia for the return of the vibrant baseball culture of his childhood. He often muses about whether 1934 will be the year that brings baseball back to Chatham. Amidst the All-Stars' winning streak in August, Calder proclaims with hope and conviction that "baseball in Chatham has every chance for a mighty revival."

In the years the All-Stars played, teams and leagues came and went, flourished and folded in much the same way they do today in response to finances, availability of players, and the willingness of sponsors to support teams. While the All-Stars, by all accounts, had to cobble sponsorship together, the support of the East End never wavered.

In June, in spite of the quality of play the All-Stars offered, we see the beginnings of what will become a familiar refrain throughout the 1934 season: fans need to come out and support the City League. Calder and the *Chatham Daily News* sports editor William Scurr, who also covered local sports, frequently mention that Chatham City League offers fans high-quality baseball. In his "Sport in Short" column from June 8, Scurr relays, "Last night's defeat was the first time this season that the Stars have finished on the short end of the count. After the experiences of the last two starts perhaps some of the fellows in close touch with baseball in Chatham who have the idea 'the league doesn't mean a thing' will change their opinion." Part of the motivation to get fans out is clearly financial. The City League struggles, as it had from its inception, to make ends meet, and Calder contributes quite a bit of column space to encouraging Chathamites to support this local league. Of the game on June 26, 1934, for example, Calder reflects that "the City Baseball League game [between Braggs and Duns] was about the best to date . . . There's plenty of action in the games and in the crowds at the Park Street lot and any evening there is well spent. When the games are as good as last night's you can count on getting your money's worth several times over at a City League game." Calder continues, "Tonight the Braggs will be trying to make it two straight wins when they meet the rocketing Stars . . . This game will be worth an early meal and a dash to the park." One consistent theme in Calder's plea for fans to come out and see the games is that if you miss seeing the All-Stars play, you are missing some incredible baseball.

Boomer Harding, nd. Courtesy of the Chase family.

Earl Chase Sr and Earl Chase Jr, at their home in Chatham. Courtesy of University of Windsor, Archives and Special Collections.

Boomer Harding, nd. Courtesy of the Milburn family.

Ross Levera Talbot. Courtesy of Mr Douglas Talbot.

King Terrell in Taylor ACs uniform. Courtesy of the Chase family.

Jack Davis, Joseph "Happy" Parker, and Thomas Holden. Courtesy of Chatham Kent Black Historical Museum, nd.

King Terrell in Chatham Arcades uniform. Courtesy of the Chase family.

Earl Chase off the field, Chatham. Courtesy of the Chase family.

Gouy Ladd in All-Stars uniform. Courtesy of the Chase family.

Scurr's and Calder's urging fans to come attend the game seems
at odds with how the East End residents recall the crowds attending
the All-Stars games and the huge following the team had. Blake
Harding remembers his father describing how Stirling Park was
"filled with everybody" and how fans would "park all the way down
the next street, and the next street over . . . There were no empty seats,
no empty places to stand." Given that Calder's assumed *Chatham
Daily News* readership was almost exclusively white, Calder's columns then are urging white baseball fans to come and see this team.
Why some white fans in Chatham might not attend All-Stars games
is a matter of conjecture, but it is more than likely that some of them
believed the All-Stars played a "different" kind of baseball. In this
instance, "different" wasn't the kind of baseball they wanted to see.

Towards the end of June, the season of stellar baseball that Calder
yearned for seems to be shaping up: "Though pressed to do it, the
Stars continued their winning ways in the City Baseball League
when they took last evening's twilight affair from the Duns by a
7–6 score at Stirling Park. Hard hitting and smart base running
accounted for the Stars' victory and though it was a squeeze at the
finish they led in most of the departments of the game." His excitement over the quality of play is clear in paragraphs like this:

> A sparkling pitching duel in which Stirling and Chase
> tangled for seven strenuous innings, saw the Duns hold
> the Stars to a 1-all tie at Stirling Park last night. The game
> was one of the best of the current season and after the first
> inning neither team was able to score. Chase allowed but
> three hits and all came in the opening frame when a trio
> of singles pushed across the Duns' only run. A double and
> a single accounted for the Stars' sole counter in the same
> stanza. Besides hurling great ball . . . Chase obtained two
> of the Stars' four hits. His strike-out victims numbered ten
> while young Archie Stirling whiffed six.

Under the headline "Interesting Game," Calder reflects on the base-ball seen in June:

> An attraction which promises to draw the largest baseball crowd of the season is the Stars–Merchants exhibition game which is carded for Stirling Park on Saturday of this week. There has been considerable controversy among fans of the city as to which team was playing superior ball and the game which has been arranged should just about decide that question.
>
> Both teams have high-class pitching staffs and smooth defences while both have taken it on themselves to break out into rashes of base-hits at different times during the season. That augers well for a smart contest and few fans who care anything for the game will be missing this one.

While the other three teams in the City League seem to be fairly competitive, the Stars' abilities on the field appear to have had a particularly strong appeal and excitement is building around the team.

In the month of June, the All-Stars play ten games: Of these ten, one is called due to darkness with a 1–1 tie and they have one loss to the Duns. Including their 6–4 contested victory against Kent Bridge, the All-Stars score fifty runs and allow only thirty-one over those nine full games. On June 21, 1934, the All-Stars boast a .777 winning percentage and their players dominate the statistical leader-board. Of the top eleven batters in the league, six are All-Stars, and the top five of those have averages ranging from .406 (Chase) to .526 (Len Harding). Three of the four players who lead in stolen bases are All-Stars (Washington, Olbey, and Talbot); Terrell leads the league with two home runs, Chase with two triples. Chase, Washington, and Len Harding are three of the four league leaders with doubles, at seven, five, and four respectively. The league's top four pitchers include three All-Stars: Chase with four wins, Terrell and Talbot with two. It's no wonder that the All-Stars make a rare appearance on the front page of the *Chatham Daily News* on June 26, 1934. Placed in the lower right-hand corner of the front page, the story describes the previous evening's game with a headline reading: "Talbot Hurls Loop Leaders to Victory: Stars Continue String of City League Successes Defeating Kent Bridge." At the end of June 1934, the All-Stars are, without a doubt, the team to beat.

★ ★ ★

The All-Stars' winning record and their style of play was an attraction to fans in and around Chatham. In their early days, the All-Stars were often initially seen as a kind of novelty or, in the words of Blake Harding, "a freak show." But when people watched the All-Stars, they soon learned they were a high-quality baseball team. In a 1980 interview, King Terrell reflects on the All-Stars visiting neighbouring towns: "We had a good ball club and sure, people acted funny when you went there, look at you as though they were looking at a bunch of clowns, more or less. That's what it looked like: they looked at you as a bunch of clowns. But when you got out on the baseball field . . . They knew how to play baseball and they played baseball." Their fast style of play was sometimes used in advertisements like this one from the *Chatham Daily News* from May 30, 1934: "Exhibition Baseball! Walpole Indians vs Chatham Stars, Canada's Fastest All-Coloured Team." Their fast, aggressive style might have attracted spectators, but it did not always serve them well outside of town when the All-Stars beat white teams, which they often did.

King Terrell recounts a particularly chilling anecdote about one such incident: "There was never a place that we played baseball that we couldn't go back and play again, except one place . . . We beat West Lorne and they run us out, they run us out of the town. They had clubs, and hoes, and rakes, and everything else. We got everything all packed up before the game was over because we knew there was something going to happen anyways. So, we just got the game over. When that last man was out, we all got in the cars and took off and we never went back. And we couldn't go back to play ball there no more." In 1984, Ross Talbot also shared memories of playing that once in West Lorne describing how "we caused a small riot . . .

Boomer was going [to] home [base]and knocked down their catcher and people snatched boards off the fence, but we came out of that all right." Olbey remembers insults from some of the fans: "One or two loudmouths would make some remarks and they stood out in the crowd ... It was quite bad sometimes, but we just kept on playing and tried to ignore it." "As for heckling," Talbot reflected, "we just had to take it ... At that time we had to live with it." In the same interview Talbot recalls playing in Strathroy. "They wrote on the sidewalks, 'the n___s are coming' and the 'black clouds are moving in,'" Talbot said, a tear coming to his eye. "That was the worst thing we ever came across." An interview with Boomer in the 1970s describes the same incident: "Messages were scribbled on the park fence and sidewalks referring to the colour of the team and suggesting that they go home." According to Fergie Jenkins Sr, the events were not reflective of the players or the Strathroy community as a whole, and other players like Talbot and Don Washington agreed. Washington, who moved to Strathroy to captain their baseball team in 1935, stated in a 1984 interview that while he remembers some of these events and was the only Black person in town, says he was treated well by everybody.

Nevertheless, fifty years later, these players remembered these events. Jenkins's interview with Boomer's sister Wanda in 1980 does convey something of what it must have felt like to play out of town and to beat the home team. Jenkins says, "And we beat them and then something happened at home plate ... and we had to get out of Strathroy." Len Harding "picked up the ball and hit that guy where he shouldn't of been hit and then we had to run [out of the park] across the little footbridge." When Wanda follows up with "You mean you had fights?" Jenkins responds, "Oh fights, always. There was arguments in baseball years ago ... it didn't come to blows but there was always a lot of discussion and cussing. We were talking to people what the right thing was. And being coloured, it was that you had to beat any team by ten runs pretty near." Blake Harding is one of the rare interviewees from the *Breaking the Colour Barrier* project who remembers hearing these stories directly from his parents. He recounts his father telling him about playing a game in a community outside of Chatham where the people were mean, kids were mean. They were cruel. One story, and it's a community that's not that far out of Chatham, heading toward London, they played and they basically, after they had won the game, kids, you know, six and seven years old were spitting at them and throwing rocks at them, encouraged by their parents. To keep your dignity and your pride was difficult.

It wasn't only the All-Stars on the field who were subjected to racist taunts. In interviews from the 1980s, two of the Harding sisters told stories about how they were targeted by local fans when they travelled to support the team. Beulah Harding Cuzzens describes going to Blenheim to watch the All-Stars: "I taught down in Shrewsbury, so I got there a little early and the kids along the road said, 'Well, I see the darkies are arrivin'.' That was me. [laughing] And a little later on our team came along and we were called all the names that they call people in those days. But once in a while we do a little about it." These interviews provide numerous examples of the Harding sisters not only being victims of racism but also doing "a little about it." "We had to fight our way through," Beulah recalls. "We went to the integrated schools, but if you could fight, you got along a little bit better. Not fighting all the time, but just fighting to make them know that you were a person. I didn't do much fighting. I was a young'un. My sister [Georgina] was the fighter . . . She would help us in any of our problems." Wanda Harding Milburn also appears to have been a fighter, as evidenced in a comment she made while interviewing King Terrell. After Terrell talked about the team getting run out of West Lorne, Wanda followed up with this incident:

Inez [Andy Harding's wife] and Joy [Boomer's wife] and I and Olly, Ken's sister, hitchhiked to Bothwell to watch the All-Stars play ball. And some kids were calling us names and throwing apple cores and stones at us. I finally got tired for one and got up and chased the little boy and when I caught him I beat him. And I beat him so hard that they had to stop me. They stopped the ball game and sat me on the bench with the ball players. And they came over behind the bench and started and the ball players ignored it. When I went to get up again, my brother Len slapped me down on the bench and made me sit there. But they chased us out of Bothwell too.

Some of the *Breaking the Colour Barrier* interviewees describe players as well as fans responding directly to acts of overt racism. Pauline Parker Miller, daughter of Happy Parker, recalls that the All-Stars "had a tough time with Tupperville. Because they were really prejudiced. And they called them everything, you know. All the names you could think of. And [Happy Parker] had a time keeping the boys under control. Yeah. Trying to keep the two American boys [Don Washington and Don Tabron] under control . . . Oh yes. And there was always a lot of little fights after a ball game."

Racial taunts were not limited to away games. Occasionally the All-Stars and their fans experienced racist attitudes in their own neighbourhood. Beulah Cuzzens recalls one incident that happened on Scane Street: "I can remember being in Stirling Park one time when I think Aby Scott was up to bat and some little white boy sitting in the stands calling, 'C'mon black boy.' And I remember Duddy Milburn getting up and walking over—Duddy was lame and he had a certain walk—he walked deliberately over to this boy, slapped him in the mouth, walked deliberately back and sat back down." Likely Milburn would not have responded in this way had he not been amongst the East End crowd, where Black fans would have outnumbered white fans.

For the most part, the All-Stars appear to have attempted, as Blake says, to "change hearts and minds" of the Chatham community by hard, tough, skilled, and entertaining baseball. Instances such as those described above, however, suggest that there were times— on the field, in the stands, in the media, and in the other towns and at their home field—where there was a tipping point for the players and fans. As a Black team, the Chatham Coloured All-Stars faced challenges that white teams did not.

The June 4, 1934, game hints at things to come later in the season and beyond, and to the events that led to the teams' demise in 1939. At various times teammates experienced racist verbal and physical abuse at games and were denied food and accommodations while on the road. Many of the players never forgot these incidents, remembering them in vivid and precise detail decades later. Even fifty years later, the memories of these events could still bring a tear to the eye of Ross Talbot.

JULY
1934

IN THE FIRST WEEK OF JULY, THE SUMMER AIR SMELLS
of heat-baked soil and it's easy to imagine the corn growing taller
before your eyes. These long, hot days are occasionally punctuated
by thunderstorms, like the "near-hurricane storm" that cancelled
the All-Stars' first games of July. They did not play until July 9, this
month, giving them a rare lull in their season. The *Chatham Daily
News* still reported on their activities at the ballpark this week, but
as spectators not players. Scurr writes, "Flat Chase and Ross Talbot
were on hand to lend vocal encouragement to the Merchants' cause
on Saturday and Chase claims responsibility for coaching in the four
Chatham runs with oratory from the bench. He was to have lined
up with the Merchants on Saturday but no uniform to fit him could
be found."

At the beginning of July, the All-Stars lead the City League
with an impressive .923 winning percentage with twelve wins and
one loss. In second place were the Braggs with seven wins and seven
losses, the Duns in third with five wins and seven losses, and Kent

Bridge in last with one win and ten losses. Writing about their first game in July, Scurr suggests once more that the All-Stars are the team to beat. "The Duns," he writes, "think that the Stars' winning streak is a little too extended." In other words, July would be an important month for the 1934 Chatham Coloured All-Stars since the games would start to test whether their .923 winning percentage was a fluke or indicative of something larger.

★ ★ ★

If the month's coverage is anything to go by, the All-Stars would have been a fun team to watch. The write-up from their first game in July casts the All-Stars as unstoppable. The headline summarizing the July 10 game reads: "Stars Gain Thirteenth Win: Five Inning Game Goes to Leaders as Duns Collapse: Chase Hurls Three Hit Ball and Stars Pound Four Pitchers." In his "Sport in Short" column, Scurr declares, "The Stars were 'on' last night as they roundly walloped the Duns. Chase was hurling masterful ball all evening and when he wanted to bear down the Duns were practically helpless." Words like "pound," "walloped," and "masterful" pepper the descriptions of the All-Stars in the July 11 sports pages and exude the respect and admiration the team is garnering. Phrases like "collapse" and "practically helpless," used to describe their opponents, set the tone for the month the All-Stars will have in July.

July is also the month where Calder starts to document the strengths of the team and its individual players. Calder's stories offer descriptions of the players' individual skills and their distinctive playing style. We learn how they respond to challenges on the field and, occasionally, off. As the season progresses, Calder crafts an understanding of the All-Stars as athletes and men, not just names on a roster or box score.

On July 13, a *Chatham Daily News* sports page headline nicely summarizes the strengths of this team: "Stars Romp to Victory Against Dresden: Six Runs in Second Frame Aid Chatham Nine's Cause. Terrell Turns in Masterful Job of Relief Pitching, Allowing No Hits in Last Three and One-Third Innings Here." We can start to see all the moving parts that make up this juggernaut. Like all successful baseball teams, the All-Stars had a range of strengths: "What they lacked in fielding finish they made up for in hitting and effective pitching. Tabron started the game on the mound for the Stars and while he was wild, he held Dresden hitless and scoreless for two innings while his mates were scoring seven big runs to give him credit for the win." The story that follows shows the varied tools in the 1934 team's arsenal:

> With three runs in and two men out, King Terrell took over the hurling duties, struck out the last man and allowed neither a hit nor a run for the rest of the game. He struck out four and walked only two in a brilliant exhibition of relief hurling. Only eighteen men faced Tabron and Terrell in the six innings, for the Stars were picking off men right and left from base-paths. Dutch Scott lined up with the Stars for the game and played a big part in their win. He scored the first run after doubling to deep centre field. He pounded in the opening counter in the big push of the second inning with a double to the same spot and scored on Terrell's single. Hits by Harding and Chase and a bit of bad infield judgment brought Terrell and the last-named pair home and Washington stole home to cap the momentous rally.

At their best, the 1934 Chatham Coloured All-Stars have a winning combination of a strong and deep bullpen, solid hitting, smart base-running, and skilled fielding.

Almost certainly the game recaps and summaries don't capture the full excitement the East End would have experienced at these games. But Calder gives us a glimpse of what it must have been like to watch the All-Stars live, and perhaps there was no more exciting prospect in 1934 than to see the incomparable Earl "Flat" Chase in action, in both the batter's box and on the mound.

★ ★ ★

Mention Flat Chase's name anywhere in the East End and you'll still hear stories about him. But outside of Chatham, whenever I've spoken about the 1934 Chatham Coloured All-Stars to baseball historians and Canadian sports history scholars, invariably, someone raises their hand and says, "Why don't we know about him? Why has history forgotten Flat Chase?"

As we've seen, the All-Stars worked to field a more competitive team in 1933 by drawing on regional connections beyond the Chatham-Kent area and "importing" players from outside the county. Importing players as a practice was not always sanctioned, but nevertheless occurred with some frequency. That the Chatham Coloured All-Stars would look towards Windsor and Detroit isn't surprising, given both the established baseball culture in these communities and the tight connections within the Black community in this region. Chase appears to have joined the All-Stars in 1933, shortly after his twentieth birthday. His arrival is announced in the *Chatham Daily News* on August 24, 1933: "Chase, a hurler from Windsor who has been working in the Riverside league, will also play with the Stars." His talent was clear at a young age, and he quickly built a reputation as one of the finest ball players in Southern Ontario.

Born in Buxton in 1913, Chase moved to Windsor with his family while a young child. At the time, the Chases were a considerable presence in Windsor, and the city directories from the early 1930s list numerous families by that name living on and around Mercer Street. Mercer was at the core of the McDougall Street corridor, the centre of Black life in Windsor and that city's equivalent of Chatham's East End. Flat's family lived across the street from Wigle Park, a vibrant community space in this predominantly Black neighbourhood. A park not unlike Stirling, Wigle had a baseball diamond and other recreational facilities. Chase's son Earl Jr recounts that Flat "grew up in the park across the street." At the age of fifteen, Chase was playing baseball for teams such as the Second Baptist Church and the Detroit Church League Champs. Flat Chase not only played against teams from Detroit, he often played with them. Earl Jr says they would "just come over, and they would get him to come play with certain teams on weekends, or if they were in some type of, I don't want to say back in them days you call them a tournament, but they would have games in a different city or different town or something like that. He travelled when he was a teenager, according to the aunts, his sisters." The chance to play as much baseball as he did, and to play in Detroit against a much broader spectrum of players, undoubtedly gave Flat Chase many more opportunities to hone his skills and refine his level of play. In the early 1930s, Chase and Fergie Jenkins Sr both appear in the Windsor newspaper box scores playing for the Windsor Stars, a Black team occasionally called the Coloured Stars.

In 1933, the Chatham All-Stars needed, as Boomer Harding recollects, "a little reinforcement," so Len Harding went to Windsor to scout players. Chase and Jenkins would both come to Chatham, partially for baseball but also for economic reasons. According to Boomer, "Work was kind of scarce in the Windsor district so this is how we got most of our players. Times were tough and they'd play just for a house [or] some place to stay." Chase and Jenkins came to Chatham that way, and both stayed with the Harding family: "Our home was their home. We all lived in a big house in the East End. When the boys come into town there was no accommodations so we always had room for them in the house. They seemed to appreciate it, and they played their ball and finally they'd branch out and get a house or else get a room some place and made Chatham their home for two or three seasons. Some permanently." Chase remained in Chatham from 1933 onward, and Jenkins would come and go depending on the availability of work, but Chatham would eventually become his permanent home.

The newspaper coverage from the 1933 Wanless Trophy series hints at what Chase would offer Chatham throughout his playing career. Coverage of the October 1, 1933, game describes how "Chase was on the mound for the Stars in the first game and the Merchants were unable to do much with the offerings of the Buxton boy, six hits being the sum total collected off him, two of which came in the first frame and two in the last." When the All-Stars won the Wanless Trophy, defeating the Chatham Juniors 5–0 and then 9–6, the *Chatham Daily News* columnist offered this explanation: "It was simply a case of too much Chase, who worked on the mound in both games. This was especially so in the Saturday afternoon tilt, in which Chase allowed the Juniors one lone hit, a single by Kistler in the seventh." In 1934, and beyond, these sorts of stories can be found almost every time Chase plays.

At different points in the season, Calder calls him a "smoke-ball artist of the Chatham Nine," "the speed ball demon," and the "smoke-ball king of the City League." Perhaps the most significant descriptors of Chase for the 1934 season are these: the "mainstay of the All-Stars' pitching staff" and "one of the hardest hitters in amateur ball." Sporadically posted throughout the season, the published City League standings continually list Chase in the top spots for batting and pitching. Using every box score I could locate for the 1934 season, including league play, exhibition games, and playoff games, I have calculated Chase's batting average to be .470 for the 1934 season. Modern pitching statistics like ERAs (earned run averages), wins, saves, and losses were not recorded, and it is difficult to ascertain precisely how many games Chase's pitching won for the All-Stars. One thing that is certain, however, is that much of the success of the 1934 team was reliant upon Chase's abilities to pitch hard throughout the season and his unstoppable, legend-making bat.

Flat Chase was indeed the stuff of legend—as a player, as a batter, as a pitcher, and as a man. This refrain can be found in every retrospective piece about the Chatham Coloured All-Stars and every history of Southwestern Ontario baseball from the 1950s to the present day. Perhaps the most incisive comment about Chase comes from Archie Stirling, who reflected in 1960, that "if Flat Chase were as good [today] as he was when he first came to Chatham, the Detroit team would pay him thirty thousand dollars to sign with them." At the time Stirling made that comment, Major League Baseball had only been integrated for thirteen years. While Stirling could imagine Chase playing for the Detroit Tigers, such a thing would have been impossible and perhaps even unimaginable to Chase himself. In the summer of 1933, it would still be thirteen and a half years before Jackie Robinson and Larry Doby would break the colour barrier and another twenty-five before the Detroit Tigers would sign Ozzie Virgil, their first Black player, in 1958.

Like many of his teammates and baseball players in this era and league, Chase played multiple positions not only throughout the season but also within a single game. The 1934 box scores show some players at one or two positions throughout the season, but Chase can be found everywhere except first base, catcher, left field, and right field. The fact that he did not play these positions is likely not indicative of any limitations but, rather, reflected the reliable availability of Boomer Harding to play first, Washington to catch, and a crew of outfielders at the ready. Routinely, Chase played two or three positions per game. Unlike most other baseball players, then and now, Flat Chase had the rare combination of being a superlative pitcher, a strong consistent hitter, and a formidable base runner—skills he was able to sustain throughout his playing career. The box scores and game recaps help document what Chase contributed to the team game by game. The reflections of his teammates, however, flesh out those statistics and show us exactly what a powerhouse he was. It is in these interviews where we really get to see the reasons why he has become such a legend.

Chase's long-time teammate King Terrell says that he got the nickname Flat because "it looked like he had flat feet. And he could run." Terrell further describes him in this way:

> He was a power hitter. He could hit home runs just about
> as easy as the rest of us could hit singles and doubles and
> triples . . . He was a spray-hitter. That means that you can
> hit a ball in any park over the field. Nine times out of ten
> if he hit a ball south, the ball would be going direct over
> right field because he was a power hitter. A spray-hitter
> means that you can spray a ball in the outfield. Because
> that's when you don't know where it's going to go. He was
> one of those kinds of guys: you didn't know where the ball
> was going to go.

Boomer Harding offered similar reflections about Chase's skill at the plate:

There's no doubt about it . . . he could hit a ball low and he could hit it high . . . there's no weak spot. He could hit the ball where it was pitched. If they thought, well, we'll pitch him outside—he'd hit it hard, he'd hit it out of the park, in left field just as easy as in Stirling which was small. But he'd still hit it further out of the park than a righthand batter would hit it out. So, he was strong in any field and he'd hit it like it was pitched.

Chase was equally strong, though occasionally wild, on the mound. Ben Talbot was not the only one of his former teammates who recalled that no hitter wanted to face him at the plate: "Chase threw the ball so hard some players in the City League didn't want to pinch hit against him." Nor did his teammates want to catch for him. King Terrell remarked, "ask him for a curve and he's liable to throw you a fast ball, which I know all about—his fast balls and his curves— because he darn near killed three of us in one night." Terrell continues:

Donise was catching this night and he asked Flat to throw a pitch. And instead of Flat throwing the pitch he asked for, he threw something else and he bruised Donise Washington's fingers. Donise couldn't catch, so your brother Len took over catching. I'm pretty sure it was Len. Anyway, he ruined Len and Len had to come out of catching. And there was nobody else to catch.

The legend of Chase's skills lives on in the next generation. All of the sons of the players I have talked to can tell you stories about Flat Chase as a baseball player. Fergie Jenkins Jr, who grew up watching Chase play, offers this assessment: "Flat Chase was probably the best pitcher, and the best catcher, and the best hitter of the ball." Donald Tabron Jr, too young to have seen or met Chase, summarizes what his father told him about watching Chase play:

He admired Flat Chase as the best hitter that he ever saw in real life . . . he talked about it just over and over again how he would hit balls and you would just kind of see them go off into the distance and how just a fantastic hitter he was. I've heard many, many stories about that.

Much more could be written about Chase's baseball legacy beyond the All-Stars as he was a strong and highly competitive ball player until his untimely death in 1954. After the All-Stars disbanded, he played for the Taylor ACs, the Chatham Shermans, the Chatham Hadleys, the Arcades, and the Patterson Cars in Chatham. But he also played on teams around the region such as the Windsor City League Champions and the Windsor Stars. In 1939, the *Windsor Daily Star* offers this succinct description of his reputation within the region: "Flat Chase, Chathamite, was not only the leading hitter of the day, but by far the leading fielder of the day and one of the classiest to be seen in these parts in quite some time. He is not only a smart shortstop, but Chatham's leading flinger and to cap his great day, it was he who stemmed an Aylmer rally in the eighth to save the game." In 1944, he played for the London Majors, steering them towards their victory in the Canadian Sandlot Baseball Congress championship. In 1946, Doug Scurr comments that the thirty-three-year-old Chase can "still throw his blazing fast ball and wicked crossfire as well as hold down any position in the infield." The most comprehensive list of teams Chase played on is long and likely incomplete as he played whenever and wherever he could, and, as time passed, increasingly on integrated teams.

The stories about Flat Chase can, at times, border on hyperbole, but at their core is an element of truth. As Boomer Harding said, "Flat is a story in and of himself. He's a legend as far as I'm concerned." Chase's legendary status begins early with stories like the following from Calder in 1935, which has an almost mythical "Casey at the Bat" feel.

Strathroy people will talk for many days of a home run clouted out there on Thursday afternoon by Flat Chase, who deals in home runs and shoe-shines. The particular blow—it was one of two circuit swats made by Chase during the game—travelled over the centerfield fence, it not only travelled, it flew through the stratosphere.

The occasion was the first on which any player had laid the ball over that particular section of the fence in the five-year life of the Strathroy Park. Fans have been waiting for someone to accomplish the feat all during that time and a mighty whoop went up when the ball sped on its way. Only slightly less remarkable was the manner in which the ball bounced when it hit the ground on the opposite side of the wall. Estimates of those who watched were that the height of the bounce was anywhere from fifty to two hundred feet.

The differences of opinion are quite natural for the mighty Chase has caused many baseball followers to go overly eloquent in days gone by. Frank Stover, one of the sponsors of the Stars this year, was eating peanuts when the crash came. Excited, as was everyone else in the stands, he swallowed the shells of four peanuts by mistake. And threw the kernels away.

The most-told stories about Chase are about his home runs. In 1984, fifty years after the All-Stars' victory, Don Tabron recalls, "Every park Chase played in, he had the record for the longest ball hit."

When asked about Flat Chase, many former players tell the story of Welland and his most legendary home run. Boomer Harding recounts how, at every OBA affiliated ballpark,

we'd all look to right field to see how we were going to get along in the long hits because Flat was our power man. There was few parks that he never knocked the ball out of. We were kind of doubtful when we got to Welland because the fence was a good 320 or 330 feet back and [the park] had about an eight foot fence around it. Plus, behind there, there was a big building; a one and a half story building. The first time at bat, Flat proved his power. I was standing on first base and all I did was look. He got hold of it and the ball went over and it was still rising when it was going over.

Boomer calls this home run "one of the greatest moments" and remembers it vividly: "I was on first base when he hit it. The ball not only cleared the right field fence, it cleared a building way behind the fence. People in Welland later said the ball ended up downtown." King Terrell also had vivid memories of this home run: "I remember there was a tree dead center of the baseball diamond and Flat Chase hit a home run that cleared that tree. And we talked to different people there and they had seen baseball games there and said they'd never seen a ball hit that far or that hard in their lives before." Chase's home run wasn't just remembered in Chatham, it retained legendary status in Welland as well.

Boomer Harding remarked in 1978, "If you were in Welland today and told anybody you were from Chatham, the first thing they'd tell you would be about the home run Flat hit there one day." In 1987, Horace Chase confirms Harding's statement, recalling that "one time we went to Welland to see the locks and an old fellow asked me my name. When I told him Chase, he asked me if I was related to Flat Chase. I told the fellow Flat was my dad and he started telling me about the home run Dad hit there one day." He continued, "They put up a marker and we went around to see it. That was really something." Chase repeated his long-ball prowess wherever he played: a newspaper column from 1944 claimed that Flat had, and perhaps still has, the record for hitting the longest ball at Sarnia, Strathroy, Aylmer, Milton, and Welland.

Over time, the stories about Flat Chase started to feel like urban legends, as with this 1967 recollection from All-Stars scorekeeper Orville Wright: "Flat hit [a baseball] in Chatham I don't think they've found yet. It cleared the centre field fence at Stirling Park, went over the trees and houses on Park Street, cleared the road and the houses on the other side and landed in a back yard on Wellington Street." There is even a local legend, believed by many, that Flat Chase caught for Satchel Paige. Horace Chase recounts,

> My dad told me he even caught Satchel Paige down at
> Wigle Park down in Windsor, when Satchel Paige's catcher
> got stuck in the traffic in the tunnel coming over for the

game. The coach went to the other team goes, "Do you have anybody that can catch Satchel Paige," he says, "cause our catcher's stuck and we wanna get the game going." And they looked at Flat and says, "You want to catch him?" He goes, "Yeah, I'll catch him." So, he caught him for six innings, I was told by this gentleman. And there's a write-up in the Windsor paper, and I think that was back in about 1928 or '30, around that. But I couldn't find the article. I went to the *Windsor Star* but I'm not that good with their machines and checking archives to find this kind of stuff.

I have not been able to find this newspaper article nor confirm that Paige was in Detroit or Windsor around this time. However, the specificity of details gives me enough reason to believe there may be something to this story. Regardless of our inability to fully verify it, what is important is that the community believes the story to be true. Moreover, they believe if anyone would be called in to catch for Satchel Paige, it would be none other than Earl "Flat" Chase.

We get a few more details of who Flat Chase was in the newspapers of the 1930s. Sometimes there are mentions of Chase's showmanship, such as his doing "something of a rumba" when he steps up to the plate or step-dancing in post-game celebrations "with the same effect he employs when throwing them 'down the alley.'" Or this story from the playoffs of October 1934 of how he got Pete Gilbert's coat:

Flat was without a jacket after he had warmed up prior to the game. [Team backer] Pete [Gilbert] loaned him his coat and when it fit said he would give it to Flat if Chatham won the game. "That's my coat," Flat was heard to remark after he walked out to the mound for the opening pitch. When the game had ended, Penetang was defeated and Flat had a new coat.

These passing mentions in print and the brief recollections of the team's off-the-field antics corroborate what everyone who knew the

1934 All-Stars said: these players were young men playing the game they loved and having the time of their lives.

Chase married Julia Black at the end of the 1934 season and they would soon have four children. Baseball wasn't Chase's entire life, but it came close. Horace Chase summarizes his father's life in this way: "Go play ball, go to work, look after us." Reflecting on the role of baseball in his father's life, Horace says, "I think that was his only thing, was to play ball. Live to play ball, eat, sleep, and enjoy life. Horace further describes the centrality of baseball in his family:

> My dad was like a supervisor for the city [in the sanitation department], he had about three or four guys who worked for him. And my mother was a stay-at-home mom, because they had four children in five years, so that kept her busy looking after them. She worked a little bit at the little bean factory, a little part-time, helping out on weekends when they needed it. Then, most of the time my dad actually played ball, tell you the truth, his love of the game was phenomenal because that was his sport. In fact, when all four of us children was born, he wasn't there for the birth, he was playing ball. That's how much he played.

Unlike the Hardings, who pursued a range of sports, the Chases were a baseball family: "We weren't what you'd call a much outside baseball family," says Horace. "We liked our baseball."

In speaking with Earl Jr and Horace, it's clear that baseball played a major part in the way that Flat Chase connected with his sons. Horace recalls, "If we had a game he'd come out to the game there and he'd cheer for us. I remember once that I was pitching against my brother, and he was behind the backstop and I was trying to figure out who's he gonna cheer for? My team, or my brother's team? He was cheering for both teams every inning." Horace describes how his father was

> always talking to my brother, Earl, and myself about sports
> . . . he always told us when we got out on that field, he says,

"Do this, do that, play this, watch this, watch that." He could coach us from the sidelines or at home, and tell us how to play the game ... And I really, I grew from watching them ... I might ask my dad, I said, "Why is so-and-so doing this, why is so-and-so doing that?" He says, "Because of this, you do that because of that, you cover this man, whenever the ball's hit everyone moves. In the infield, whether it's hit to you or not, you go for cover, to a base, everything." And when I managed, I taught my team the same thing. When the ball's hit, everybody's got a position to move to. You gotta cover. That was the main issue he always used to tell me.

In 1954, Flat Chase died suddenly when Horace and Earl were still young men, and baseball seems to be one of the ways they carried on their father's legacy. Earl Chase Jr recalls that his father "got a job working for the City [of Chatham], and that way he could get time off so he could go play ball, stuff like that. He was working with the City until '54. When he passed away, I took his spot. The City hired me and I come in and took his spot, needed a job, so I was there from '54 to '92. I left out of there in '92 and I'm sitting here looking at you in 2016, and still playing ball!" When I talked with Earl in the summer of 2020, he sheepishly admitted that he'd just retired from baseball at the age of eighty-five. When he said that, Earl's wife, Shyla, caught my eye from across the room and gave me a look that seemed somewhere between relief and incredulity.

Most of the discussions Earl and Horace had with their father about baseball seemed to have been about the nuances of the game on the field and not what happened off of it. As Horace describes, "When I played ball he'd come to the game and he'd tell me what I'd done wrong. How to pitch, where to throw, and things like that. Teaching me the game, but not so much about his history of his life." When asked if his father ever talked about racial hardships or struggles, Horace replied that his dad "didn't do a whole lot of talking about things like that. No, if he did he might have talked with my mom about it, but like I say, when you're a little kid you don't get into adult conversations. So, no, I don't remember him talking about something like that."

Later in our interview, Horace vaguely recalled a few stories his father told:

> I think he mentioned one time they had a problem with accommodation, getting food, and I think Happy Parker had to go into the restaurant at the back, and the people at the back, I think the cooks, they were Black, and sent them sandwiches out to the guys on the bus to eat, for their lunch, to get something to eat because they couldn't go into the restaurant. And I think he just talked about that once, and I can't remember where it was, but I know that it happened like that.

Aside from these few vague comments, Horace observes that his father "didn't get into too much of that because I think he loved the game too much, that he just had to put up with it. It was a way of life, so we had to put up with it." Further, he never talked about "the Black community and sports, how it affected people. He just went out and played the game, and enjoyed the game. We never sit and talked, and he never said, 'Well you can't do this because you're Black, or you can't do that because it's just for the whites.' He'd just go on out there and do the best you can, whatever sports you're in." Just as Jennifer Miss said her parents shielded her from some of what had happened, it appears that Flat and Julia Chase also tried to protect their children. And understandably so.

One afternoon in February 2020, after spending several hours vigilantly watching me digitize his family's scrapbook at the Chatham-Kent Black Historical Society's Black Mecca Museum, Earl suggested he and I go for lunch. We ended up at a restaurant in what was once part of the Merrill Hotel, constructed around 1903, not far from the East End, but across the tracks. We talked through lunch about baseball, the Chase family's long history, and how his mother could trace her lineage to the brother of Robert E. Lee. The lunch crowd had dispersed as Earl Chase Jr talked about his parents and growing up in their house. At one point he said, "They only talked about the good times. Only the good times." He ended his sentence with a thoughtful silence that seemed to echo through the empty hotel dining room, and I followed his gaze out the window.

Although Horace and Earl have only hazy recollections of their father talking about the colour line, it is highly unlikely that Flat Chase didn't think about it. Chase turned thirty-four in 1947, the year Jackie Robinson would break the colour barrier. Too old, in all likelihood, for him to try to make it in the Majors, but Jackie Robinson's signing must have offered hope that his sons might have opportunities denied to him. Horace Chase recalls,

> we were so happy in '47 when Jackie Robinson broke the colour barrier. But like I say, that was about seven years before my dad died. That all happened, and it was quite a thing. But Dad admired him and I told him, "I want to be like Jackie Robinson when I grow up. I want to play second base." He says, "You watch how he plays it, swing and everything else." So, we all kind of started to model ourselves after different guys on the team that we'd seen play.

As it happens, neither Horace nor Earl made it to MLB, but both played baseball throughout their lives, as their father likely would have done as well. One son of the 1934 team, however, did make it to the major leagues. And he did it like no other Canadian had done before.

In the box scores for the All-Stars exhibition game against Dresden on July 11, 1934, a Jenkins appears on the All-Stars roster. This Jenkins is almost certainly Ferguson Jenkins, who would officially join the team in 1935. Better known as Fergie, he was born in 1909 to Joseph Jenkins and Gertrude Holmes in Windsor. Jenkins, like Chase, grew up in the McDougall Street corridor playing baseball in Windsor and Detroit. As many of the players recall, it was Chase who suggested the Stars round out their roster, initially with Jenkins, and later Tabron and Washington. In his interview with Milburn and Chavis, Jenkins recalls that he came to Chatham in the winter of 1933 to play ball. When Chavis asks, "Why did you come in the winter? Did they scout you?" Jenkins responds, "Oh yes, well you had to . . . with being an amateur ball player, . . . your name had to be on the contract with the rest of the ball players in the district and that's the only way." Prior to coming to Chatham, Jenkins worked as a cook on Great Lakes freighters, occasionally out of Windsor. After moving to Chatham, he became a chef at the William Pitt Hotel, where many of his teammates also worked. Later he also worked as a chef and chauffeur for the Houston family, who owned a sugar factory in Chatham. As he recalls, "It was the greatest thing that ever happened to me coming to Chatham. I didn't realize it until about three days after I was here." Jenkins's recollections of coming to Chatham are filled with memories of the warm community, especially the Harding family: "I had relations here I hadn't seen in years so, but I didn't even know. And everybody was calling me Cousie, that's how I got that Cousie business, calling everybody cousin . . . And I stayed, I met the Harding family, which was outstanding." It was there Fergie met his wife, Delores Jackson of Chatham, who was a descendant of the freedom seekers who came to Canada via the Underground Railroad, and they were married in September 1937.

Although Jenkins appears sporadically in the box scores in 1934, playing only nine games in July and August, he became a more consistent member of the All-Stars lineup in 1935. Fergie Jenkins Jr notes, "My dad was a centre fielder. He's left-handed. He hit left-handed, threw left-handed. I think he had pretty good speed. He could catch the ball. He always told me that he was a good out-fielder when I was growing up." Boomer Harding describes Fergie as a player "that could get on base" and a "very good base runner." Harding recalls Jenkins "was a left-hand batter and any pitcher that was throwing him a curved drop always hit Fergie on the toe. This way, he was a sure base runner. If there's a record kept he would have had it by getting hit on the foot or the leg and wobbling down to first base." King Terrell conjures up a similar version of Jenkins: "Say we were in the ninth inning, or something like that, and we needed a run or something to get somebody on base—I can just see it like it happened—that Fergie would come to bat. And if he didn't hit the ball, he got on base anyway by being hit by the baseball. And then we always had somebody to bring him around." Terrell continues, "Fergie was a good old player ... I've seen him catch balls out in the outfield that you'd swear up and down that he would never even get close to. He would dive and catch balls, and catch balls over his head, and all kinds of things. He was good." In his conversations with Wanda Harding Milburn, Terrell comments, "He could've been in the Major Leagues," to which Milburn responds, "Well, his son did make it." The son Milburn mentions is none other than Ferguson—or Fergie—Jenkins Jr, who was born in December 1942.

Around the time of his son's birth, Ferguson Sr was working as a chef at the Montreal Hotel and the family lived at 221 Colborne Street. As anyone in Chatham will proudly tell you, Fergie Jenkins Jr would go on to play major league baseball and become the first Canadian player elected into the Baseball Hall of Fame in Cooperstown, New York, in 1991, for his stellar pitching career. Over his nineteen-year career in the major leagues, most of which was with the Chicago Cubs, Jenkins pitched 664 games and 267 complete games. He accrued 284 wins and 226 losses, with a 3.34 ERA, and 3,192 strikeouts. In addition to making three All-Star teams (1967, 1971, and 1972), he won the National League Cy Young Award in 1971.

Until fairly recently, most mentions of Fergie Jenkins Jr's family would describe how Ferguson Sr would follow Fergie's career in great detail and attend his son's games with Delores, who had gone blind years before, listening to the games on a portable radio so she could follow along. More recently, however, it is also mentioned that Jenkins Sr also played baseball for the Chatham Coloured All-Stars and was a talented player in his own right. In addition to any natural talent Fergie Jr might have inherited from his father, growing up watching the former All-Stars playing in the 1940s might also have shaped his career.

Stirling Park was an important place to Fergie Jenkins Jr. He recalls listening to his father reminisce "a lot of times about Stirling

Park . . . And I've played some baseball there myself. But my dad used to reminisce about playing centre field there in Chatham." Jenkins Jr's contemporary Dorothy Wright Wallace cites the existence of Stirling Park as one of the key factors in his success: "As far as I'm concerned, Fergie Jenkins should be very much thankful to Mr Stirling. Because he had that mound over there that was two or three doors down from where he lived and he could throw that ball and practice and practice and practice. And you see where it got him." Jenkins Jr mentions several times that his father never pushed him into baseball; his passion for baseball was supported and encouraged by his father: "My dad, basically was just a hard-working individual, worked for the Houston family, and he worked, as I said, for the William Pitt Hotel, and later on the Holiday Inn. And he just made sure—I was an only son, only child—he made sure I got all the right equipment, if it was hockey, or basketball, or baseball." Jenkins Jr recalls, "He didn't push me into the sport, but he just said, 'Hey, I'm gonna get you the right equipment.' He would say that all the time. 'What you need, let me know. I'll get it for you.' Which really worked out well." Jenkins Jr's comment that things "really worked out well," is, of course, an understatement. In 2016, Andy Harding's daughter Tracey told us her father "was best friends with Fergie Jenkins Sr, so he spent a lot of time following Fergie's career. That was very important to him." All the interviews done with All-Stars players in the 1970s and 1980s reveal a tremendous pride in Fergie Jenkins Jr's successes in the major leagues. That pride is still strong in Chatham today.

As we've seen with Blake Harding, Earl Chase Jr, and Horace Chase, and will see again with Donald Tabron, sports were one of the important connections Fergie Jr had with his father: "He'd seen me as an individual, and I wanted to be a professional athlete . . . He encouraged me to do the best I could, and I think this is the reason why I wanted to be such a good athlete, because I got the encouragement from my father." Undoubtedly, the community support of baseball, particularly Black baseball in Chatham's East End, was influential on the young Fergie Jenkins growing up in the 1940s and 1950s as local teams became increasingly integrated. Equally important would be the larger shifts happening in Major League Baseball at this time.

★ ★ ★

Fergie Jenkins Jr was four years old when Jackie Robinson and Larry Doby broke the colour barrier. Unlike his father and the rest of the All-Stars, Jenkins Jr grew up seeing players who looked like him playing major league ball. Moreover, he would have seen from a very early age that a career in the MLB was a possibility, something none of his father's teammates would have had growing up.

Chatham's proximity to Detroit allowed opportunities for Fergie Sr to take young Fergie Jr to see professional baseball up close at Briggs Stadium, where the Tigers played. Significantly, Fergie Jr grew up seeing men of African descent playing in a major league ballpark. This proximity to Detroit and the efforts of both of his parents to get him to games enabled Jenkins Jr to see Larry Doby and Satchel Paige, who were both playing for the visiting Cleveland team, in person. As Jenkins Sr recounts to Wanda Milburn:

> Fergie's seen Larry Doby bring him the ball ... when I
> started working for Miss Houston and he was about six, I
> was down at Russell Woods, that's down near Windsor.
> And Delores would put him on the railway, on the train
> with a ticket on him and she'd call me up when they left,
> when the train left, and the conductor would put him off
> in Belle River. And I'd pick him up and we'd go to Detroit.
> And he had a little crazy glove on [laughs] and he was
> dressed the whole bit. The short pants and he saw Larry
> Doby and 'oh!' and Satchel Paige too, they were on the team
> ... we had box seats and he could see them you know. And
> he 'oh!' I couldn't keep him off the playing field ...

Not surprisingly, both Jenkinses talk about legends like Jackie Robinson, Larry Doby, and Satchel Paige in a range of interviews. Jenkins Jr told me that when his father worked as a chef and chauffeur for the Houston family, the family and their staff would often go to Florida, where Jenkins Sr was able to see Jackie Robinson play in Vero Beach. In his 2022 interview with filmmaker LeSean Harris, Jenkins Jr recounts his father taking him to see the Tigers at Briggs Stadium and seeing Larry Doby hit two home runs: "The crowd cheered for him. I said to my dad, 'Dad, maybe I want to play baseball.'"

In his conversation with Wanda Milburn, they both describe the impact of seeing the colour barrier breaking down in baseball. When Milburn observes, "There was a future in baseball for coloured players. But in the other sports there didn't seem to be too much at that time," Jenkins agrees, noting, "Football came on later. And just like ... it was the greatest thing ever happened, you know .. . if you have a quality Negro player playing on a team, the people go see the Negros play. I don't know, and that was outstanding."

In spite of Jenkins Sr clearly seeing the injustices surrounding the colour barrier in sport, Jenkins Jr does not recall his father talking about the hardships he faced. In his interview with me, Jenkins Jr's comments are remarkably similar to those expressed in interviews with the other players' children. When I asked if his father ever talked about any challenges or difficulties playing ball, either in the community, or elsewhere, Jenkins Jr replied, "Ooh, not really, no he didn't bring that up." Still, when sportswriter Jordan Bastian spoke to then seventy-seven-year-old Jenkins about the seventy-third anniversary of Jackie Robinson breaking the colour barrier, Jenkins makes connections with his father. Whenever Jenkins Jr heard a slur or saw an act of hatred, his father's voice would come to him: "He would tell me, 'Son, if you're going to be a professional athlete, you've got to carry yourself as a professional. A lot of times, you just can't strike back. You've just got to hang in there,' which a lot of times I did." In this memory, Jenkins echoes what Blake Harding said about the lessons he learned from Jackie Robinson as well as from his father and his uncles.

Later in the same interview, looking back over his own legendary career, Jenkins Jr circles back to his beginnings in Chatham and to his family:

Five generations of Canadians in my family. Back from the
1800s . . . After I came back and now I'm in the big leagues,
I was starting to see all these different celebrations they
were having for all these different athletes and where they
came from, and then that really struck home with me. Who
I was. Where I came from. And my parents had to struggle.
I don't think I had that much struggle. I didn't suffer a lot
of abuse. I was very fortunate when I came up through
baseball.

Even so, in his interview with LeSean Harris, Jenkins Jr recounts
that when he signed with the Phillies in 1962, he and the other players of colour were still encountering some of what his father and his
teammates encountered on the road. He recalls how when he went
to Miami, Florida, as a minor leaguer there were still places where
he and the other players of colour couldn't go: "we couldn't go to
Miami Beach, we couldn't eat in certain restaurants. We used always
to eat late after ballgames in a Trailways bus station . . . On the
road, we couldn't stay with the white players. They'd drop us off at a
small hotel outside of town." Jenkins mentions that sometimes he
and the other players of colour were housed in unusual places: "We
stayed at a brothel, we stayed at a funeral home." Stories like Jenkins
Jr's are constant reminders that though the official colour barrier in
professional sports had technically been "broken" in 1947, significant
barriers and limitations still existed and, indeed, continue to exist.

In his Baseball Hall of Fame Induction Ceremony speech,
Fergie Jenkins Jr shows the difference a single generation made, as
he movingly shares this tremendous honour with his father:

My father played baseball from 1925 to the 1940s in
the Ontario baseball league . . . His opportunity to
play professional ball was limited by the history of that
era. Fortunately, he outlived history and witnessed this
change. His sacrifice in baseball has been my reward by my
achievements. This day belongs also to my father. He was
my first teacher. He inspired me. He was a great outfielder.

He was known as Hershey. It was my father who taught me
to be conscientious and responsible. It was my father who
instilled a love of baseball in me. So, on this day, I am not
only being inducted alone, I am being inducted, on July 21,
1991, with my father, Fergie Jenkins Sr. Hershey.

The video footage of the speech shows Fergie Jenkins Sr retrieving a
handkerchief from his pocket and wiping away a tear. It is difficult
to watch this speech and Jenkins Sr's reaction to it and not think of
the other players who were also, as Jenkins Jr says, "limited by the
history of that era."

Juxtaposing Fergie Jenkins Jr's baseball career with those of
players like Earl Chase, King Terrell, Boomer Harding, and count-
less others, it is tempting to imagine what baseball history as well as
their own personal histories might have looked like if they had been
given a chance to play in the major leagues.

★ ★ ★

Leading up to the league playoffs in August, much of July's coverage
of the All-Stars' game is akin to this section from the July 21, 1934,
Chatham Daily News, which highlights the type of fast, skilled, and
exciting baseball the All-Stars provided. Calder's own excitement
comes through in his prose:

A trio of extra-base hits and an error in the first inning gave
Chatham Stars a four-run lead and from that point they
proceeded to shut out Blenheim intermediates at Stirling
Park last evening in a six-inning exhibition game, the final
score standing at 6–0. Flat Chase scattered four hits and
four walks over the rout and was scarcely ever in danger.
Smart base-running and good fielding played big parts in
the Stars' victory but Chase's hurling was the real feature
as he fanned nine men in the six frames and three of them
in a row in the fourth . . . Len Harding opened the game
with a bounder down the third base line that hopped away
from McPherson's glove for a two-base error. King Terrell

brought him in with a ground hit–triple which bounded off
the fence in left. Terrell remained on third when Boomer
Harding grounded out but Chase's double allowed him
to trot home putting the Stars two up. Another error by
McPherson after Washington had grounded out brought
Chase home with the third run and Ross Talbot's mighty
drive over the left field fence produced the fourth counter
... In their half of the sixth the Stars showed a bit of good
base running that brought them two runs. Boomer Harding,
first up, doubled. Chase hit to Gray at short who tried
to throw out Harding going into third. Ayres ran down
to third from the place to take part in the run-down, but
Harding slid into him to knock the ball out of his hand
and reach third safely. Chase took second on the play. As
Ayres turned to toss the ball to Phair, Harding hit out for
home and reached it easily. Chase scored from third when
Ayres tossed the ball away returning it to the pitcher a few
moments later.

We can see why the Stars are 15–1: the team possesses multiple
strengths and contributions are made by almost all the players on
the roster. Virtually any championship baseball team must have the
right combination of hitting, pitching, and fielding, and the All-
Stars had it all.

By July 21, though the All-Stars' official record is 15–1, if their
exhibition games are included, their complete record from May to
the end of July is twenty-one wins, two losses, one tie, and one nullified victory, for a .913 winning percentage. The exhibition games are
particularly important to consider because more often than not these
are the games from which we get a fuller picture of the depth of the
All-Stars' skills and a more complete sense of the strengths of the
team than their four-team City League season conveys. Exhibition
games were often played against more competitive or challenging
teams, like Walpole Island or, as we'll see in August, the Taylor's
Stars of Detroit. In their 5–3 win against Walpole Island on July 18,
1934, we see two more evenly matched teams:

King Terrell and Shognosh hooked up in a stirring battle
on the mound that saw honors about evenly divided. The
Stars scored in each of the first and third innings, their runs
coming mainly as a result of bases on balls. In the fourth
the game rout gave the visitors a tally and a walk, an error
and a single enabled them to draw up on even terms with
the Stars in the fifth. Terrell drove his home run with one
out in the fifth and then, with Boomer Harding on first as
the result of an error, Chase drove out his.

As of July 23, 1934, statistics in the *Chatham Daily News* for the City
Baseball League reveal five of the top eleven batters are All-Stars:
Chase (.525), Olbey (.379), Len Harding (.351), Washington (.350),
and Boomer Harding (.350). Reporting on the league's pitchers' wins
and losses, three of the top five are All-Stars: Chase 7–0, Terrell 4–0,
and Talbot 3–1. Yet while the team does seem to be coming together
in important ways, a close look at the box scores later in the summer
reveals still other factors worth noting.

July and August's box scores show significant absences of key
players for weeks or even months. Fergie Jenkins Sr, as noted earlier,
appears on the roster sporadically over the summer months and then
disappears entirely after September 15. Gouy Ladd only plays one
game between June 30 and August 30, and Ross Talbot is absent
from the roster between July 12 and September 3. It's easy to overlook
these roster changes on a game-by-game basis, but taken collectively they reveal important things about the economic realities players navigated. In her interview with King Terrell, Wanda Harding
Milburn makes this clear when she asks if "the reason why you had
so many imports and local boys at the time too was because nobody
really had a steady job?" When Terrell responds, "That's right, yeah,"
Milburn wonders aloud, "Maybe the reason why they missed some
ball games is because if they had a day's work, they had to work." Just
as the team's roster benefitted from having under-employed players,
it also suffered when players needed to travel or move for work.

In spite of their ever-changing roster, Calder's coverage suggests that the All-Stars are really coming together as a team. "The

Stars," he observes, "are drawing big crowds because they are playing together constantly and are a well-knit machine." Under a heading that reads "Chatham's Most Ambitious Team," Calder also corroborates what our interviewees told us about the team's competitiveness and work ethic:

> It's a wonder Chatham Stars, leaders of the City League, aren't all hobbling on crutches with charley horses that whinny pretty loudly. For if ever there was an amateur team that loved to play ball and play ball and then go out and toss the ball around a bit for fun it's this same Stars aggregation. A week isn't a week to them if they don't play five games. Up and down and around the country they go and everywhere they draw big crowds. They're an attraction and they should be. They're a good ball team—a team that's trying all the time and throwing as much colour into the game as possible. Those qualities are necessary to an outfit that's going to break even in these days of strain and stress.

As the subsequent weeks prove, the All-Stars are not a team to break under the strain and stress of an intense playing schedule. If anything, they seem to build an even stronger momentum.

As August approaches, the financial situation of the City League begins to have an impact on how the league thinks about the playoffs, or, as Calder mostly calls them, playdowns. On July 28, 1934, the *Chatham Daily News* announces that

> there will be a meeting of the executive and team managers of the City Baseball League at Stirling's store Monday evening following the scheduled game. Considerable business of importance is due to be discussed and all concerned are asked to be on hand ... The City Baseball League playoffs are soon to be arranged and a winner determined to enter further play in the OBAA. The schedule may have to be cut short for attendances and collections are falling and the league cannot afford to

go behind much further. There should be a pick-up in
attendances when play-off time arrives.

On July 31, the results of that meeting are reported in Scurr's column: "At a meeting of the City Baseball League team managers last
night it was decided to continue the series until either the Braggs or
the Duns have been eliminated. The team which emerges will play
the Stars in a three-out-of-five series for the championship and the
right to continue in the OBAA." A few columns over on the same
page, Calder writes, "The League is in financial straits and needs the
aid of all fans who can attend the games. Tonight's will be a hotly
contested affair and all who are able to be present should watch the
Duns struggle to reach a playoff berth." Without losing a game since
early June, the Stars end July knowing they will be contenders for
the Wanless Trophy, the City League championship. Further, going
on to the OBAA playoffs is a very distinct possibility. Since the
viability of the league is at stake if fans do not attend these games,
it makes a lot of sense that Calder and Scurr tempt fans with the
promise of good baseball.

Given Calder and Scurr's loaded enticements, it's easy to dis-
miss the advertisements and write-ups about the Stars' exhibition
games over the August Civic Holiday weekend. However, these are
exhibition games and attendance only benefits the two teams playing, doing nothing for the ailing City League. In this way, Calder's
promise of great baseball appears a little more sincere. August will
prove Calder correct.

AUGUST

1934

AUGUST IN SOUTHWESTERN ONTARIO IS SULTRY, THE
air humid and heavy. These are the dog days of summer and of the
baseball season, when both seem never-ending. On August 1, 1934,
just down the road, the Detroit Tigers were narrowing in on their
post-season hopes with a 60–37 record; they ended August leading
the American League with eighty-three wins and forty-three losses.
Meanwhile in Chatham, *Chatham Daily News* sports editor William
Scurr wrote in his "Sport in Short" column, "The Stars should be
tuckered by the time they get through their game with Braggs
tomorrow evening. Four games in three days is a grind. The team
has a reliable hurling staff now however in Chase, Talbot, Terrell and
Tabron." If Scurr thought they should have been tuckered out by the
first of the month, by month's end they should have been exhausted,
playing at least fourteen games over August. But they were not. By
August 31, the All-Stars seem unstoppable as they look towards the
OBAA playoffs set to start on September 6.

From our vantage point, the All-Stars going onto the OBAA playoffs seems like a foregone conclusion. But, as Calder reminds us, at the beginning of August the All-Stars still have a lot of baseball to play: "Optimistic supporters are calling them to win an OBAA title but the Stars realize they've got to hurdle a lot of good teams— including the Braggs—before that goal is reached. Still, it's possible." In baseball, every month is a long month and nothing is ever certain.

As the regular season began to wind down, the team looked towards the City League playdowns as a way of making it to the OBAA championship series. They solidified their lineup, worked on weaknesses in their play, and navigated a range of obstacles encountered on and off the field. If the season's early months of May, June, and July were for exploring their potential, August was where that potential was tested and measured. Through their wide range of games—from league play to exhibition battles—we learn more about baseball culture in this corner of Southwestern Ontario. We also gain more insight into what it meant to be a Black team in Canada in the 1930s.

As of August 1, the Stars' winning record assured them of a spot in the league championship. All that needed to be determined was who they would play. As the *Chatham Daily News* reported, "After being held scoreless before Archie Stirling's [Jr] slants for the first two innings, the Stars found the Duns' good young left hander for six runs in the third inning and proceeded to take a 12–6 decision from the league's third place team last evening. The result of the game all but finishes the chances of the Duns to reach the playoffs and if they are beaten in one more game the Braggs and Stars will automatically go into the final round for the league title." The "Sport in Short" column noted, "The Stars were not at full strength for last night's encounter but they fielded some capable reserves. The regulars who live in the country were not able to be in town for the game last evening." Names we haven't seen on the roster before like Browning (second base), Morton (left field), and Parker (right field) rounded out the roster alongside Terrell, Boomer Harding, Chase, Washington, Tabron, and Jenkins. In August, some of the regular players were absent from the roster, likely away for seasonal agricultural work.

The Stars emerged as a team willing to play anytime and anywhere they could. The August 9 *Chatham Daily News* carried a story about the West Lorne team getting caught up in some league complications and the All-Stars being asked to fill in for a tournament at the last moment:

> Thus when, at about one o'clock yesterday, local baseball
> officials were certain that West Lorne was not going to
> be on hand, they got in touch with the All-Stars of the
> Chatham City League, who, even at that late hour said that
> they would be only too glad to gather up a team and give
> the spectators their money's worth ... had the All-Stars
> known sooner that they were going to play here yesterday
> they could have come better prepared and even as it was
> they were forced to play without King Terrell, Talbot,
> "Boomer" Harding and others.

A few days later, William Scurr wrote, "The Stars don't mind playing ball day after day. Right in playoff time they play four games in four days. Monday and Tuesday of this week they played Walpole Island and are meeting the same team again at Kent Bridge today. Tomorrow they resume their series with the Braggs for the right to enter the OBAA playdowns."

"The Stars," he continued, "are in constant demand in all parts of the district because they're so good a drawing card. Happy Parker, manager of the team, says he's soon going to restrict the Stars to about two games a week so they'll be ready for OBAA Playdowns." As the playoffs drew near, the Stars became the team to stop, by whatever means.

In addition to their City League games, the Stars played a range of other regional teams in August, including teams from Detroit, Wheatley, Blenheim, Walpole Island, Tilbury, and the Delaware Nation at Moraviantown. These "barnstorming"—or exhibition— games were vital to the development, maintenance, and success of the team. The August 13 advertisement in the *Chatham Daily News* for the Kent Bridge tournament on August 15 lists a twenty-five-cent ticket price (though ladies are free), which is a higher admission than the usual OBAA games, which are listed as five or ten cents. The higher ticket price is probably because "the winners play for a cash prize," adding a financial incentive for a victory and the promise of strong, competitive baseball. It is not clear from the extant coverage who won this tournament; it is known the All-Stars won two of their three games, but no score can be found for their third scheduled game against Walpole Island.

Exhibition games, such as the Kent Bridge tournament, were one certain way teams could generate income, and there was a significant incentive to play strong, entertaining baseball. The better they played, the bigger the crowd, and the better the gate revenue. Aside from the financial benefits, barnstorming also allowed the All-Stars opportunities to test and show their mettle against different and, in many cases, stronger teams. Barnstorming also took them into different communities and had them playing in front of new crowds. These new crowds would present some challenges for the team in the coming weeks.

The All-Stars' first game of August was a doubleheader against the Taylor's Stars of Detroit, as part of Emancipation Day celebrations. That the Chatham Coloured All-Stars were part of events that celebrated the talents of people of African descent in this region was not accidental, given they were the pride of the neighbourhood. In both 1933 and 1934, the Emancipation Day celebrations included a two-game exhibition series in Chatham between the Taylor's Stars of Detroit and the All-Stars. In August 1933, the Taylor's Stars were "considered one of the best teams in its class" and in 1934, the All-Stars split the series before "the largest crowd to watch a baseball game here this year." Anticipating the series, Calder writes, "Two fast affairs are assured Chatham fans ... The Stars are fresh from a string of victories in exhibition and the Motor City nine will have to play thoroughly good ball to pull out with a victory in either of tomorrow's games." Elsewhere on the page, Calder anticipates the games will "be a superlative sort" since the visiting team is "the best of Detroit's amateur clubs and the Stars are the best coloured team in Canada."If the box scores and game recaps of the Chatham-Detroit games are any indication, this was indeed some of the best baseball the region could witness. Calder's unproven claim that the All-Stars are the best Black team in the nation is almost certainly something he wrote to entice fans. But this statement is important because it is the first overt mention of the All-Stars' race I have found in Calder's 1934 baseball coverage, most likely because the games are part of the Emancipation Day celebrations.

These celebrations were what historian Natasha Henry calls, "the most anticipated days of the year for Black Canadians." Commemorating the end of slavery in the British Empire on August 1, 1833, these day-long or weekend events featured parades, speeches, lunches, banquets, balls, concerts, church services, and, of course, baseball. As we've seen, baseball was frequently part of gatherings in Black communities, but nowhere was this truer than during Emancipation Day. In the 1930s, Chatham had a full slate of Emancipation Day activities. A *Chatham Daily News* story from August 2, 1932, describes how Emancipation Day events were held in the East End "on the spacious grounds of the Woodstock School on King Street East and in Stirling Park."The amount of press given to these celebrations suggests that some white residents took part in the festivities. For Black communities across Southwestern Ontario, Emancipation Day was an occasion to bring the region's people of colour together, strengthening the connections between and within Black communities.

Emancipation Day in Chatham was a day that marked and celebrated the abolition of slavery, but, perhaps more important, it was also an occasion to mark, share, and celebrate the talents, skills, and strengths of regional community members as well as the accomplishments of renowned people of colour. Some parts of the festivities, like displays set up at the Woodstock School grounds in 1932, were overt in their intention to demonstrate "the progress and achievements of the coloured people" by highlighting "the proficiency attained by men in the various trades" and the "adeptness" of women's needlework and fancy work. Other parts highlighted athletic skills and other aptitudes and talents. Coverage from 1932 provides the winners of various contest like foot races for boys, girls, married men, married women, and "fat men"; boys' standing broad jump competition; and a mother and daughters needle race. The "interesting typewriting contest" was won by a Miss Williams. In the evening, an arts program at the Woodstock School featured solos, quartettes, and dialogues. Emancipation Day celebrated and documented the various contributions, skills, talents, and accomplishments of people of colour within the neighbourhood and globally and put them on display for the broader Chatham community.

Emancipation Day was also something noted, if not celebrated, by the white residents of Chatham. In the first week of August 1933, the hundredth anniversary of the abolition of slavery within the British colonies, the paper describes an event where a white man lectured about emancipation to a group of other white men. Regional historian O.K. Watson "delivered an intensely interesting, entertaining, and instructive address to the Chatham Rotary Club," revealing a "deep fund of knowledge regarding the progress of the abolition of slavery, not only on this continent and in the British Isles, but in other countries of the world." When focused on abolition, Emancipation can be read as the event that completes a chapter in the history of people of African descent, rather than part of an ongoing story with long, lingering impacts within the Black community. Whether the all-white Rotary Club of Chatham made connections between Watson's mention of British abolitionist Thomas Fowell Buxton (1786–1845) and the settlement bearing his name established by and for formerly enslaved people fifteen kilometres away from Chatham or between the lecture and the lives of the descendants of formerly enslaved people living across the tracks in the East End are certainly matters for conjecture.

Lectures to Chatham service clubs were also part of the 1934 Emancipation Day celebrations, but this year they were provided by a Black man, the Reverend Dr W. Constantine Perry of the Campbell AME Church. He addressed the Kiwanis Club on July 31 and the Chatham Rotary Club on August 1 on the topic of "Negroes' contributions to world civilization since Emancipation." The August 1 edition of the *Chatham Daily News* offers this summary of Reverend Dr Perry's talk to the Kiwanis Club:

> Contributions of the negro race to culture, science, music, art, and religion have been outstanding and have proven their ability, intellectually, spiritually, and physically . . . Coloured men have taken their place in all spheres of life, said the speaker. He pointed out that they had fought side by side with white men in defense of their country during the Great War, and declared, just as emphatically, they would do so again.

On a different page, another article about Reverend Dr Perry comments that "the freeing of the negroes from the bonds of slavery in the southern United States is remembered by few of the negroes in the Kent settlements, although they are direct offspring of the Canadian terminal of the 'underground railroad' which delivered the negroes to freedom in Canada after they had escaped." The article then mentions the nearby settlements at Buxton, South Buxton, Shrewsbury, and Dresden—the racialized geographical context for the celebration. This distinctively local content not only reminds *Chatham Daily News* readers of the connections between this region and the legacy of slavery but the ways in which slavery had an impact on the lives of their fellow community members and neighbours.

The talks the Reverend Dr Perry gave to the Kiwanis and Rotary Clubs are noteworthy as they show a Black man speaking to white men in a public context about racial inequality, the need for recognition of Black accomplishments, and the need to have Black history taught in schools, ideas that were part of larger cultural discussions happening amongst Black American thinkers, writers, and intellectuals during the early parts of the twentieth century. It was thought that highlighting the achievements of Black Americans would not only counteract negative stereotypes but also contribute to a sense of racial uplift and movement towards racial equality.

These Kiwanis and Rotary Club speeches, and the publication of stories about them in the local paper, are notably progressive, and likely would not have happened in many other communities in Canada and the United States. But, at the same time, they were also limited by the biases and constraints of the era. The Rotary Club speech, for example, occurred in the William Pitt Hotel, an establishment that, like many of its time, employed people of colour, including many of the All-Stars, but would neither seat nor serve them. While many Canadians know of discriminatory segregationist practices related to restaurants and hotels in the US, few Canadians seem aware such practices also happened in Canada. It wasn't until 1954, twenty years after the All-Stars' barrier-breaking season, that the Act to promote Fair Accommodation Practices in Ontario was passed to prevent discrimination in services, facilities, and accommodations. The setting of this lecture is especially important since we know that a number of the All-Stars were working at the William Pitt Hotel during the 1934 season, and possibly even during these lectures.

A little over a week after the reports of Emancipation Day celebrations, lectures, and events were printed, a story about another event on Emancipation Day is printed in the August 10 edition of the *Chatham Daily News* towards the bottom right corner of page six. In a wire story from nearby London, Ontario, the headline declares, "Beer Service is Demanded: Colored Man Claims He Has Been Refused Drink in Chatham."

> Edmund Odette, liquor commissioner, has been asked by *The Dawn of Tomorrow*, a paper published in London in the interests of the coloured people, to give a ruling as to the rights of that race drinking in the beverage rooms set up under the new act.
>
> The issue started when a coloured resident of Raleigh township, Kent County, was refused service in a hotel in Chatham on Emancipation Day, August 2. According to the story he was in company with a white friend and was refused service by the waiter.
>
> To test the law in London a coloured man resident of London, R.A. James, 519 ½ Richmond Street, desired to

find out for himself if the beverage rooms are refusing to serve coloured persons. According to Mr. James he met with the same experience as the Raleigh township resident and was at first refused service in a London hotel beverage room.

Mr. James says he was later served but only when he said he would wire the liquor commissioner at Toronto. *The Dawn of Tomorrow*, in explaining the incident to Mr. Odette, says the hotel proprietor finally complied and directed the waiter to serve him, but in doing so added, that it was because he was a "British subject." This does not satisfy *The Dawn of Tomorrow*, which asks what is the position of coloured Americans touring in Canada. *The Dawn of Tomorrow* winds up its letter to Mr. Odette as follows:

"To avoid any such unhappy experiences occurring to coloured visitors from across the border or elsewhere we are asking for your ruling. This might exonerate your department in the eyes of the National Association for the Advancement of Colored People in America, the local voice of the negro people, and at least prove for once that the Canadian Government does not approve of discriminating practices."

The letter is signed by C.E. Jennings, proprietor of *The Dawn of Tomorrow*.

These two events in Chatham during Emancipation Day—a lecture celebrating the accomplishments of Black people and an incident of denying them service—illustrate how discussions of race exist on multiple co-existing and often contradictory planes.

★ ★ ★

In the Emancipation Day doubleheader, Chatham and Detroit split the series. Detroit took the first game 9–6 and Chatham took the second 7–6. Of the second game, Calder writes:

Flat Chase put a thrilling finish to an exhibition encounter with Taylor's Stars of Detroit last evening as he pitched and batted his team to a 7–6 decision over the Motor City Team. Chase's screaming double to right field drove in two men in the eighth with the tying and winning runs after Detroit had gone one run up in the first part of the eighth inning. The result of the game evened up the day's doubleheader as Detroit had taken a 9–6 verdict in a morning snowfall of errors and heavy hitting. Six home runs were slapped out of Stirling Park in last night's tilt and the fourteen hundred fans on hand were treated to an all round entertaining spectacle.

In his regular column on the same day, Calder muses, "Maybe last night's game between the Stars and Taylor's Stars of Detroit was just a criterion of what is to come. Fourteen hundred fans—and they've been panning me for conservative estimates—were on hand to watch the Stars, a great ball team, win in spectacular fashion." We see a different kind of team when the All-Stars play Detroit. Taylor's Stars of Detroit is a stronger, faster team than the All-Stars' City League competitors, and they test Chatham in a way few other teams do. Competition of this nature causes the All-Stars to raise their game and refine their approach: "The Stars were a little off in their fielding yesterday but maybe that's just as well for they know where they must improve now and the system will be made a little closer to perfection." Against Detroit, we see the All-Stars alongside perhaps the strongest team they've encountered to date. Calder comments: "When it is considered that the Detroit Nine was picked from the 180,000 colored residents of Detroit, where baseball is going better than ever this year, Chatham fans must realize that the Stars are a pretty nifty team." These games against the Detroit Stars dispel the notion that the All-Stars' stellar record was solely due to the weakness of other City League teams. This was indeed a team to be reckoned with.

The All-Stars' fairly frequent match-ups with Detroit and the connections between several players and Detroit baseball link them with the larger history of Negro Leagues baseball. There are few mentions of Canadian teams within the almost exclusively US-focused scholarship on Black baseball but there are nevertheless important connections. The term "Negro Leagues baseball" has a number of working definitions that would exclude the Chatham Coloured All-Stars, since they did not play within the organized Negro Leagues. However, the Center for Negro League Baseball Research (CNLBR), believes it is "important to recognize everyone's contribution to the history of Black baseball in America"—and, one assumes, that this would include Canada. In addition to the formalized Negro League teams, the CNLBR's definition includes travelling barnstorming, independent teams, Negro "minor" league or regional leagues, winter league baseball (in places like Cuba, Puerto Rico, Mexico, Panama, Venezuela, and Colombia), local town teams and industrial league teams, Black military teams, and Black college teams. The Chatham Coloured All-Stars would probably fall within the CNLBR's independent team category.

The CNLBR's more inclusive definition helps to position the history of the All-Stars and Black Canadian baseball within this more established area of research. Even so, Donald Tabron Jr, resident of Detroit and son of player Don Tabron, notes that even though Detroit and Canada are only separated by a river, few people in Detroit know about the All-Stars: "Most people here have heard of the Detroit Brown Bombers, most of the people here have heard at least of the Detroit Stars" but "there's not enough recognition, or even knowledge of the story of the Chatham Stars. Even though locally, there were at least a couple of guys from Detroit that made a pretty good impact on that team." While there are obvious reasons why the All-Stars are not part of the story of Black baseball in the US, including them and other border teams opens new areas of inquiry for a more inclusive and nuanced history of Black baseball in North America.

The presence in Southwestern Ontario of Black baseball teams from Detroit predates the All-Stars' Emancipation Day doubleheaders by several decades. One scholar has found references to cross-border games as early as 1869, when the Goodwills of London played the all-Black Rialtos of Detroit. Stories as early as 1920 in the Windsor newspapers show how frequently Black American teams crossed the fluid border between Windsor and Detroit. A wire story from Chatham printed in the September 18, 1920, *Windsor Star* shows the Detroit Stars playing a white team at Tecumseh Park. On the Detroit Stars roster was future Baseball Hall of Fame member John Preston "Pete" Hill.

Because of its proximity to Detroit, Windsor offers significant connections with the US Negro Leagues and the informal network of African American baseball teams in the Detroit area in the 1930s. Mack Park and Hamtramck Stadium—the main ballparks where Black Detroit teams played—are both roughly twelve kilometres from Wigle Park. Separated by the Detroit River, the two cities had long been connected by a regularly running ferry. The opening of the Ambassador Bridge in 1929 and an under-river tunnel in 1930 made this international border more fluid and crossable, as can be seen in the even more frequent match-ups between teams in Ontario and Michigan after this time. In spite of this fluidity, the study of Black baseball in the US has, by and large, stopped at the Canadian border, even in this border region where we should know better.

Because of the opening of the bridge and tunnel, the 1930s were particularly active in terms of cross-border Black baseball. During the August long weekend of 1931, a reported two thousand fans came to Windsor's Wigle Park to watch the Detroit Colored Stars beat a team 18–5 that included former Detroit Tigers Bobby Veach and Bernie Boland. The box score lists most of the Detroit Stars 1931 roster, including Turkey Stearnes, who scored four runs in five at-bats. Some other Black American teams playing at Wigle Park in the 1930s include the Saginaw Michigan Colored Baseballers (1930), the Ecorse Colored Giants (1930 and 1936), the Hamtramck Colored Stars (1931), the Philadelphia Colored Giants (1931), the Wolverine Colored Stars (1933), the Quinn's Colored Stars of Detroit (1935 and 1939), and the Detroit Colored Stars (1936), among others. It has proved difficult to track these teams down in any newspapers or other printed materials of the time. More than likely, these were informally organized pickup teams that were not part of the formal Negro Leagues, though there were almost certainly cross-over players. These brief mentions in the Windsor papers add to the still evolving understanding of the Black baseball tradition in the Windsor-Detroit area in the 1930s.

Black baseball in Detroit had a significant impact on the Chatham Coloured All-Stars. Much of the success of the team came from bringing in players like Chase and Jenkins, who honed their skills watching Black baseball in Wigle Park and then playing for and against Detroit teams. It was also through Chase's and Jenkins's connections to Detroit that the All-Stars recruited players Don Tabron and Donise Washington, both of whom made considerable contributions to the 1934 victory.

Calder's coverage in August 1934 shows a number of players hitting their stride. Don Tabron, in particular, catches Calder's eye for his steady improvement and contributions to the team over the season. In the story headlined "Don Tabron Leads Stars to Easy Win," Calder writes, "Paced by Don Tabron, Chatham Stars won a decisive victory over Wheatley at Stirling Park Saturday 9–1. Tabron hurled the first eight innings of the game for the Stars and after the opening frame shut out the visitors. He contributed a home run to the Chatham cause." In the next day's paper, Calder continues his reflections on Tabron, noting:

> I never saw Don Tabron play ball before this year but when I attended the first game in which he played this season I wasn't overly impressed with his work. He had a good arm but only a fair sense of direction and a poor hitting eye. Today he's one of the greatest threats of the Chatham Stars, one of two teams who will meet in the City League playoffs beginning Saturday afternoon at Athletic Park. The arm is more deadly and he's a surer man on ground hit balls. But more. He's developed a batting eye and in recent games he's

knocked two home runs out of Stirling Park. Tabron has been taking a turn on the mound too and may yet develop into quite a pitcher. But he's a real source of strength to the Stars today as a hitting shortstop.

According to the recollections of various All-Stars, Tabron came to the team sometime in May. The All-Stars were scheduled to play an exhibition game on the Victoria Day weekend and needed a couple of extra players. In an interview in 1984, Ben Talbot recounts how "Flat said he knew a guy in Detroit that he played with in the Church League . . . So Len Harding and I went over to Detroit looking for this guy. Flat said the guy was a good fielder but couldn't hit a bull in the behind with a shotgun. Len and I went over and we looked in every pool hall on the East side . . . We finally found our shortstop about two in the morning." This shortstop was Don Tabron, who brought along catcher Don Washington. Donald Tabron Jr tells a similar version of this story:

> Some recruiters came from Chatham to Detroit and
> had heard about my father being able to play baseball.
> And so, one way or another they found their way to his
> neighbourhood and began to ask around about him. And
> several people said 'well, hey, if you wait 'til about eleven
> o'clock at night, go to that house right there, you'll see a
> young man in a bow tie and a suit and that'll be who you're
> looking for.' And so, they circled back around and that's
> how they found my father, because he was running the
> card tables at his sister's house rent party. So, they asked
> him to come play a couple of exhibition games and he
> ended up staying.

When asked if his father played in the church leagues that Chase played in, Donald replies, "If there was baseball to be played, he was involved . . . so I'm more than sure that he probably did participate in the church leagues." He further adds that Jenkins and Chase "were two of my dad's good friends. So, if they were coming over to play,

I'm sure Dad was playing right with them." Although Tabron played only two full seasons with the All-Stars, the impact of playing on that team stayed with him his entire life.

In his interview with the *Breaking the Colour Barrier* project, Donald Tabron Jr recalls that Don Tabron was born in 1915 in Princeton, Indiana, but moved to Detroit at a young age after a tornado destroyed the town where he lived. He was the youngest of ten children, and his mother had passed away soon after his birth. Don was raised primarily by his oldest sister, Myrtle, who moved the family to Detroit sometime after the tornado. The Tabrons arrived in Detroit in the early days of what is called the Great Migration. Between around 1916 and 1970, an estimated six million African Americans left the Southern United States and headed north and west to cities like Los Angeles, New York, Chicago, Philadelphia, Pittsburgh, and Detroit. In the first decade of the twentieth century, 90 percent of the African American population in the US lived in the south. By the 1970s, almost 50 percent of African Americans lived in the north and the west. Between 1910 and 1930, the recorded Black population in Detroit went from 5,741 in 1910 to 40,838 in 1920 to 120,066 in 1930—roughly a 1,991 percent increase.

In Detroit, the Great Migration contributed to the development of the Black Bottom residential area and the Black-owned business and entertainment district called Paradise Valley. Paradise Valley offered a range of businesses and services to Black citizens as well as nightclubs, theatres, and gambling. But the Great Migration also had a tremendous impact on Black baseball in cities like Detroit. As noted historian of African American baseball Lawrence D. Hogan writes, "The rise of black professional baseball teams in the early 20th century coincided with increased migration, and the institutional racism that contributed to the development of Black business districts in American cities." Prior to the Great Migration, "black baseball clubs played for essentially a white clientele." The rise of neighbourhoods like Paradise Valley and Black Bottom was "too important for [Black baseball] to ignore. A new generation of both black and white baseball entrepreneurs would attempt to tap into this growing market." The Detroit Stars played, for example, in the middle of Hamtramck, which was at the time a predominantly Polish working-class neighbourhood.

Upon their arrival in Detroit, the Tabrons lived in the Black Bottom neighbourhood. As Tabron describes, "Detroit was very, very segregated in the early 1900s. And so that segregation created a very thriving community called Black Bottom. And so, my father grew up very poor and always loved baseball. My father attended Northeastern High School and was very smart. He graduated from high school at age of sixteen but was too poor to afford the cap and gown. He did not even attend his own graduation, rather just picked up the diploma the next day from the school." Tabron graduated around 1931, amidst the Great Depression. Around this time, the Tabron family began throwing rent parties—social events where tenants provided entertainment to raise money to pay their rent. The family made and bottled their own liquor, the oldest sister made and sold food plates, and young Don oversaw gambling. Tabron had, as Donald Jr tells it, "a photographic memory when it came to numbers," so he, aged fifteen or sixteen, managed all of the card games and gambling at these parties. Donald continues:

> Frankly, he became an amazing cheater. When they first mass manufactured playing cards, he noticed that the Deuce through Ten cards had one particular cut on them, because they were just all being mass produced. And then, he noticed that Jack through Ace had a slightly different cut pattern. So, he was able to know whether the next card on the deck was going to be Two through Ten or Jack through Ace, which in cards makes a substantial difference.

Although the gambling income was certainly welcome to the family, Don was, according to his son, "always very concerned that one day him being so good at gambling and cards would catch up with him." He was "a teenager besting adult men who were going to work in the factories for a week making about a nickel an hour . . . coming to gamble and leaving with nothing."

"It's a difficult thing," Donald comments, "to have a house rent party and someone work for a week come gamble, lose their week's wages and not be fairly upset about it ... my father was always scared that in doing the different things that he had to do to make money, that it would physically be dangerous for him." When Harding and Talbot showed up in Detroit looking for him, the offer to play for the All-Stars in Chatham must have seemed like a ticket to a welcomed escape.

Initially, Don Tabron agreed to play a couple of exhibition games in Chatham. However, as his son recalls, after he "went to Chatham he saw something completely different" and "compared it to the risks that he was taking in Detroit." Donald imagines his father's response at the time: "Well, you know? I think I'm going to stay." In coming to Chatham, Tabron was able to relax a bit in "an environment where he could play what he loved to do and his basic needs were met." It is unclear what the financial arrangements were, given that this was an amateur team, but Tabron appears to have been given room and board from someone in the community. Donald recalls that his father found the East End welcoming: "The environment that Chatham provided was such a new start, a place where he could go to kind of get away from a lot of other things, play baseball, meet good people and pursue his dreams at the time ... He was able to initially meet very good people, you know Fergie Jenkins Sr, Boomer Harding ... they really welcomed him in." Tabron played with the All-Stars until other responsibilities brought him back to Detroit, but he never forgot the people in the East End and spoke highly of them for the rest of his life.

In his interview commemorating the fiftieth anniversary of the 1934 win, Tabron reflected, "That year was one of the most memorable times in my life. I was 18 and away from home for the first time, but the memories are most pleasant. I always had fond memories of that year in Chatham." Donald Tabron Jr concurs, noting his father "had friends as an adult but seemingly nothing compared to the bonds that he forged with his [Chatham] teammates. Like I said, he had friends who were in business with him, but I never really heard him speak of really anybody with as fond memories as he spoke of his teammates."

On August 11, the All-Stars and the Braggs begin the best of five series for the City League championship. The All-Stars win the series convincingly in three games: 15–8 on August 11, 7–1 on August 16, and 11–7 on August 18. The depth of the team's strengths and the weaknesses of their opposition are clear from the coverage. Of the first game, Calder writes, "A powerful early-inning attack that was aided along by a flock of opposition errors carried the Stars through to a 15–8 victory over the Braggs . . . The potent bat of Flat Chase and King Terrell's consistent hurling again undertook the brunt of the Stars' attack and came through with flying colours. Chase whacked a long home run in the first inning and followed that with three singles. Terrell allowed but six hits and fanned eleven to more than do his share towards giving the Stars the jump on the series." In describing the second game of the series, Calder points to Don Tabron as one of the keys to victory. With a headline that reads "Braggs Bow to Tabron's Great Work," Calder writes, "the good right arm of diminutive Don Tabron, ambitious young City Leaguer, carried the Stars to a 7–1 triumph over Braggs yesterday in the second game of the City League playoffs as he held his opponents to four hits, two of them scratchy, and struck out fourteen batsmen." When the Stars win the final game of the series, Calder writes, "There was little doubt in the minds of most baseball fans in the city that the Stars would go through the City Baseball League playoffs for the right to go into further OBAA play with little difficulty." The lopsided four-team City League play and their various exhibition games have shown something of this team's strengths, but not all.

One player who quietly impresses Calder throughout the season is King Terrell. It's easy for Terrell to be overshadowed by the awe-inspiring flash of Flat Chase's playing style. But his solid, consistent, steady play is a key part of the All-Stars' success, as this game recap conveys:

> King Terrell was the hero of last night's city baseball league game between the Stars and Kent Bridge, when, with two strikes on him and two out in the last frame, he got hold of one of Bus Reed's good ones for a home run over the centre field fence, with two of his mates aboard. The blow put the Stars on the top end of a 6–4 count.

In a story entitled "One of Stars' Most Reliable Men," Calder quotes an unnamed City League pitcher who says of Terrell, "There's the batter I hate to pitch to . . . I'd sooner pitch to any of them than Terrell." Terrell, Calder continues,

> is one of the League's most dangerous hitters. If that was where his work stopped however, this bit would never have been written. For while Terrell is a good man to have around when a mass attack is needed, he's also a great fielding third baseman. And game after game he's pitched for the Stars this season and won a huge majority of them. His left-handed shoots and curves are as baffling as any deliveries offered up by any pitcher in the circuit. It was he who started the Stars off in the City League playoff race last Saturday by winning the first game.
>
> As leadoff hitter for the Stars, Terrell gets on base more than half of the time. That's a handy sort of leadoff man to have playing on your ball club, Happy Parker. He was a good schoolboy athlete a few years back and today can run the bases at a smart clip. For a left-hander he plays a great game as third base and his whip across the diamond is something to watch. Terrell will probably be on the mound for the Stars tomorrow in the third game of the series. . . A visit to Stirling Park might not be amiss because Terrell is bound to furnish a great exhibition.

In October, Calder calls Terrell "the most dependable man on the team" and says his left-handed throws are "scarcely a handicap." He is "fast on the bases and usually scores the first run of the game." Terrell's left-handed fielding was always mentioned and has become almost legendary.

The *Chicago Defender* was the most prominent Black newspaper in North America, collecting community news from across the US and Canada, including Chatham. In 1936, the local contributor of Chatham, Ontario, news wrote, "One baseball player in the city who never gets the amount of credit due him is King Terrell of the All Stars. A southpaw third baseman playing under a handicap has learned to pivot in such a way that there's little delay to his throw across the diamond and he cuts off many a drive over the bag that a right-handed player would miss." The people of Chatham were still talking about the legend of Terrell in 2016. In her *Breaking the Colour Barrier* interview, Dorothy Wright Wallace tells of her brother, who has "seen a lot of people play ball. But he says you never ever saw a third baseman like that. And even to this day he's never, ever seen a third baseman play the way that King Terrell did. . . . He was so fast . . . Really, really fast. And the way that he handled the glove and the ball!" Terrell is what sportswriter Simon Sharkey-Gotlieb calls "the rarest of baseball species: a left-handed throwing third baseman." What makes being a left-handed throwing third baseman challenging is that the glove being on Terrell's right hand means he needs to field most ground balls backhanded—far more difficult to do well. Furthermore, to throw to first, a left-handed third baseman will have to pivot somewhat for enough accuracy and speed to get the out. Somehow, however, King Terrell, turned this disadvantage into an advantage, as Boomer Harding makes clear: "I caught a lot of his [throws from third] standing on first base. He could throw them around, curve the ball around the pitcher usually. He didn't have to bend over because King automatically threw a curve to first base." Boomer's statement that he caught a lot of the throws "standing on first base," suggests that Terrell's aim and accuracy was also top notch. King Terrell's glove is on display at the Chatham-Kent Black Historical Society Museum, a quiet testament to his role in the All-Stars' success.

Although the *Breaking the Colour Barrier* project was unable to interview any of Terrell's descendants, everyone who has spoken of him does so with unwavering respect and admiration, both as a baseball player and a member of the Chatham East End community. In her MHSO interview with Boomer Harding, Wanda Milburn reflects on the interview she did with Terrell and remembers he "spoke highly of just about everybody on the All-Star team. I think that's typical of his character," to which Boomer replied, "He's a real gentleman and a real good ball player." We get a sense of this gentleman ball player from Terrell's interview with Milburn when she says, "And we know that you were the left-handed third baser who was really quite unique, very good," and he responds, "Well, I ain't going to brag about what I did, myself, or anything like that, because that wouldn't sound right." From Boomer's interview with Milburn we know that Terrell, along with Chase, was one of their "entertainment men." Boomer recalls that after the game, whether the team won or lost, "Terrell would get on the piano and Flat Chase would do the dancing. Win or lose, and we had a real good time and relieved all our tears and woes." He also remembers that, on their road trips, "going and coming from a place like Owen Sound, five and six would get in a car and the same King Terrell could tell jokes all the way to Owen Sound. Then when we got ready to come home and never tell the same joke twice. He'd just keep us in stiches all the time."

In his 1980 MHSO interview, Terrell sits beside Wanda Milburn with the 1934 team photograph between them and they talk about each player. As the sister of Boomer and the rest of the Harding ballplayers, Milburn knew everyone, and the conversation they share sheds much-needed light about players who don't often appear in the game recaps in the *Chatham Daily News*. Terrell recalls that Stanton Robbins was "a right fielder; he played right field a lot. And he had an arm about as strong as any one of the ball players on the team, because he cut many a guy down from right field going into second base and third base, as nice a throw that you'd ever want to see. He got his share of hits too." Hyle Robbins "played in the outfield. He didn't play with us very much. He played a little bit, but not very much. I don't know whether he was working the majority of the time that he couldn't get in to the baseball games or what, but he didn't play with us too much. But he was a good fast runner."Terrell recalls that Ross Talbot "was a good ball player. He played first base quite a bit. He wasn't a real fast runner. He got his amount of hits about the same as the usual bunch of us got" and that Sagasta Harding played the piano: "Yeah, he used to play a piano too. I played lots and lots and lots of times with him. I used to love his playing."This interview also provides us with the only extant information we have about Jack Robinson, the young boy in the middle of several team photos. When Wanda Milburn asks about Robinson, Terrell says "Yeah, the mascot, our mascot. He was a little guy, real small. No matter where we went, he went with us 'cause he was young, he went to school, and he wasn't working at the time when we was playing quite a bit of our baseball. He went with us to a lot of our baseball games. He was always there, getting up to bats, and getting up to gloves, and this, and that, and the other. He was a busy little dude."

The players are more forthcoming with Wanda Milburn than they are with newspaper reporters. Terrell's description of the All-Stars being "run out of town" with "clubs, and hoes, and rakes, and everything else," for example, comes from his interview with Milburn. These are the kinds of memories that the players appear not to have talked about with their children. When we asked Hyle and Stanton Robbins's niece Pauline Williams if her uncles faced any racial challenges playing baseball, she replies: "If they did, they didn't mention it . . . I mean, if anybody said anything cruel to them they never came home and bragged about it. They might have gotten name calling or I don't know, they never said. They would never say nothing like that. Not to us anyway."

Like several other All-Stars players, Terrell worked at William Pitt Hotel. Unlike many of his teammates for whom this was a temporary job, Terrell worked for the hotel for over forty years, as everything, including bell boy, bell captain, general handyman, switchboard operator, and elevator operator. He was credited with saving multiple guests' lives when he was working on the switchboard. At this time, hotel work and sleeping car porter work were two of the few options Black men could rely upon for employment. The connection between Black men, baseball, and hotels is even deeper,

*King Terrell and Flat Chase
in Taylor ACs uniform.
Courtesy of the Chase family.*

*A postcard from the 1940s showing the William Pitt Hotel where a number
of the All-Stars worked. One of the 1934 victory celebrations was held here.
Courtesy of University of Windsor, Archives and Special Collections.*

however, since many Black players in the US, like members of the Cuban Giants, were also employed by hotels to play baseball in addition to their hotel duties. In Southwestern Ontario, there are brief mentions of Black hotel teams in regional newspapers of the 1930s. In Chatham it appears there weren't Black hotel teams, though many of the All-Stars, as we have seen, worked at the William Pitt.

The next generation of Black Chatham residents had a few more job options than hotel and sleeping car porter, but many of them began their working lives at the William Pitt Hotel. Dorothy Wright Wallace, born in 1943 and thus a generation younger than Terrell, recalls his influence helping younger members of the Chatham's East End community: "He helped me get my first job. I ran the elevator. You're only going up four floors, but [laughing] I ran it anyways. Blowing fuses as I went." Dorothy recalls that her brother Eddie also worked at the William Pitt and got to know King Terrell quite well, working alongside him as a bellhop. "He kind of mentored Eddie a bit," Dorothy remembers, "but, you know, [Terrell] made, I think, my brother realize that there's more to your life than just this bell hopping. I guess my brother listened to all the mentoring along the way because it was successful for him."

The brother Dorothy Wright Wallace talks about is Eddie Wright, the first Black player on the Chatham Junior Maroons hockey team. From there, Eddie went on to play NCAA Division I hockey for Boston University. In 1970, he was hired as the head coach for the SUNY-Buffalo hockey team, becoming the first Black coach at the university level. This is yet another example of the far-reaching legacy of the 1934 team.

★ ★ ★

As in previous months, the *Chatham Daily News* sports pages are full of encouragement for fans to come out and support the teams. On August 2, Calder writes, "Baseball in Chatham has every chance for a mighty revival. Every follower of the game should get behind the teams and shove." Throughout August, Calder seems disappointed with the fan turn out. On August 10, he writes, "If Sarnia and Blenheim fans can turn out in large numbers for games in which the

Stars play, there's no reason why a lot of the stay-at-homes shouldn't at least investigate. Baseball is still a living thing here and will continue to thrive. A little extra shove on your part wouldn't hurt the upward climb at all." Speaking directly about the All-Stars, he adds: "Your presence added to that of many others will encourage the boys who are Chatham's hopes in the OBAA playdowns and who have brought about a revival of baseball in a once widely known baseball centre." It is unclear why Calder's tone gets more pointed, specific, and hortative at this time, but it does:

> It shouldn't be necessary to have to appeal to the people
> of Chatham to attend a baseball game. In days gone by
> the mere mention of a not-so-hot exhibition would have
> brought out the fans in droves. Even many of the practices
> drew larger crowds than some games have been attracting
> this year.
>   It seems that some former followers of the game are
> convinced that baseball as today's youngsters play it isn't
> just the same as in the "good old days." I promise you
> not that tomorrow's affair will be as good as that game in
> which St Thomas' Danny McPhee shut out the Briscos 1–0
> when Blake McCoig was holding sway on the mound for
> Chatham's famous nine. But the boys are playing good ball.
> There can't be many places in the entire dominion where a
> city league is providing such good ball.

It is not entirely clear what is behind Calder's critiques of the "stay at homes" who yearn for the baseball of "the good old days," or Calder's other critiques of local fans. Blake Harding's recollections from his father's stories, however, might offer some additional context.

By all accounts, Black and white citizens of Chatham were coming out to watch the All-Stars and, in this way, as Blake Harding summarizes in his conversation with LeSean Harris, "it brought a unity to the city." But, Blake is quick to add, "Not everybody in the city liked them. Not everybody in the city cheered for them. But almost everybody in the city would come out to see them. They would either come out to see them succeed or fail." Here Blake draws attention to a subtle but significant distinction: attendance at games did not necessarily equal respect. Blake continues: "there was a lot of prejudice in the city of Chatham, there was a lot of racism in the city of Chatham. And [the All-Stars] were bringing with their type of play an excitement where you just had to come out and watch them. And they were beating everybody that they played. As per anything else but people of colour, back then, they had to be better than who they were playing or they would have been a joke. As it was, a lot of times people perceived them as a joke. Either out of resentment for winning, or if they did lose, then, 'you had no business playing' type of thing." As we shall see, the further the All-Stars go in the playoffs, the more support they gain within the white community.

Within the broader OBAA playoffs, Calder comments that the skills of the All-Stars stack up well against a broader competitive field: "Ardent followers of City League ball are looking for the Stars to go far in the provincial series. The opposition to be encountered is not especially strong. The team is entered in the Intermediate B series but already such class A teams as Blenheim and Sarnia Red Sox have been beaten by the Stars." The Stars have a strong team, but they have limitations too. In a game described as the Stars' "Warm Up for Playdowns" Calder observes, "Seventeen errors, the greatest number in a game here this year, marred what promised to be an outstanding baseball bit at Stirling Park yesterday afternoon." Though Chatham defeated Tilbury 8–5 in a game that "was a good exhibition of hitting and well-pitched ball," the All-Stars' success in the playoffs is still far from certain by this point in the season.

In the final days of August 1934, the All-Stars play one last exhibition series: the "Indian Fair" tournament at what is now known as Walpole Island First Nation. A story titled "Three Ball Games at Walpole Fair" describes how

> three snappy baseball games have been arranged for the
> days of the annual Indian Fair at Walpole Island this week

... On Thursday afternoon, the Wallaceburg "All-Stars" will play Jacob's Braves. The game is to commence at three o'clock and Shognosh, well-known Indian hurler, will be on the mound for the Indians. Waubuno and Walpole Island Seniors will play on Friday afternoon and Chatham Coloured All-Stars will meet the Walpole Island All-Stars on Saturday afternoon.

This series is important to this story for a few reasons. First, it hints at the vibrant Indigenous baseball activity at this time, and second, it mentions Wellington Shognosh, a player who will join the All-Stars in 1935.

★ ★ ★

Wellington Shognosh, an Ojibwe man, was born February 28, 1914, in Walpole Island and died there in February 1982. Little is known about his early life, but he appears to have grown up playing in the rich baseball culture of this First Nations community. He may have lived in Detroit at some point and is rumoured to have tried out for the Detroit Tigers. In contrast to how rarely Calder mentions the All-Stars' race, Shognosh's Indigenous background is consistently referenced in most mentions of him, usually in ways that would strike us as regrettably stereotypical. In 1935, for example, Calder calls him the "erstwhile Walpole and Waubuno Walloper" and "The tall Indian flinger."

Shognosh joined the All-Stars around the same time as Ferguson Jenkins, and a deep friendship developed between these two men. Boomer Harding recalls that "Willy and Fergie were the Mutt and Jeff of our team. They roomed together that year and you'd see them any night walking the streets. Willy was very quiet. The most you could get out of him was 'ug' for a long while. Fergie and Willy got along very well together in their early days."

Stories of Shognosh's stellar pitching abilities appeared in the *Chatham Daily News* in the early 1930s, making him seem like a local media star, even though he wasn't playing for a Chatham team. In the June 13, 1932, sports pages, we learn he struck out seventeen

Chatham Juniors players and on June 18, it is stated he "pitched excellent ball" in a game against Ridgetown. On July 20, 1932, it is noted that he has great potential to be a "bang up hurler" but runs the risk of ruining his arm with over-use. When the All-Stars play Walpole Island, Shognosh is a formidable opponent for the All-Stars' hitters. It is not surprising then, that he goes on to be recruited to play with them in the 1935 season.

Shognosh appears to have been brought in to offer some depth to the All-Stars' pitching staff and to give Chase's arm some rest. It is logical that, when looking for pitching help, the All-Stars would look to Shognosh, who had so often challenged them as they stepped up to the plate. In 1935, Calder describes what Shognosh brought to the team in this game recap: "The Stars have met with in-and-out fortune all along the way. Their work of today, however, is marked by an improvement over anything the club has previously shown. This is due, in great degree, to the increased effectiveness of Willie Shognosh, Indian pitcher, who came to the team this year from Waubuno and Walpole Island." These descriptions of Shognosh's skills are reminders of the strong tradition of good baseball within First Nations communities in this area and the diversity of the story of baseball in this region.

Although his focus is always on Chatham teams, Calder's journalistic lens in the 1930s captures something of the history of Indigenous baseball in this region. This history merits considerably more attention than it has received. Nevertheless, the box scores of games where the Chatham Coloured All-Stars played Walpole Island records their team's roster, providing some print documentation of the team and its players.

The Indigenous players occupied a curious space within the formal colour barriers that formed around baseball in the US and the informal—but no less real—barriers in Canada. The Archie Stirling story quoted earlier about telling the American players that the Black players in Chatham were Indigenous so they could play against them reveals something of the racial space Indigenous players occupied in Canada and the complexity of the racial climate of the era. While Indigenous players undoubtedly faced racism and discrimination, their formal exclusion from professional baseball hadn't been as explicitly codified as it had been for Black and African American players.

As August winds down, the All-Stars' record of thirty-two wins, five losses, and one tie gives them a .864 winning percentage. The lopsidedness of this winning percentage raises questions as to whether the All-Stars were that good or the league was simply weak. These questions get answered as the team heads into the playdowns.

SEPTEMBER
1934

THE DAYS ARE STILL HOT IN THE FIRST WEEKS OF September, but there's an occasional hint of a chill in the evening air. In the first week of the month, rains play havoc with baseball scheduling. Calder writes, "The elements more or less scrambled things on the sports map yesterday, causing postponements and the necessity of making arrangements for double-headers. Chatham, Detroit, and New York, three great sports centres, all suffered but we all expect more favorable conditions today." The signs of fall are evident in the sports pages of the *Chatham Daily News* as the baseball and softball seasons start to wind down. Early in the month, Calder's coverage often bounces between the Detroit Tigers' playoff run and the Stars' OBAA championship drive, as hopes and expectations surround both teams.

The All-Stars play nine games in September and lose only two of them. In Calder's columns in the early weeks of September, every game becomes a case study of the team's strengths and weaknesses, a prognostication of how they might do in the OBAA playoffs. In their Labour Day exhibition game with the competitive Taylor's Stars of Detroit, Calder remarks of the victorious All-Stars, "The game marked the return to fielding brilliance of the Stars. They made only one error up until the ninth when two tumbles nearly spelt disaster. Spectacular catches in the field before that had given the big crowd a good deal to shout about." Defense is an area in which the team improved over the 1934 season, as Calder describes:

> The Stars have progressed remarkably on the defensive in recent games and are about due to turn in an errorless game. They have a fly-hawk outfield that will cut off many runs before the OBAA campaign is finished and Donise Washington and Donald Tabron are the spark-plugs of a well-knit inner wall. All four pitchers alternate in the infield and when they are working on the mound know just what to do with a bunt or a slow roller.

Throughout the month, Calder maintains a measured optimism about the All-Stars' chances at an OBAA championship.

The first round of the OBAA playoffs is a quick series for the All-Stars. On September 8, they beat the Sarnia Red Sox 8–3 in the first match. The second game, scheduled for September 13 at the Chatham Athletic Park, reveals some of the precarities of amateur sports and the challenges many teams had even filling a roster. The September 14 *Chatham Daily News* sports pages headline reads: "Exhibition Game Taken By Red Sox: Sarnia Cannot Field a Team and Chatham is Awarded OBAA series." As the story recounts, "Several members of the Sarnia team are engaged in drilling for the coming football season and when a full team could not be rounded up to make the trip to Chatham yesterday, the Red Sox brought along a player who was not signed with their club and played the game under default." What was therefore scheduled as a playoff game became an exhibition game when Sarnia defaulted, and even though the All-Stars lost 7–3 they still went on to the next round of the OBAA championship.

Although the All-Stars beat the Braggs to go on to the OBAA playoffs, the All-Stars play the Braggs again in another City League series, this time for the Wanless Trophy. They win a game 8–7 on September 15, and then no other record of a played game appears in the papers. I have found references to the All-Stars being awarded the Wanless Trophy in 1934, but no press coverage describing championship games. The Wanless championship series games appear to have been cancelled due to rain or the OBAA playoffs. The All-Stars may have been given the trophy for having won the league.

While some of September's games show the All-Stars at their best, we also see a team capable of less than stellar play. Calder describes their fielding in the September 13 game against Sarnia as "erratic" and notes, "At times their lackadaisical playing drew the ire of the crowd. Flat Chase and Gouy Ladd were the only members of the team who were outstanding on the defense. Chase made three beautiful catches at shortstop, a position which he took when Tabron went to the mound." A week later, the All-Stars play their first game in their OBAA series against Welland and lose 17–7. "Welland," Calder declares, caught "the Chatham Stars on one of their off days— the worst they have experienced this season, [and] handed the locals a 17–7 drubbing." Calder offers this reading of this loss:

> Chase the pitching ace of the Chatham Stars and considered by many local fans one of the best amateur hurlers in this part of the country was far from his usual form. When this became apparent right at the start of the proceedings, the fact unnerved the local lads and before they could get settled down to anywhere near their usual form, thirteen visitors had scampered across the plate and Washington the regular catcher had shed the receiver's armour in favor of Harding and assumed the mound duties himself.

Calder explains these two losses in the larger context of the All-Stars team and season. When they lose the exhibition game to

Sarnia, Calder reminds readers not to despair: "those fans who have been following them all season know how the team can play ball. And others who were at the game saw a flash of the team's real form when those three runs were pounded across in the eighth."

★ ★ ★

Rather than sending Calder to cover the more distant away games in the OBAA playoffs, the *Chatham Daily News* begins to print wire stories or other towns' newspaper coverage for the All-Stars games outside of Chatham. In so doing, we lose Jack Calder as our primary narrator for the remainder of the season. Piecing together the out-of-town games through these vague, unsigned wire stories reminds us that Calder was not simply a documentarian of sports scores and statistics, but a true sportswriter. In discussing what made the esteemed Roger Kahn (1927–2020) such an exemplary and consummate sportswriter, journalist Bill Dwyre points to qualities like "phrase-making and insightful storytelling," the ability to capture "the souls and personalities of baseball players," and a flair for memorable summation. Dwyre wrote that great sportswriting can be "magical and spell-binding, a sensory treat for a reader." All of these qualities are present in Jack Calder's writings about the Chatham Coloured All-Stars. Those of us trying to understand the 1934 season are indebted to him for creating a record so vibrant, detailed, nuanced, and observant.

John Philip Sargent Calder, or Jack as he was called, was born February 4, 1915, the same year as Boomer Harding. The second son of Archibald Clement Calder and Mary Agnes Harding Calder, Jack was born in Regina while his father was a rector in Qu'Appelle, Saskatchewan. The family moved to Southwestern Ontario where Archibald Calder was rector in Wallaceburg and later at Chatham's Holy Trinity Church. Archibald was Kent West's Conservative member of the Ontario Legislature from 1926 to 1934. Jack Calder attended Chatham Collegiate Institute, where he wrote for the school newspaper. It is unclear when Calder began writing as a sports columnist for the *Chatham Daily News*, but in 1933, when he was only eighteen, he contributed to "Casual Comment on Current

Sport," a regular column that brought together small news items and commentaries about local, regional, and, to a lesser extent, professional sports. There are unsigned articles written about the All-Stars in 1933 that sound very much like Calder, with his particular cadence, commentary style, and thematic interests, but it is difficult to say for certain whether these are indeed written by him. In 1934, the "Casual Comment on Current Sport" column appears to have been replaced by two new columns, Calder's "Analyzing Sport" and sports editor William Scurr's "Sport in Short." By 1934, attributing columns to Calder becomes much easier through this two-column arrangement and the emergence of his distinctive writing voice. Calder continues writing for the *Chatham Daily News* sports pages throughout 1935. In October 1936, a wire story from Sarnia states that Calder "announced he was leaving for England next week with a view to writing hockey news for English papers." In the spring of 1937, a story by Calder covering hockey in Toronto is printed and his name appears in national and regional newspapers as a Canadian Press Staff Writer.

While he continues to write about sports, the focus of his writing shifts after he joins the Royal Canadian Air Force in May 1940. While serving in the military, he writes for the Canadian Press and publishes articles in the *Toronto Star*, *Globe and Mail*, and *Maclean's* magazine, about the war and his various adventures, including his first plane crash and his time as a prisoner of war in Ireland. Calder smuggled a news story out of the camp through his brother and it was published in *Maclean's*. He later escaped from the camp. Jack Calder was killed in action in July 1944, at the age of twenty-nine, after his second plane crash. Upon his death, a wire story observed, "Colleagues remember him as a tall, quiet redhead with an acute sense of personal responsibility. Sports editors across Canada knew his byline meant a studied story with a touch of class. When Jack Calder left a [Canadian Press] desk to join the R.C.A.F. in 1940, fellow workers were sorry to see him go." A Jack Calder Memorial Cup softball game was planned in Chatham, where funds were raised to purchase a plaque to be placed in the school he attended. The Western Ontario Sports Writers Association created a Jack

Masthead for Jack Calder's "Analyzing Sport" column, 1934. Courtesy of University of Windsor, Archives and Special Collections.

The image from a news clipping saying that Flying Officer Jack Calder is back in England and "safe again." Windsor Star, July 8, 1943. Courtesy of Patricia Calder.

Game advertisement for game against Walpole Island, calling the All-Stars "Canada's Fastest All-Coloured Team." Chatham Daily News, May 30, 1934. Courtesy of University of Windsor, Archives and Special Collections.

Game advertisement for regional tournament, featuring a cash prize for winning team, dancing in the evening, and free admission for ladies. Chatham Daily News, August 13, 1934. Courtesy of University of Windsor, Archives and Special Collections.

Calder Trophy to be given as an annual award to the outstanding high school boy athlete in Western Ontario.

Calder's published war pieces remain remarkable in their narrative detail and evocative, brave storytelling. It is not surprising to see these qualities in his later writings, as the stories he published as a nineteen-year-old, covering the Chatham Coloured All-Stars, also had this careful yet pointed fearlessness about them. As a sportswriter, he seemed unafraid to take people to task when he did not agree with them, whether they were players, community members, or league officials.

It is important to remember that the young Calder's writing was almost certainly mediated by at least one editor, if not more. His sports columns, as we have seen, occasionally contained outbursts of impetuosity, and editors may have attempted to rein him in now and then. Inevitably, the question will arise about Calder's positions on race and his potential role in breaking down barriers. We know very little of his thoughts regarding race, and we haven't got enough unmediated Calder to draw any conclusions. As a journalist, as opposed to a diarist or a personal letter writer, Calder was required to be constantly aware of his public readership. As Boomer Harding told Dan Kelly, Calder knew he had to be careful about what he said or he could lose his job. Sports page advertisements in the *Chatham Daily News* suggest without a doubt the assumed readership was white, male, and middle-class, although we know that the Black residents of Chatham also read Calder's column. As a later chapter will describe, at least one of the East End residents was not afraid to remind Calder he was a white man writing about a team of Black men.

★ ★ ★

Given the number of games the All-Stars played over the summer and the number of innings Chase pitched, it's not surprising to read in early September that Chase is having some issues with his throwing arm, poetically described by Calder as "the cold in his arm." Chase, however, emerges as a formidable competitor who does not give in to adversity of any kind, as conveyed is this description of a playdown game versus Sarnia: "Flat Chase was credited with twelve strikeouts and twice a victim of his third pitch was Dutch Schaefer, once one of the hardest men in this district to fan. Chase's index finger became badly blistered early in the game and near the finish the blister broke to leave a red patch of unprotected flesh. So the big fellow was labouring under difficulties when he pitched his way out of a deep hollow in the eighth frame and then retired the Sarnians in order in the ninth." Chase's fierce competitiveness is a key factor in the success of this 1934 team. Equally important was that when Flat Chase had a rare off-day or an injury, there were others on the team able to step up.

In addition to Chase, "the smoke-ball king of the City League," the Stars also had Tabron, Terrell, and Talbot. Calder called Don Tabron's rise to prominence in the City League "phenomenal," noting,

> Only a fair-fielding, weak-hitting shortstop at the start of the season, he transformed himself into an able, all-round player by constant work. He and Don Washington have toiled for hours together in the mornings whipping themselves into shape for the OBAA campaign. After he had developed a good throwing arm at shortstop, Tabron tried his hand at pitching. In the first game he was wild and had to be removed. Then he lasted the route and scored a victory, though again his control was bad. Gradually however he has mastered the art of finding the proper spot. On Monday Tabron defeated Taylor's Stars of Detroit, one of the strongest coloured teams in the world. He allowed only seven hits and two walks and he fanned seven.

While Terrell is the team's only left-hander, Calder comments "he would be a one-man pitching staff by himself. His work was largely responsible for the Stars' success in the finals for the right to enter further OBAA play." Talbot, too, can be "counted on to turn in a good job if called on." Gouy Ladd, who returned to the roster in

September also impresses Calder: "Ladd, who may soon be placed nearer to the top of the batting order, walloped the longest one of the day, a triple that refused to stop til it hit the fence. Ladd has never been noted for his hitting—he's an exceptionally good centre fielder—but his stick work of late has been a big aid to the Stars."

Towards the end of the month, Calder offers what might be the most accurate precis of the Chatham Coloured All-Stars' 1934 season: "They've developed from a team with only three or four outstanding players to an all-round clever organization. They've done it by hard work. Inexperience in actual playoff competition accounted for the poor showing of the Stars here last week. Winning spirit placed them back in the running."

One player who quietly and consistently embodies that winning spirit is Donise—or more often Don—Washington. By the end of the season, his batting average is .319 in the thirty-three games he's played, mostly as catcher. Only Terrell and Chase have played more games, with thirty-five and thirty-four games respectively. Under a "Washington the Hero" subheading in an article about the All-Stars' 17–7 loss to Welland on September 20, 1934, Calder writes: "Washington finished the game on the mound. This lad was the hero of the game as far as Chatham was concerned. Despite the fact that it was a hopeless cause the way his mates were going and the scoring splurge the visitors had staged, Washington worked hard and gave the best he had." Washington's main contributions appear to be the kinds of things that cannot be recorded in box scores or game recaps. Throughout September, Washington gets more attention from Calder for his steady presence behind the plate and his leadership on and off the field, characteristics that will be vital in the 1935 season.

★ ★ ★

Originally from Detroit, Don Washington came to Chatham with his friend Don Tabron. As Boomer Harding told Dan Kelly, "Washington came from Detroit, but we passed him off as Windsor. It was kind of a sin [against OBAA regulations] to play if he was from another country but from Windsor, that was just Canada." Washington did not have the flash and power of a player like Chase, but he emerges as a quiet guiding presence on the team. After the Stars' 11–7 victory over Braggs on August 18, Calder describes Washington as "a fine target and good at picking men off the bases." Early in September, Calder writes, "Don Washington, catcher of the Stars, is the best in the city and is the brains of the team. He is a great target and an able handler of pitchers. Though he has an awkward batting stance he is a hard and consistent hitter and regularly bats in fifth position." On the eve of the OBAA finals against Penetanguishene in October, Calder asserts "the Stars are a remarkably good ball team. They're led by a master of the diamond, Don Washington, who really knows baseball. He has brought along his pitchers this season in admirable style and he has done his share of work offensively and defensively too." Washington's strength and addition to the team may have been overshadowed by the legend that was Flat Chase. But almost all legendary pitchers owe something to their catchers. And Chase is no different.

Catchers are important to baseball teams, but their skills are often not as attention-grabbing as ace pitchers. However, as sportswriter Leonard Koppett puts it in his *Thinking Fan's Guide to Baseball*, aside from the pitcher, the catcher is for obvious reasons the most important player in the game: "He handles the ball all the time, he calls pitches (thinking along the same lines as the pitcher), he quarterbacks the infield (since he is the only player on his team facing all the others), and when called upon, he must make the most important put-out of all, the one that prevents a run." Sometimes, it's hard to see the impact a catcher has on a particular pitcher until someone else is catching them.

Such was the case at the end of August when Calder describes Chase pitching without Washington: "Chase was without his regular catcher, Don Washington, and the game showed just what Washington means to the club." Catching for Chase, as we've previously seen, was not always an easy task. Terrell recalled another occasion when he was asked to catch for Chase:

> This ball game was on and we wanted to win . . . The last
> batter had come to bat. I think Flat had two strikes and

two balls on this guy, and I told Flat to throw me a curve ball on the outside corner. And like I said, Flat would never remember what you asked him to throw. I asked Flat to throw this ball on the outside corner. And his curve ball would naturally curve into a right-hand catcher because he was a right-hand pitcher. Instead of him doing what I asked him . . . he threw a straight ball, right, straight down the middle. And I knew there was no way in the world that I could get back fast enough to get this ball, to keep it from going to the back stop, so I grabbed it with my bare hand. I didn't use my bare hand for about three days afterwards because it was paralyzed.

What aren't as well documented as his abilities behind the plate are Washington's leadership abilities on and off the field. As King Terrell remembers, "Donise practically run the ball club, you know what I mean, he run the ball club." Because of Washington, Terrell continues,

we knew from week to week what we was going to do and when we were going to play. But when we played in Stirling Park in the City League, we had a schedule and we knew about the schedule, when to play. And everybody knew it and what time they was going to play. But to top it off, Donise, he practically kept the team together and made all the arrangements for everything, to travel, and everything like that.

Memories of Washington's skills lingered on for many years after the 1934 season. In a 1967 interview, scorekeeper Orville Wright recalls some of the good-natured tensions between Chase and Washington on the field. Wright said Washington would get frustrated when Flat threw "junk and slow stuff . . . Donise used to get so hot at Flat he'd throw the ball back a lot harder than Flat was throwing it in . . . Donise used to throw stingers back at 'im." In the 1980s, comments from teammate Ben Talbot put Washington's skills into a broader historical context, observing that "Chase was a great pitcher but Washington was just like another [Roy] Campanella." King Terrell offers a similar view in his interview with Wanda Milburn:

> Donise Washington was a catcher, but I don't think there's any catcher in the major leagues, the national leagues, the international leagues, any league, could catch any better than Donise Washington could catch. I've seen Donise Washington cut guys down on second base when he was on his haunches; he wasn't even standing up straight. He could throw a guy out just as easy as he could if he was standing up straight. There was very few balls went by; he could trap a ball. Talk about guys coming into home plate, he wasn't a rough guy, but nobody tried to rough him up, because he stood his ground. And he let everybody know, wherever we played baseball, that he was our catcher.

Terrell concludes his reflection on Washington with a familiar lament: "And you heard all over, wherever you went to play baseball, saying that it was too bad that he couldn't get into the major leagues." "He was the wrong colour at the time," Wanda Milburn reflects. Terrell concurs, "He was the wrong colour at the time."

Perhaps what is most interesting about Don Washington is that his life story diverges from many of the other All-Stars players who stayed in Chatham and continued to play with the All-Stars in the 1930s. For reasons unknown, Washington left Chatham in 1937 and went to play and coach in Strathroy. A wire story from Chatham describing his departure is printed in the *Windsor Daily Star* in April: "Don Washington, catcher and captain for the Chatham Coloured All-Stars for the past three years, has left to join Strathroy, O.B.A. champions for 1936." According to Art Cartier, Washington was recruited by Strathroy, "the first town in the district to import a coloured ball player," where he quickly became a fan favourite. This move is particularly interesting given the history the All-Stars had with Strathroy in 1934 and 1935, where messages and drawings that referred to the All-Stars were chalked on sidewalks and fences along with suggestions that the team go home. When Dan Kelly asks Boomer Harding about the differences between playing in Chatham and playing out of town, Harding responds,

> They were coming to see us get beat. . .When we went to Strathroy they used to write on the sidewalks that we was coming to town. But I guess, and everything else they were out to beat us, but they attracted big crowds and people come, you know, would give up their work and everything . . . Well, you didn't know how it was going to happen in a game. Something was going to break loose before somebody could hold us for a little while. Then the bats would break loose and we'd make some little excitement some way. Run the bases or something else. And you didn't know what—it wasn't—we weren't really coached well. Everybody'd done his own thing. And with the advice we could get from this Don Washington and a few others, well, it turned out all right.

While Washington was certainly not blind to what was happening, he would later reflect about his time coaching and playing in Strathroy: "I was the only negro in town . . . I remember the sidewalks being painted but when I lived there everybody treated me well." It's not entirely certain what Don Washington did after his two or three years playing and coaching in Strathroy. The interview with Boomer Harding suggests that Washington returned to Detroit and ran a bar on the east side, but not much else is known about his later life.

Comments in various interviews across the decades convey something of Washington's character. All point to someone who showed calm leadership skills. Clifford Olbey's brother, John, has distinct memories of Don Washington, calling him "the solid heart of the team." While writing about a tense event that occurred in Strathroy in 1935, Calder describes Washington not only as a "clever player" but also a "philosopher and diplomat."

★ ★ ★

"Welland Beaten in Playoffs: Stars Even Round with Clever Win" is the headline of the wire story from Welland which ran in the *Chatham Daily News* about the second game in the series: "Chatham's Stars in a startling reversal of form surprised 2,000 fans here Saturday afternoon by defeating the Welland Terriers 4–2 . . . "Flat" Chase, hard-hitting shortstop for the Stars, supplied the biggest thrill of the afternoon when he drove a mammoth drive far over the right field fence in the sixth for a home run. It was the longest drive in the history of the local park. Welland errors gave the Stars two of their runs. It is expected the third game will be played at London or St. Thomas." The mention of the location of the third game being in London or St. Thomas, cities partway between Chatham and Welland, suggests an OBAA impulse, though not always a practice, towards selecting equidistant neutral cities for playdown rubber matches. Just as the *Chatham Daily News* started to rely on other town's sports reporters for coverage of All-Stars games, presumably, other papers began publishing Calder's coverage of their hometown teams because his stories start to take on a "wire story" feel, as if he's writing for a new and non-local audience.

The only out-of-town playdown coverage we have from Calder is when he goes to London and witnesses the All-Stars' series-winning 11–7 victory against Welland. His coverage is, in most ways, classic Calder: "Flat Chase, who was the first to face Shupe, nailed the Welland moundsman's first delivery on the button and the crowd sat fascinated as the sphere threatened to vanish into the heavens. When last seen, the ball was disappearing over the large sheet metal shed outside the right field fence. Chase was given a standing ovation by fans for his performance. It was easily the longest hit ever made in the park." In other ways, however, it is distinct from virtually all his other columns in his highly racialized depiction of Chase: "Again it was big Flat Chase, who played at shortstop for the Stars yesterday, who predominated on the attack. The Kolored King of Klout rapped a triple, a double, and a single in five attempts." This is only the second mention of the team's race I have found in Calder's writing, and in both cases he was writing for a larger, non-local audience. The other instance is when he writes about the first game of the OBAA playoffs against Sarnia: "Chatham Stars, coloured baseball team of this city, will oppose Sarnia Red Sox here tomorrow afternoon at Athletic Park." It's not certain why Calder, or his editors, included mentions of the team's race here. Likely it was the excitement or challenges of writing for a broader audience or that other communities would not have known this was a Black team.

Mentions of the team's race, while rare in Chatham coverage, are almost always included in out-of-town stories about the team. Usually, it's a descriptor, as we see throughout the region's newspapers in the 1930s of teams like the Ecorse Colored Giants and Quinn's Colored Stars of Detroit. In the September 25 *Chatham Daily News* they reproduce parts of the *Welland–Port Colborne Tribune* coverage about the first game in the series, when the All-Stars lost 17–7. These segments provide insight into how other towns viewed the All-Stars. Significantly, their race is the first thing noted: "A word about the coloured lads." The quoted sections then go on to describe how

they made a big hit with the crowd. Especially Percy "Feet" Parker who coached at first base and was a whole show in himself. His "my, my, my," observation after close decisions went against Stars kept the crowd in high glee. Flat Chase's home run brought down the house and every good play by the visitors was applauded. Catcher Washington proved to be a backstopper of no mean ability and all in all, the crew performed in a style that caused general bewilderment in view of the top-heavy score the Terriers registered against the Chatham Club last Thursday.

These segments reveal the All-Stars were seen as an entertaining, skillful, exciting team, even when playing the hometown team. The recurrent mentions and, in many cases foregrounding, of their race in the out-of-town coverage of the September and October games is a reminder that the further the All-Stars go from the known confines of Chatham, the more they need to navigate a racialized world in unfamiliar communities.

This short passage from the *Tribune* reveals a number of things that connect the All-Stars with a larger history of Black baseball in North America. In addition to the exciting style of play and the skill of the players, the mention of Percy Parker being "a whole show in himself" highlights white expectations that Black players and coaches be entertaining on the field. From its earliest days, Black baseball was known for having an element of on-field entertainment. Lawrence D. Hogan describes the common practice in the 1880s of Black touring baseball teams "clowning" during pre-game practices and even during the games to keep the paying customers amused. One popular amusement was "shadowball," where players would perform "elaborate fielding pantomimes with invisible baseballs during practice." Pioneering Negro leagues player Sol White recalled that "Every man on a team would do a funny stunt during a game back in the eighties and nineties." There was also a "low burlesque" bantering from the players from the sidelines of the games and a fair bit of "comical coaching" between the first and third base coaches. Hogan, noting that "black teams more often than not were playing for white fans," argues that some of their antics were the team's way of delivering what white fans expected of Black baseball players. In Hogan's words, "Making a fool of oneself on the diamond was part and parcel of taking admission money from as many white folks as possible." By the time we get to 1934 in Chatham, however, there appears to be very little left of this clowning in the games. Nevertheless, there are some residual traces to be found in the newspaper coverage of the time, especially in descriptions of Percy Parker, the All-Stars coach.

Percy Parker was born in 1898 in Raleigh Township, Ontario, to Alfred J. Parker and Geraldine Henry, one of twelve children. He married Bertha Holden in September 1923, when his occupation was listed as "labourer." In the 1934 Shepherd's city directory for Chatham, he is listed as working at the Canadian Fertilizer Company on King Street East. Primarily a third-base coach for the All-Stars, he was perhaps best known for amusing the crowd with catch-phrases and comments.

When Dan Kelly talks to Boomer Harding, he asks about Percy Parker. Kelly says, "They said he used to clown around a lot being third base coach. There was a whole write up in there about him and Flat Chase and their antics. Like, if the game were slow, they'd kind of entertain the crowd by doing these stupid things." Boomer responds, "Oh—'ain't that beautiful.' That was one of his sayings. Somebody'd make a good catch, or good throw, and he'd say 'Ain't that beautiful.' It was one of his favourite expressions. And then he had three or four more that all during the game he'd crack you up." In his 1985 interview with Wanda Harding-Milburn, King Terrell recalls that Parker had "one of those original chants, too, didn't he? . . . Percy Parker used to 'yatateeyat'—what was that yell? Can you remember that yell that he used to give? He was loud, you could hear it all over the East End."

Parker's antics were sufficiently notable that they received several mentions in Calder's columns. Calder describes how during the September 8 game against Sarnia, "Percy Parker gave Sarnia fans a treat with his yellings and antics in the third base coaching box. 'Lovely, boys, lovely, lovely,' Percy would holler and the fans alternatively yelped approval and disapproval." Calder calls Percy Parker "the human foghorn" and describes how Parker "turned to the big crowd and, cupping his hands, announced, 'The big left-hander, Mr. Joe Allen has ree-tired.' And Joe grinned from the bench." Several days later, Calder calls him the "third base coaching box vaudevillian of the Stars' organization," and describes how Parker "puts on a little floor show by himself during the game. Saturday he had the Sarnia fans in high glee throughout the contest. He earned the name of 'Feet' as he went through his version of a highland fling." Out-of-town coverage of the OBAA playoffs often note Parker's entertainment from the sidelines, and Doug Scurr recalled that it was "hard to forget [Parker's] rasping voice and 'rat-it-tat-tat,' which never failed to rattle any hurler." In addition to and entertaining fans, Percy Parker's performances may have served a dual purpose of rattling the opposing team's players while also keeping the All-Stars calm, focused, and relaxed.

★ ★ ★

There were always City League players who were absent, presumably for work, at some point during the season, and September was no different for the All-Stars. Early in the month, Calder reports Ross Talbot "has just returned to the city after an absence of several weeks." Towards the end of the month, Calder comments that "it's doubtful if Don Tabron will be with them again this season for he could not obtain work here and had to go to Windsor." Tabron's name is absent from the box scores of the first games of the Welland series, but the *Chicago Defender* reports that "Messrs. Washington, Ladd and Robbins, members of the Chatham Star baseball team, made a trip to Detroit to get Don Tabron for Wednesday's [September 6] game." These small details, made in passing, are reminders that while the All-Stars played with a particular kind of professionalism, this was amateur baseball, and it's unlikely that players received financial remuneration. Though there might have been some under-the-table money or in-kind offers that made it possible for out-of-town players to move to Chatham, players would still have had other responsibilities. There were certainly occasions where work or family demands had to overtake baseball as a priority. Individual players, many of whom were seasonally or precariously employed, would have had to prioritize working and supporting their families over baseball, even during an OBAA championship run, especially within the economic climate of the 1930s.

In September and into October, the expanded playing sphere of the All-Stars' playoff run also meant increased financial strain on the team for travelling expenses. Although the All-Stars would have received a share of gate proceeds from exhibition games and almost certainly something from league games and playoff games, these funds would have barely covered team-related expenses in a struggling league. In late September Calder writes that if the Stars make the finals, they will "have some long travelling to do on the meagrest of finances. Their share of the gate yesterday was one fin—five green dollars—not enough to pay the expenses of grooming the diamond for future play." An advertisement a column away draws attention to a fundraising exhibition game for the Stars:

Tilt Arranged to Aid Stars. The Stars and Braggs will
meet Saturday afternoon at Stirling Park in a game to
aid the Stars to go east for the OBAA finals, according to
arrangements completed late this morning.... It is hoped
that fans of the city will attend Saturday's game at Stirling
Park in good numbers for the Stars are sorely in need of
finances.

No documentation about the team's finances exist, but Blake Harding
recalls that the All-Stars "didn't have the financial backing that a lot
of the white teams had." Instead, Blake recalls,

they would have to pass the hat at games and take a
percentage to just, you know, get from point A to point B ...
And I don't know how true it is, but my dad used to say they
used to borrow somebody's car from somebody's driveway
or somebody's flatbed truck from somebody's driveway and
drive to a local community to play their away games, and
then put it back when they got home.

These early worries about finances and the financial strain of playoff
appearances will remain a perennial concern for the team, coming to
a dramatic head in the last weeks of their final season in 1939.

Throughout September, Calder returns often to an idea that he's
been considering all season: Chatham is on the brink of a new era
of baseball glory, and fans need to help bring this about through
their enthusiasm and their admission fees. With youthful optimism,
Calder writes often of his hope that that the All-Stars can bring
baseball glory to Chatham after a long drought: "The Stars have
had a remarkable season, winning games all over the southwestern
counties against strong teams. They loom as one of the best teams to
be developed here since Briscos held sway at Athletic Park." Early in
September he writes wistfully,

It took the Stars to do it. Baseball finally comes into its own here tomorrow when Chatham Stars engage Sarnia Red Sox in the first game of the second round of the OBAA intermediate B finals. Not in half a dozen years have prospects for a championship OBAA team been so bright here. It's just as well that so colourful a crew as the Stars will be the revivalists in the big push here. They'll instill in the minds of some of our delinquents the idea that baseball can be made most attractive when energy and drive are injected.

Even with the impending playoff run, the success of the All-Stars, and the All-Stars management's predictions of a crowd of three thousand fans, Calder still seems anxious about fan support:

There's scarcely any need to tell baseball fans of this city just what is due to be staged at Athletic Park tomorrow. Chatham Stars have been largely responsible for a revival of baseball interest in this city and they're making a name for themselves throughout Western Ontario. Before they finish their OBAA campaign they hope to extend their fame over the entire province and to widen their local reputation as "Canada's foremost coloured team."

"Children in arms may stay at home if they wish," Calder continues, "but they're the only ones who will be excused."

The one crowd that didn't need to be persuaded to support this team was, of course, the East End residents. This neighbourhood didn't need to be told why these games were important or that they needed to get behind the team. The East End residents understood that the All-Stars were not just playing for Chatham in the OBAA playoffs, they were representing the neighbourhood and the region's Black community on the provincial stage. Every time the All-Stars took the field, much more was at stake than simply sports excellence.

OCTOBER
1934

IN EARLY OCTOBER, THE DAYS HAVE GROWN SHORTER and the warmth of late summer is beginning to fade. On Monday, October 1, the *Chatham Daily News* sports pages publish the time and place of the second game in the city's Church Softball League final. A story about the final game of the City Softball League is in the same column as the MLB final standings and is given the same amount of space. Much of this day's coverage is dedicated to the Detroit Tigers, undoubtedly Chatham's major league team, in their first World Series run in twenty-five years. In his "Analyzing Sport" column, Calder writes: "Maybe I am going to be a little cruel on local teams this week by using a lot of space in the Tigers' behalf but I want to string along with the potential champions." The fact that Calder feels compelled to apologize to readers for privileging a professional baseball team over local church and amateur league teams reveals a lot about the importance of local sports in Chatham.

Amidst the World Series coverage, it's easy to miss a smaller story in the October 1 sports pages about another group of "potential champions" tucked in the bottom right-hand corner of the page. Above an advertisement where a British bulldog and Scottish terrier discuss the merits of shaving with Rolls Razors, a headline states: "Chatham Stars Will Go East." This story and one a few days later are reminders of the resources needed to send the team to the play-offs and finals.

Just as Archie Stirling had supported the team in various ways in its formation, another white local businessman, Pete Gilbert, stepped up to pay for the team's travel and other expenses for the semifinals. Calder writes, while "supporters of the Stars were doubt-ful if financial backing for this team could be secured," Pete Gilbert, "enthusiastic baseball fan, has assumed their expenses and will send them in three cars." In this way, we see the support for the All-Stars coming from the broader Chatham community, not just the East End. The fact that Gilbert offering financial support for the team makes the *Chatham Daily News* sports pages suggests that there had been doubts about if and from where the All-Stars would get backing. Calder's numerous mentions of their travel expenses sug-gest that these are recurring concerns, ones that Chatham organiz-ation raised with the OBAA: "No definite word was forthcoming from the OBAA headquarters [about locations of the games] but followers of the Stars said it seemed hardly fair that the Chatham team should have to travel to the far east twice in order to win an OBAA title." Who has to travel and incur those expenses—and who doesn't—is a controversy that builds in the 1934 finals and resurfaces again in 1939. Undoubtedly, Archie Stirling was a strong advocate for the team.

An advertisement for the first game in the OBAA playdowns appears in the October 2 *Chatham Daily News*: "Milton vs Chatham All-Stars at Athletic Park. Thursday, October 4th at 2:45 PM. The World Series will be broadcast at the park." Admission was twenty-five cents, about $5.35 in today's dollars. Calder uses this opportunity to not only reflect upon the team's performance this season and pos-ition them for the series but also to talk about their contributions to the Chatham community: "A huge crowd is expected to throng to Athletic Park for Thursday's game, for never since the organization of the OBAA has a Chatham team made such progress as the Stars of this year. They are a fast, colourful team with a smart pitching staff and a row of heavy hitters. While they have looked bad in their two playoff games at home, they have created a great deal of favourable comment in the outside centres and are determined to play their best ball against Milton."

This day's paper also has a small wire story about the other OBAA division semifinal between Meaford and Penetanguishene, describing the special meeting of an OBAA subcommittee to "consider the protest of the Meaford club against the umpire's ruling on interpretation of ground rules in the game against Penetang . . . Umpires and witnesses from both towns were present and gave evidence. The protest was not upheld and game stands as played, a tie score. Both games in Penetang were tie scores, Meaford winning in Meaford, and to try and break the tie, the OBAA has ordered the next game for tomorrow in Penetang . . . neutral umpires were appointed at the request of the clubs." A story like this reveals a great deal about the seriousness with which communities approached local sports.

What is noteworthy about this controversy is that the tie-breaking game was not played in neutral territory between Meaford and Penetanguishene, as might have been expected. This move is ever stranger when one considers the fact that two of the three previous games had been played in Penetanguishene. Though I have been unable to find an OBAA rulebook for this time, this series does seem to be evidence that there was no set policy that tie-breaking matches be played in neutral cities. Where to play a deciding game would soon become controversial in the All-Stars' road to the championship. The fact that their rubber match was played in a neutral city may speak to the importance of having Archie Stirling, a powerful supporter and OBAA convenor, in their corner.

The coverage of the October 4 game reveals that the All-Stars' roster is nearly identical to the first games of the season: Len Harding, King Terrell, Boomer Harding, Flat Chase, Don Washington, Ross Talbot, Don Tabron, Gouy Ladd, Sagasta Harding, Clifford Olbey, and one of the Robbins brothers. Calder's coverage of the All-Stars' 10–9 victory over Milton in front of the hometown crowd fills nearly half of the sports page, considerably more than the first game of the Tigers-Cardinals World Series match-up. It's unclear whether Chase's arm was still causing him issues, but Tabron was on the mound for the first nine innings and Terrell closed the tenth. Chase, nevertheless, was the hero with his game-winning RBI: "With the count knotted 9–9, two men out in the last half of the tenth and [Boomer] Harding perched on first base, Chase got hold of one of K. Clement's good ones and the ball sailed into deep centre right field for a circuit drive, sending Harding across the plate with the winning counter." Although the Stars win this first game, Calder comments, "if yesterday's affair is any criterion, the second joust will be a real battle . . . the Chathamites will have to play all the time to nose out a victory on the [Milton] diamond. In fact they will have to play 'heads up' ball all the time, something they did not do yesterday especially in the ninth inning." Calder's comments turn out to be portentous, as this headline from an October 9, 1934, wire story recounts: "Stars Badly Beaten in Semi-Final Game. Milton Evens Playoff With Chatham Team. After First Inning Stars Look Bad and Lose By 21–4 Score." The wire story from Milton is three short paragraphs and begins: "In a free-hitting semi-final fixture of the OBAA playdowns, Milton swamped the Chatham Stars to the tune of 21–4 yesterday." The box score reveals that Chase, Terrell, Tabron, Talbot, and Washington all pitched, the All-Stars got eleven hits and made seven errors. With the series tied one game apiece, the rubber match was set for Thursday, October 11, 1934.

Calder's "Analyzing Sport" column of October 11 begins wistfully with "Another splendid season in summer sports is all but completed as softball has finished the sifting stage and baseball playoffs reach the final games. Today the All-Stars are in Milton for what Chatham fans hope will be the game that sends them into the provincial finals . . . They can play spotty ball but they can also play a very high class of ball and if they should be having a good day today there will be no stopping them."

Calder's column is again portentous as the All-Stars come from behind to beat Milton 8–7 and win the series. The only coverage of this game comes from a sparse wire story from Milton recounting that Ross Talbot's bases-loaded triple in the seventh put the Stars ahead to win: "Clearly outplaying their opponents after a shaky start, the Stars were convincing in their triumph. An air-tight infield; three members of which are included on the Stars' pitching staff, helped Flat Chase along the way." The wire story also notes one big change to the team's chances for the OBAA finals: "Chase, big Chatham pitcher made a remarkable return to form after several poor performances to hold Milton to nine hits." As Calder says in his "Analyzing Sport" column that day, "as [Chase] goes, so go the Stars." With Chase back from "a bad cold in his arm," Calder predicts, "if he's ready to go against Penetang in the finals, the Stars should land us a provincial championship." Calder also adds, "Now is the time to think about a civic reception for the Stars. They're the first Chatham team to ever reach the provincial finals and as such they deserve all the praise and honour we can give them. Plus a banquet."

Having won against Milton, the All-Stars went on to face the Penetanguishene Spencer Foundry Rangers for the OBAA championship. A town on the southeast tip of Georgian Bay, roughly four hundred kilometres from Chatham, Penetanguishene is far enough away in our own era of fast, reliable cars and smooth, wide provincial highways to cause problems for a home-and-home series, but this was even more the case in 1934. Considering the logistics and the financial and community advantages of having both games in one place, Penetanguishene reportedly sent a telegram to Archie Stirling, the OBAA convenor, asking what sum the All-Stars would want to play both games in Penetanguishene. Boomer Harding recalls that they were offered $200. "Here," writes Calder, "was a chance for the team to make sure of paying off debts and making sure of a well-equipped outfit for next season. A meeting was held in the afternoon but there was little sympathy for the proposal that both games should be played away from home and the man on the street who wanted one of the games to be played here was taken care of." The OBAA then decided the first game would be played in Penetanguishene on Monday, October 15, and the second game in Chatham on Thursday, October 17. As the All-Stars declined the offer from Penetanguishene so that they could play at home, Calder pleads for the community to come out and support them: "Chatham people asked for one of the games. Now it's up to them to support the Stars who know how to play really brilliant ball. Attendance at the game in large numbers in essential and a little help in the financial campaign will be welcomed." Organizers must have anticipated a large turnout as the game is scheduled at Athletic Park, not Stirling. Calder concludes his article reminding his readers, "There's considerable time before the staging of the game but now is the time to arrange to be at Athletic Park."

The first game of the series is on October 15 in Penetanguishene, and though Calder does not travel with the team, his mind is clearly preoccupied with the All-Stars and their chances of bringing Chatham an OBAA championship. "Chatham's own constellation, the Stars, are in Penetang today," he writes in his October 15, 1934 column, "for the first game of the OBAA finals. They have gone further than any Chatham team has ever done [before] baseball was put on a properly organized basis in the province. This evening the Stars will be either one up or one game down in their quest for the title." The rest of the column weighs the team's strengths and weaknesses, and considers their evolution as a team over the season. In so doing, Calder has compiled the most complete, frank, and compelling overview of the 1934 Chatham Coloured All-Stars and their barrier-breaking season on record.

Whether the All-Stars are a match to the good or "on the losing end of a 25 to 0 score makes little difference," he writes. Having watched them keenly all season, Calder reflects, "The Stars are a mysterious team. Their infield this summer turned in better games than any amateur ball team in this district ever did." Yet, at other times, "Boomer Harding, the Stars' first base, was stretching down and low, far and wide trying to haul in glaringly bad throws" while the infielders were dropping "pop flies and messing up ground hit balls." "But," Calder continues, "the Stars are a remarkably good ball team."

The All-Stars, Calder continues, are "led by a master of the diamond, Don Washington, who really knows baseball and has brought along his pitchers this season in admirable style and has done his share of work offensively and defensively too. In a district where good catchers are rare indeed, Washington looks to be just about the best that is. He bats in fifth position and has hit hard and regularly all year long." The All-Stars have "just about the only four-man pitching staff in the OBAA." Chase is generally their starting pitcher with Terrell, Tabron, and Talbot as relief. Of Chase, Calder writes, "When he is right he has a terrifically fast ball. Cold affected his arm for a good deal of the latter part of the season but at Milton the other day he finally turned in an effective game and looks ready for the series. He swings a mean bat and hits in fourth spot." Absent for much of the summer, Ross Talbot returns to the roster in the beginning of September. He was "shifted this year from first base to second and the change seems to have done him good. He is hitting and fielding better than before. It was his single with the bases loaded that guided last week's important game in Milton." Calder calls Don Tabron "the city's most improved defensive player. He has a great underhand whip from the shortstop position and he's almost sure death on the hardest of grounders. He has been known to hit home runs this season and his average in hitting has steadily climbed." Third baseman King Terrell, Calder writes, "leads off the batting order and is the most dependable man on the team. He throws left handed and this is scarcely a handicap to him. He is fast on the bases and usually scores the first run of the game." Combined Chase, Tabron, and Terrell "add variety to the Stars' pitching offerings for Chase's deliveries are fast, Terrell's sweeping from the left shoulder, and Tabron's and Talbot's are mixtures of curves and fast-ball deliveries. They are great fielding pitchers."

At first base, Boomer Harding's "fielding and batting have been big factors in the Stars' march." Batting in third position, "he is a hard man to keep off the base-paths. He has a good reach and races far to the left or right to cut off hits." Len Harding is in left field and one who "covers acres of territory and who brings a two-base bat. Harding's collection of doubles is the envy of many City League players. Harding is especially good at cutting off runners at the plate with long throws from the outfield." At centre field are Gouy Ladd and Sagasta Harding, though "Ladd has been seeing more work of late because of his ability to cover ground. Next to Tommy McKie, Ladd is the city's best ground-covering outfielder." Sagasta Harding is noted for "hitting in the pitches and he may be used to hit for the weaker batsmen on the team if crises arise in the Penetang series." In right field are Stanton Robbins and Cliff Olbey. Olbey, Calder writes, "has the faculty of turning in hits at all needed times while Robbins, because of his short stature, is frequently walked. Both men do their fielding jobs well."

On the first day of the series, Calder ends his column on a realistic but hopeful note: "The Stars are liable to be beaten today. If that dismays anyone, he doesn't know the Stars. They have come back time and time again to make rival teams eat their bantering words and Penetang will be just another team to them . . . The Stars have, true enough, been disappointing in home engagements but they are going to fight for the title. And a provincial baseball final will be an innovation for Chatham people."

The top of the October 16, 1934, sports page features a headline reading "Stars Beat Penetang in First OBAA Final." Calder begins his "Analyzing Sport" column that day with, "The Stars did it. And now they're just a game away from a provincial championship in baseball." He ends by reflecting that "it's gratifying to see them do so well after calling them to go far this season. They won't miss now with the title so close at hand." Without Calder at the game, the *Chatham Daily News* coverage is reliant on a wire story recap. The coverage is cursory, lacking key details such as which of the three Hardings hit the two-run single to beat Penetanguishene 4–2 in the tenth inning. The details on the game are not plentiful, but the piece does note that Phil Marchildon, Penetanguishene's pitcher and future major league hurler, outpitched Tabron while fanning nineteen. In a short capsule story to the left of Calder's column is another story, likely penned by Calder or Scurr: "The Chatham Stars arrived home from Penetang about eight o'clock this morning after an all-night drive, tired but happy and confident that they will be crowned provincial champions after the game with the northern lads here Thursday afternoon. The trip from the northern town was somewhat hazardous as fog blanketed the highways most of the way through. The boys left here Sunday afternoon and remained in Midland for the night, proceeding to Penetang yesterday morning. They report having received courteous treatment from the northerners." Nothing else is said about why the team stayed in Midland instead of Penetanguishene, but interviews with players and their descendants in later decades shed some much-needed light on the subject.

As we saw earlier in the events around Emancipation Day, it wasn't uncommon for restaurants and hotels to refuse service to people of African descent in Ontario in the 1930s. While people within the Penetanguishene region have disputed the players' claims that they stayed six kilometres away in Midland because they were denied accommodation within Penetanguishene, numerous players corroborate that this in fact happened. In his interview with Dan Kelly, Boomer Harding talks about the road trips to Penetanguishene and Guelph for the 1934 series. He says,

> You know there were quite a few places we couldn't even
> stay at . . . We stayed at a main hotel in Midland, but we
> couldn't stay in Penetang. They wouldn't have us. They
> were very prejudiced. That was the trouble. And then
> in Guelph on that day, we moved into the same hotel
> [Penetanguishene] were [at] and they moved out as soon as
> they found out . . . They wouldn't stay in the same hotel with
> us.

In 1984, on the fiftieth anniversary of their OBAA championship, Boomer Harding adds a few more details about accommodations on this 1934 road trip:

> When we went to play Penetang in the first game of the
> series, we arrived there late on a rainy night. We had driven
> from Chatham 35 miles per hour and it was a long trip.
> When we got to the hotel we were told all the rooms had

been sold so we had to drive another three miles over to Midland. When we got to Midland the people understood our problem and welcomed us with open arms. The next day they wished us luck and some of the people followed us to watch the game.

In his 1980 MHSO interview, King Terrell adds some key details to this story: "The first time we went to Penetang to play ball we got there around midnight, around eleven o'clock at night. And we went to Penetang and they wouldn't let us stay there. So, we called up Midland, which is just about six or eight miles from there." He recalls how they called the hotel in Midland and explained their situation to the manager: "And he said, 'How many is there?' And we said, 'There was 17.' He said, 'Bring them all down here.' So, we went down to Midland and they put us up for the night. And then we drove back to Penetang to play ball the next day."
Don Tabron's 1984 recollections reinforce those of his teammates:

It was cold in Penetang in the middle of October but when we went to Midland the people sort of adopted us . . . They told us the people at the Penetang hotel lied to us. They said there wasn't three people in that hotel. The next day half of Midland went back with us to watch the game. There was between 50 and 100 cars going to Penetang. It was just like a parade.

Some have used Calder's claim that the team received "courteous treatment from the northerners" as a way to contradict the All-Stars' descriptions of discourteous treatment in Penetanguishene. Harding, Terrell, and Tabron, however, all specify it's Midland who treated them well. Why one Ontario town would treat the All-Stars differently from another a mere six kilometres away is uncertain. What is certain, though, is that the effects of that treatment lingered with the players for the rest of their lives.

In 1980, Terrell recalls that "the fans down there—they had baby dolls all painted black, and they had watermelon, and they had marshmallows, and they called us all kinds of names, and every-thing like that." But then, Terrell recounts, once the game began, things started to change: "Flat Chase hit a ball so hard" that the centre fielder saw "the ball going over his shoulder and he took off running and I know that that ball was hit too hard from the catch. But he'd come up with the baseball and showed them he had it in his hand and the umpire called Flat Chase out." Despite the begin-nings, Terrell concludes, "when the ball game was all over, we had beat them four to two. And, you know, those people—about the middle of the game you didn't see a watermelon, you didn't see a doll, you didn't see anything. Everybody found out that we was decent and respectable people." It's worth noting here Terrell's connection between the calibre of the All-Stars' play and the respect their skill brought them. Prowess on the field had, as Blake Harding said, the power "to change hearts and minds," and we see this change happen-ing during the first game in Penetanguishene. "When the ball game was over," Terrell recalled, "they wouldn't let us go back to Midland. They made us stay right there in Penetang. And they took us all to the hotel down there and I never drank so much beer in all my life as them people had up there." As a follow-up, Wanda Milburn concludes: "They turned out to be quite hospitable." Terrell concurs, "Yes, sir. They was really nice, after that." These incidents of kindness and generosity may well be the ones Calder referenced and that the community remembers. Their existence, however, doesn't mean that the team did not experience other acts of racial discrimination.

The amount of coverage the team receives in the *Chatham Daily News* in mid-to-late October shows the level of excitement the OBAA playdowns brought to the city. For the first time all season, the All-Stars appear on the front page of the paper. The day before the second game in the series, a headline on October 17 announces: "Club to Honour Baseball Team: Rotarians to Make Presentations to Coloured Stars": "It was decided to invite the team to a Rotary lunch-eon, and at which each of the members of the club will be presented with a wind breaker." Another front-page story appears on October

19 and tells of how the Stars are "banqueted by Church folk." The sports pages feature multiple stories of varying lengths that also capture the excitement: "Chatham Stars Can Take City's First OBAA Crown By Defeating Penetang Intermediates Tomorrow," "Huge Crowd Predicted for Contest at Athletic Park," and "City Council's Committee Plans Parade and Game-time Holiday." The planned parade is no small affair: "According to tentative plans the Kiltie Band will head a parade which is to start from the War Memorial shortly after 1:30. Retail merchants are to be petitioned to close their stores during game time and merchants and members of service clubs were asked to join in the parade along with baseball executives." While civic victory parades for championship-winning professional teams are regular occurrences today, it's hard to imagine amateur sports generating this kind of response or cities declaring game-time holidays, especially for championships they have yet to win.

Calder is in his element and his pen is in fine form: "Their bats poised for the final killing, Chatham's meteoric Stars laid final plans today for their bid for Chatham's first OBAA title." Calder worries whether Chase will be the opening pitcher, as he appears still to have some issues with his arm, particularly in cold weather. "If the weather is warm," Calder writes, "Flat Chase, big fast-ball merchant, will probably go to the mound." Calder also positions Tabron as the hero of game one: "The Stars give most of the credit for Monday's victory at Penetang to little Don Tabron who curved the home team out of the series leadership." Even if Chase cannot be their starter, the All-Stars have Tabron or Terrell, the "smart southpaw," who could take the mound. Anticipating this could be the final game of the All-Stars' season, Calder again grows reflective of what the team has brought to Chatham. Ticket sales are reported to be "brisk" and "interest all over the city in Chatham's first crack at an OBAA championship is great." Calder also reports that the OBAA is making plans in case a third and deciding game is required: "Neutral grounds would probably be selected by the OBAA." Auspiciously, he also notes, "Tomorrow's game will commence at 2:30. The OBAA is taking no chances that the game will have to be called because of darkness."

In the October 18 game day coverage, Calder remains uncertain about the condition of Chase's arm: "Whether Flat Chase could smoke over his fast one in cool weather was another matter," though "Chase was named last night as the probable pitching choice for the Stars." Calder concludes once again writing elegiacally about the All-Stars 1934 season and its impact on the community: "Today's game brings to a conclusion one of those good seasons, Chatham's best year in baseball since way back [in 1928] when Leamington edged out the city team. And more players have taken part in baseball this year than in the past eight seasons. Playground baseball has been revived and has been highly successful."

The parade in Chatham would have to wait as the All-Stars lost the second game in the series 10–9 in what Calder called "a wild, queer affair." The prospects were for a warmer day and Chase was expected to start for the Stars, but, with a game-time chill in the air, it was Terrell and Tabron who took on pitching duties: "The two teams warmed up in almost stony silence. At the end of the Stars' fielding practice, Don Washington, catcher and captain of the team took Flat Chase and King Terrell to one side of the field to throw a few. Chase pitched about five balls and walked to the dugout. His arm was sore, he complained, and Terrell went on warming up. Terrell pitched." Calder summarizes the game thusly: "a daffy, errorful marathon contest that extended over three hours of a drear October afternoon that was better fitted for football." Twice in the game, the All-Stars were ahead and "the Stars had sufficient breaks and clubbed enough honest-to-goodness base hits to win the ball game and capture Chatham's first OBAA title. But an amazing record of stolen bases made the home team over-zealous and some unforgiveable errors in judgment robbed the Stars of a chance to win out then and there and sent the series to the limit." The All-Stars, Calder admits, "did look bad in those last few minutes and to make it worse the game had been going along for nearly three hours. But it's going to be hard to convince any season-long follower of the Chatham team that Penetang boasts the better ball club.

A pitcher they have and that's about all." This pitcher was twenty-year-old Phil Marchildon: "a curly-headed boy with two deliveries" who "had thirteen whiffings to his credit." In his sportswriterly prose, Calder describes how Marchildon "pitched with all the semblances of inexperience and poor handling but he pitched from the heart and his grit finally won him the decision. He combined a submarine delivery, like that of Eldon Auker with an over-arm swing. His curve baffled the best of the Chatham batsmen but it hit three of them and was responsible for seven free trips to first base." Calder added that Tabron and Marchildon "waged a colourful battle over most of the final part of the contest and both compiled good strikeout marks." This second game not only shows the team's inconsistencies, it also demonstrates that toughness they became known for in both positive and negative ways.

As the day's subhead suggests, tensions simmering between the teams started bubbling to the surface: "Chatham Team Beaten By 10–9 Score as Fists and Tempers Flare over Close Lays on Bases: Good and Bad Base Running in Chatham Attack." Calder writes that, down 10–8, the Stars "refused to acknowledge defeat as they took their last turn at bat." By all reports, the game was rough and both teams seem intent on winning at any cost. Calder focuses on two different altercations, both related to disputed calls in the final half inning. Under a subheading reading "Close Decisions," Calder reports that "tempers flared and fists flew twice during the mad ending to the game." In the first incident, Ross Talbot, who had been walked, was thrown out by the umpire for trying to steal second. Calder continues, "It was then that Talbot whipped an uppercut that missed its mark and he had to be pulled away from Umpire McFadden." "The decision," Calder concedes, "was disputable and the majority of the fans felt the arbiter had erred."

After Tabron singles to score Washington, who had been hit by a pitch and then stole second, the Stars narrow Penetanguishene's lead to one run. With Olbey at bat, Tabron steals second. When Olbey is also hit by a pitch, the All-Stars have the tying and the go-ahead run on base with one out. Tabron attempts to steal third while Sagasta Harding is at bat, and he is initially called safe by McFadden. But, for reasons neither apparent or recorded, the call is then reversed, and Tabron is tagged and called out. And then, as Calder recounts, "the melee was set off." Calder does not elaborate on the exact nature of the melee but notes that "someone connected with a blow that McFadden must feel today." Then the call is reversed again, Tabron is ruled safe, and the game continues. The final two outs of the game come when Sagasta Harding's strike out botches a hit-and-run play and Tabron is called out at home.

Some of this game's most tense moments appear to be due to the fact that "someone neglected to fasten down the third base sack and for that reason the runners were constantly oversliding and giving McFadden some problems to settle." Calder comments that "the cooler heads of the Stars organization kept the Chatham players fairly well in check after three close decisions had gone against the home team," but when "McFadden finally did a double reverse to call Tabron safe at third in the ninth inning he was practically forgiven."

Because this was a provincial final, we have more coverage of this game than all other games in 1934, allowing us to see slightly different versions of the same events. The *Sarnia Observer* doesn't mention the melee, but the *London Free Press* and the *Border Cities Star* each add details not in Calder's column. The London paper recounts how "a close decision at third caused the crowd to surge on the field" and suggests that the call against Tabron was, as Calder also wrote, due to the third base bag having "broken loose from its moorings." A headline from the *Border Cities Star* sports page offers a concise summary: "Dispute Delays Title Contest: Ninth Inning Decision of Base Umpire Causes Argument: Visitors Leave Field But Return to Win." The story that follows describes how "Irate players and a few hundred fans, overly baseball conscious in sensing Chatham's first OBA championship forced a delay in the Penetang–Chatham Coloured All-Stars playoff battle here yesterday. After leaving the playing field when a questionable decision by [McFadden] went in their favour making the final out of the game, and later forced to continue to play when the official decision was reversed, the Penetang athletes under protest, eked out a 10–9 win." The story told in the Windsor paper supports Calder's version where, on an attempted steal, Don Tabron is first called safe, then out, then safe again. But, as the Windsor paper reveals, "Between the changes of mind of the official, however, things happened."

The facts, as best as we can tell, were these:

The Chatham runner was safe as called in the first inning. The fact was agreed upon by both teams and the crowd in general. He was "out" when he over-slid the bag. After players swarmed Collier in arguing fashion and three hundred fans crowded onto the field, the decision was switched for the third time.

But between the first and last decisions, the Penetang squad was busy packing up to leave, quite certain that they had already won the game. According to the Penetang manager considerable "coaxing" was required to get his team back in the field to retire one more man. Manager Jim Shaw informed the umpires that the game would be finished under protest. His team, after a half-hour delay, then completed their winning effort.

While Calder has provided some details about these occurrences, he seems more interested in the bigger question of whether the All-Stars can regroup to win the championship for Chatham. He seems uncertain, at best. Sometimes he seems to count the Stars out and thinks it will be up to other Chatham teams to bring baseball glory back to town: "Chatham has a place in the baseball sun and now it's up to ball players besides the Stars to do something. The 1935 season can bring great things." At other points he seems more supportive of the All-Stars' chances: "When the Stars take the field in the third contest, interest back here in Chatham will be high and the hopes of a city will be with the Stars, a good team—an inconsistent team—but a good, trying ball team." He reminds readers that the Stars have often "looked better away from home all during the playdowns than on Athletic Park. So maybe it's a good thing they are about to go into the third game on neutral grounds." Flat Chase, for his part, seems much more certain about how events will proceed. According to Calder, "Flat Chase says he'll pitch and beat Penetang."

The third and, presumed, final game of the series was held on Monday, October 22, with a start time of two fifteen in the afternoon in a neutral city, Guelph, two hundred kilometres away from both Chatham and Penetanguishene. The start time is worth noting since, as Calder pointed out with the two thirty start time in the second game, the OBAA was cognizant of the risks of having games called because of darkness and didn't want to take any chances. Chatham was eager to finish the series and lobbied for Saturday, October 20. As Calder explains, "It is an understood fact that the northerners have but one dependable hurler. For that reason the Stars did their utmost to have the third game of the series played on Saturday so that Marchildon would have to work twice in three days. They weren't trying to pull a fast one. The logical day for any game is Saturday and the Stars figured rightfully one day was as fair to one team as another. The season had been stretched long overtime too." The move to neutral territory, far away from both teams' home regions, meant that neither team appears to have had their town's journalists in attendance to cover the third game. The extant print coverage from 1934 is limited to information from wire stories from unnamed writers. None of this coverage has the level of detail we've been accustomed to having from Calder, which is unfortunate as the events and outcome of this game, like the hotel incident in Penetanguishene, have remained controversial to this day. Was it too dark to continue playing? Or did Penetanguishene, knowing they were about to lose to the All-Stars, lobby to have the game called for darkness so they could regroup and restart the contest?

There are a few facts that are known for certain. Most of the Ontario papers, including the *Chatham Daily News*, had a version of the following wire story describing how the Stars and Penetanguishene played partway through the eleventh inning, when the game was called for darkness:

With Chatham Coloured Stars leading 3 to 2 in the
Penetang latter half of the eleventh frame, the umpires
called time in the OBAA intermediate B-1 final game here
yesterday afternoon and the score reverted to a 2-all tie. The
game will be replayed.

Yesterday marked the third meeting of the two teams,
each having won a game on the other's diamond. The
chilly weather and dull skies made conditions miserable
but a tight battle was served up and both sides had several
chances to win, but muffed them.

Errors figured largely in the scoring, although two
of the three Chatham runs were earned while both the
Penetang tallies were of the opposite variety. Marchildon,
who hurled for Penetang, fanned no less than eighteen
batters in the ten frames and got two more in the eleventh
that didn't count. He had lots of stuff on the ball and fine
control. His colored rival, Chase, fanned twelve in the ten
rounds and also struck out the only man to face him in the
eleventh, before the game was called. Chase displayed some
smart fielding around the box to greatly aid his own cause.

In the first half of the eleventh, the Chatham team
shoved over a run on a squeeze play but, with darkness
falling fast, elected to go out after more and that prolonged
the game to such an extent that there was not enough light
for the Penetang half of the round and with one out, the
game was called.

Chase stood out for the Chatham team and Crippen, at
short, did some neat fielding for the Penetang squad.

A Canadian Press version of this story appears in the *Sarnia Observer*
and the *Border Cities Star* and offers a slightly different version of
what happened:

The third game of the series was called at the end of the first
half of the 11th inning yesterday with Chatham leading 3–2,
the score reverting to the tenth inning and a 2–2 tie. A close

tussle throughout featured the game, with errors playing a big part in all but one of the four runs. The Chatham team used a squeeze play to obtain a run in the eleventh but, with one batter retired in the Penetang half of the frame the umpires called the game because of darkness. Supporters of the Chatham squad objected and a lengthy conference was held, but the decision was to have a replay held.

There are a number of factors that may have played a role in how this decision came to pass that, in spite of our best attempts, may never be properly explained. Contemporary readers are most puzzled as to why the game was nullified and replayed from the beginning, rather than continued the following day from the point where it was called, with the All-Stars leading 3–2 and Penetanguishene with one out. Were an OBAA rule book from the early 1930s available, it might explain why that happened. It's worth noting that Calder does not seem particularly troubled by this ruling, suggesting it might have been quite common at the time. The main question, which still remains the most controversial, was whether it was actually too dark to continue playing or if there was another explanation for what occurred.

At this point, it is virtually impossible to determine whether or not it was in fact too dark to finish the game—some maintain it was, others not. But if we look at what facts are before us, it may be possible to reach a tentative position. The game was slated to start at quarter past two, fifteen minutes *earlier* than the previous game's start in Chatham. The start time of that game, as Calder noted, was selected to ensure it could be completed before the sun set, at around 5:40 pm, the approximate time the sun sets in this region of the country in late October. Afternoon darkness was clearly on the OBAA's mind as they planned the series. The second game did in fact last over three hours on a "drear October afternoon that was better fitted for football." And yet the second game was not called, with the sun officially setting around 5:37 that evening, and this despite being played under less than optimal conditions.

The third game was stopped at approximately four thirty, after only two hours and nine minutes of play, an hour before the sun typically sets on that date in Guelph at that time of year. This rules out the setting of the sun as the source of impending darkness. The newspaper coverage of the game describes the weather as chilly and the skies as "miserable," suggesting the darkness could have been weather-related. In the previous game, however, the drear weather seems to have had no impact on the game or visibility on the field. Even if we were we to accept that the cause of darkness was the overcast day, it still does not explain why the game was called after the first Penetanguishene batter was retired, rather than more logically between the top and bottom of the inning. Was it suddenly that much darker after the first at-bat?

What is certain, however, is how the All-Stars remembered that game. On the fiftieth anniversary of the 1934 victory, Boomer Harding insists that there was plenty of daylight left to finish the game and that calling the game for darkness was part of a larger pre-arranged strategy by Penetanguishene. Boomer believes that the Penetanguishene players realized that "there was no way they was gonna win it that day," so they flashed a prearranged signal that the game was over. When Dan Kelly asks Boomer about this game he responds, "It's hard to believe, but I still say the two [Penetanguishene players] throwing up their arms had a prearranged signal [for the team], I guess, because they just took right out running. There was no talking to 'em. They just took to running and jumped in the car and were gone." For Boomer's story to be valid, the umpires would have had to have been part of the arrangement—Penetanguishene would otherwise have forfeited the game—which is even more troubling. But considering everything we do know about how this game proceeded, and the manner in which it was abruptly ended, it is a scenario that is difficult to rule out.

Many specifics of these games are long gone, but Blake Harding has distinct memories of growing up hearing his father and his former All-Stars teammates talking about the 1934 final series:

> I would just listen to them and hear the anxiety in the
> retelling of the story about getting to play in this game,
> which would put them ahead in the OBAA championship
> . . . And then to have [the game] called, you know, have it

suspended. And not just the idea that it was going to be suspended. But they [feared they] would have to come all the way back there the next week and start over at nothing to nothing. That story really stuck out, as long as he lived.

While we will never know definitively whether it was sunset, dark clouds, or pressure from Penetanguishene that nullified the All-Stars' lead in the final innings of the game, one thing that is certain is that Boomer Harding believed Penetanguishene wanted to beat the All-Stars at any cost. For the rest of his life, he remained convinced that Penetanguishene cheated.

We can only speculate about the conversations the All-Stars had that night as they tried to comprehend what had just happened in what should have been the final OBAA championship game. How did their lead in the final innings revert back to a tie? What precisely had happened to prevent them from winning the championship? Whatever happened, there was little controversy surrounding the decision to play the fourth and final game in Guelph the following day. The *London Advertiser* reports that "both teams readily agreed, to save expenses, there was no other alternative." But if the team was anxious before the game, it didn't show once the first pitch was thrown. According to the *London Advertiser*, the Stars "went out on a wild scoring rampage this afternoon and batted the ball freely." The game itself was decisive: 13–7 score in favour of the All-Stars. The championship was undeniably theirs.

The coverage of that final game was sparse. Numerous newspapers reprint a version of this short Canadian Press story from Guelph with a headline "OBAA Title for Chatham: Coloured Stars Slug Way to 13–7 Win over Penetang":

Chatham Coloured All-Stars are the 1934 OBAA intermediate B-1 Champions. They defeated the Penetang [Foundry Rangers] here yesterday by a score of 13–7. After playing a two-all tie game Monday the clubs went on a rampage yesterday afternoon and did a lot of wild slugging and scoring. However the teams finally struggled through the long, weary grind, as this was the last of the provincial series completed.

The difference between the two teams lay in the fact that big Flat Chase, the Chatham pitcher, was able to do a comeback inside 24 hours while Marchildon, the young Penetang hurler, was troubled with a sore arm. Marchildon started, was batted out, and later came back to the hill to hurl good ball. Chase didn't start but had to come in after Penetang had put their first three batters on the paths. He then went the route.

In between Marchildon's bits of toll, shortstop Crippen essayed to hold the coloured boys in check, but had no success, being wild and also unable to throw the ball where it couldn't be hit safely. Both teams did most of their scoring in the early part of the game, and after that they uncovered some fairly smart defensive work.

A running shoe-string catch by [Len] Harding was the best defensive play of the game, but the work of Tabron at short was outstanding. Spearn and Hale for Penetang had smart running catches in the garden."

Most of the region's papers print versions of this story, some with minor variations. The *Chatham Daily News* version refers to Flat Chase as performing an "Iron Man act" to "hurl the Stars to victory." As Don Tabron remembers, "Pitching was the reason we won ... Marchildon didn't have much of a team behind him and he was dead tired by the end of the [third] game. Chase was strong in both games for us." Even the newspapers in the Penetanguishene area conceded the All-Stars outplayed the regional favourites: "the coloured representatives of Chatham scored 12 runs in the first three innings of the fourth and deciding game of the finals ... Three runs, four runs, five runs in three consecutive innings piled up a lead that even the fighting Penetang team could not overcome." Chatham, the paper concedes, "are a team of hard hitting, fast fielding players who know their baseball."

Not surprisingly, the All-Stars' victory received a lot of coverage throughout the week in Chatham. "Chatham 'Stars' Trounce

Penetang in Final Game to Win Provincial Intermediate Baseball Championship" reads the headline of the October 24, 1934, *Chatham Daily News*. Beside the standard wire story mentioned above, Calder's "Analyzing Sport" column bubbles with pride and excitement: "At last an OBAA title is ours," he begins,

> and arrangements are already underway to do just tribute
> to one of the best road teams baseball in this province has
> known. Let Goldsmith dig his foot into that big mound
> at Southampton and mow down the rival batsmen. Let
> Fidler kick the dirt about in Strathroy while the home
> town fans applaud. Chase, Tabron, Terrell, and Talbot like
> to win their games the hard way. They'll throw the ball
> down the mouths of the hostile fans and make them like
> it. Chatham's champions. Those up and down Stars, who
> fortunately are better uppers than downers.

Calder positions the Stars within the tradition of Chatham baseball history, noting they have done what no other local team has done: "That championship for which the Constineaus, the Pencratzes, the Conniberas, the Peters, the Morgans, the McCoigs, and all Chatham's other baseball greats strove in vain was finally grasped yesterday at Guelph when our good intermediate B-1 team, the Stars, stepped all over Penetang." While Calder points out the All-Stars are the first Chatham team to win the OBAA championship, he does not mention that the All-Stars are the first Black team to play for and earn this honour. His silence on this matter isn't surprising given that Calder rarely mentioned race in his coverage of the 1934 All-Stars.

In contrast to how often the All-Stars' race was mentioned in the out-of-town coverage, the November 1934 *Chicago Defender* is the only contemporary newspaper I have found that makes reference to the All-Stars being the first Black team to win an OBAA championship. Published in a newspaper written by and for Black citizens, it's not surprising that the author describes how the All-Stars' victory is not just a victory for Chatham, nor just for this baseball team. It is a victory for the Black population of Canada as well: "Never before in the history of Canada has there been a baseball team of colour to win an OBAA pennant and in performing this feat the Chatham Stars were the first to bring this great honour to Kent County and Chatham."

Further down in this same column, the writer mentions that "At the regular meeting of the Ontario OBAA B-1 champions, the Chatham Stars, Mr Archie Stirling, a prominent merchant and backer, was unanimously voted in as a member of the team for 1935." While the team and the players are undoubtedly at the centre of this victory, they fully understand the vital role Archie Stirling played in the Black community. Respect for Archie Stirling is a thread that runs from the earliest days of the All-Stars to today. In an undated speech from the 1950s honouring Archie Stirling, Orville Wright declared: "We, the Coloured People of the City of Chatham are honoured to pay tribute to the Stirling Family—a family of long standing with character and integrity who is looked up to and respected by our community as an outstanding example of a true friendship." In the story about how the Chatham Coloured All-Stars broke racial barriers and opened doors for the next generations, Archie Stirling's role needs to be acknowledged. As Dorothy Wright Wallace told me in her 2016 interview about the All-Stars, "Mr. Stirling, he was a big part. And you can't leave him out. You just cannot. You cannot tell this story without Archie Stirling."

"When they won the series," Clifford Olbey's brother John remembers, "and they came into town they were riding on the sides of the cars and everything and the whole town was jammed at King and Fifth Street to meet them. And they just hollered and cheered them because nothing like that had ever happened in Chatham before and they had all kinds of white fans, coloured fans." Olbey was not alone in maintaining distinct memories of the victory parade that went through downtown Chatham. King Terrell recalls, "We won the Championship and when we came home from Guelph, they had a great big parade for us that night," and Wanda Milburn adds,

"I can remember that—where we all stood on 5th Street Bridge and the horns tooted and the parade came in." Pauline Parker Miller, daughter of Happy Parker, recalls people at the parade "making so much racket. I thought people went to extremes. But they were so happy." Donald Tabron Jr heard about the parade while growing up. His father "mentioned coming back to Chatham and the city meeting them when they returned. Picking all the guys up and everybody carrying his teammates through downtown on their shoulders. They made a really big deal about them winning the championship . . . he definitely talked about that memory very fondly."

The *Chatham Daily News* did make a "really big deal" about the All-Stars' championship run. Collectively, their printed accounts document the excitement and pride the All-Stars brought to Chatham. An editorial from October 24 describes how "The Daily News posted bulletins after every inning of both games in Guelph and anyone wishing to be convinced of the popularity of the Stars in Chatham should have been in the editorial room of this newspaper during the progress of the games. All telephones were kept in continuous operation answering anxious inquiries as to how the Stars were doing; and these calls lasted long into the evening." This editorial ends with words of admiration, praise, and pride for the team: "These boys deserve our homage and our tributes . . . Congratulations, Stars! The people of Chatham are proud of you." The return welcome that Don Tabron remembered is described in the front-page story on October 24, 1934. The lead headline is "Crowds Acclaim Victorious Chatham Team," and the main story is subheaded "Chatham Stars Given Great Reception on Return to the City. Tremendous Crowd Greets OBAA Champions—Enthusiastic Parade, Headed by Band and City Officials, is Staged as a Preliminary to Speech-making— Players Congratulated on their Achievement." The story describes how "amidst scenes of wild enthusiasm, the Chatham Stars were welcomed home last night" and how nearly two thousand people "gathered on Fifth Street bridge to await the arrival of the conquering heroes and form a parade, headed by the Chatham Kiltie Band." The news story is a veritable who's who in Chatham civic life and local sports. The story mentions the presence of Mayor Davis, several aldermen, Archie Stirling, Pete Gilbert, and numerous local baseball officials, and their comments are summarized in a two-column story that runs the length of the paper.

Chatham is undeniably proud of the All-Stars and the honour they brought to the city, and the stories in the *Chatham Daily News* documenting the All-Stars' 1934 victory illustrate this sort of band-wagoning that any championship team sees, even today. A few days after the parade, *Chatham Daily News* staff reporter Joe Emmett includes a verse called "Ode to the Stars" in his "Putting the Chat into Chatham" column:

> Twinkle, twinkle Chatham Stars
> We don't wonder where you are,
> Up the OBA you went
> Beating all, you weren't content
> Till the championship was "yourn"
> And in town where you were born.

In many ways, it is heartening to see white Chatham celebrating this Black team's accomplishment and treating it as a source of civic pride. In these tributes, these men are claimed as Chathamites; Emmett, for example, specifically mentions that Chatham is the town where they were born. What he does not mention is that this is a team made up of men from a Chatham neighbourhood that white residents had long overlooked or ignored. Virtually overnight, a baseball championship transformed men who had previously been invisible to white Chatham into men who were claimed, honoured, and celebrated by all manner of Chatham citizens as their own. But what is particularly troubling from our vantage point today is that once Chatham claims the victory as theirs, the players who earned that victory at considerable cost quickly became yet again invisible in the larger narrative of civic pride.

The baseball team itself is virtually invisible in the long story on the October 24 front page. The only player mentioned by name is Flat Chase, and only Happy Parker's comments are recorded. Parker is reported as having thanked the council and people for the fine reception given the team "amid much cheering." He is then quoted as saying: "We received a telegram from the mayor and we knew the people of Chatham were behind us ... We started out to win and did. We cannot attribute the success to any one player. Every man was out there doing his best. The mayor told us to bring home the bacon and we did." Aside from this brief quotation from Parker, much of this lengthy celebratory article contains only passing references to the actual game and only one passing comment about one man on the team.

This victory, however, did open doors—literally and figuratively—that were previously closed to the team. In the article describing the victory celebration, it is noted that the players and members of the City Council and other sports officials "repaired to the coffee shop of the William Pitt Hotel where the players were provided with supper. It was a jolly affair, which was concluded with the Stars passing a hearty vote of appreciation to the council and others for the splendid reception extended to them." Winning the OBAA championship has given players entrance to the William Pitt Hotel coffee shop and the chance to be served in a place in which several of them worked but none of them can normally be served. Still, it's hard to imagine that those doors would have remained open had a player and his family arrived the next day expecting to be served at the William Pitt.

The All-Stars return to the William Pitt hotel later in the month to be feted by the Rotary Club for winning both the City League and the OBAA championship. It is noted that they will receive what was described as "suitable gifts as a token of appreciation of their work. These, it is understood, are to be windbreakers." The "Chatham, Ontario" section of the *Chicago Defender*, written by someone from the Black Chatham community, offers the only contemporaneous version of the celebration from 1934:

> At the Wednesday banquet meeting of the Rotary club
> the All-Star Ontario's Intermediate baseball champions
> were highly congratulated on their fine achievement and
> presented in person with the championship medals and
> good, heavy, sheep-skin lined lumber jackets. . . . Both

championship cups won this year by the Stars were on the table.

And the *Defender* author offers this version of Happy Parker's speech:

> When "Happy" Joe Parker Manager of the All-Stars club spoke in answer to the City League cup presentation speech, he stated, "When a colored man commits a crime the whole Race is condemned for it, so now that the Chatham All-Stars have done so great a thing in winning what white teams for years back have been striving for, please give us a chance."

The local writer for the *Chicago Defender* notes that "He was given a great ovation."

This speech became legendary, and different versions get quoted in interviews in later decades. In 1966, Chatham journalist Art Cartier retells this story and quotes Parker as saying, "Thanks for the banquet. Now please give these boys a chance to work at some of the places they can't get into right now." In the 1970s, Dan Kelly asks Boomer Harding about this celebratory banquet, and Boomer chooses first to tell the story about the jackets the team received from the Rotary Club as illustrative of the event. Boomer recalls, "I never wore mine once. I took the crest off and I've got it hanging downstairs. But I gave the jacket away. It was that poor material, you know. Just kind of a washboard affair jacket. But it was something, you know, something that—some appreciation." Boomer also recalls the Happy Parker speech and offers another, slightly different version. Parker, says Boomer,

> got up and thanked the council for giving this banquet for us. And I think they made money, they made a lot of money off us. Because the place was filled and [Parker] says, "We've brought baseball back to the city of Chatham for the first time—the first championship you know, the OBA championship." And he says, "Now give the boys some jobs."

Thinking back over the decades, Boomer further reflected, "Now some of the merchants give the boys jobs. Cause all we had was hotel work, which was tips. And shining shoes and working in garages. Painting cars or something." When Dan Kelly asked if that worked out, Boomer paused and said, "Uhh, it eventually opened up. Yeah . . ." A man of few words, Boomer conveys a lot in the pauses in his answer: Employment opportunities eventually opened up for the players. But it took a while.

Whether Parker actually said "please give us a chance," "give these boys a chance to work," or "give the boys some jobs," the intention is consistent. The victory emboldened the All-Stars to remind Chatham that the glory they brought to the city was not without costs to the players and the neighbourhood. It is worth remembering these events took place against the backdrop of the Great Depression. If players had to miss baseball games to work over the summer, it could likely be assumed that some players would have had to miss work to pursue this victory. The city, Parker's comments suggest, owes much to the All-Stars.

Other than excellence in sports, there would have been few, if any, opportunities for the Black residents of the East End to have an audience with the white, upper-middle-class members of the Rotary Club. In this way, the 1934 Championship literally opened doors and gave the players a forum in which to speak and be heard.

The 1934 season thus was a pivotal moment for many East End families. As the 1921 census data mentioned earlier conveyed, the generation before the All-Stars was employed primarily in manual and domestic labour. As Blake Harding observed, "there was very little acceptance" of Chatham's Black citizens: "They went to church, or they did menial jobs." But once the All-Stars won the OBAA championship, they became "celebrities that had brought respect, through sport, to Chatham."

The victory, Blake said, not only changed how the town saw the players, it also changed how the players saw themselves: "It opened some eyes, and these guys were men. They demanded respect. And that's something I picked up just talking and knowing my dad and my uncles and Mr. Chase and Mr. Robbins and these people—they demanded respect. And so that carried on, just the way they carried themselves. So, the doors that opened, opened slowly."

Blake Harding points to some of the direct impacts of the All-Stars' victory and the respect they earned from the community:

> My Uncle Andy was the first person of colour to be a police officer in Chatham. My Uncle Ken, who was their brother-in-law, was the first firefighter, a person of colour. My dad was the first letter carrier. It opened doors later on because of their abilities and the example they set. It wasn't easy. For years in this community, we only had one person of color as a police officer, and when he retired, they hired another one.

In 2022, Blake returns to the idea of what advances made by the 1934 players mean to future generations of Chatham's people of colour: "It opened doors, and it made things easier for my generation . . . they opened doors for me [and] that made it easier for my children's generation. And now I have grandchildren. But the things still exist. It's very subliminal, I guess. But, it's still out there."

Being on the Chatham Coloured All-Stars seems to have been a life-changing experience for many players, but certainly not all. Blake recalled that his aunt Beulah came to Chatham in later years and saw one or two of the players, whom she did not name, that had played for the Coloured All-Stars. Blake recounts, "They didn't get the breaks, they didn't get life's breaks. They were sitting on that creek bed over there with a bottle of wine and a brown paper bag. It broke her heart because they had more to offer, but they didn't get the breaks. They didn't get the notoriety that some of the other team members did." "As long as they were Stars," Pat Harding reflected in 2016, "they were members of the community. When they stopped playing, they were just 'coloured boys.'"

★ ★ ★

When the doors of the William Pitt Hotel were opened to the All-Stars in 1934, it gave Happy Parker a forum to speak his mind and make his just demands. These demands led, eventually, to actions that would begin to dismantle the barriers that had limited opportunities for Chatham's Black community. Older residents of the East End still point to the All-Stars players as catalysts for the changes they witnessed in their lifetimes. As Dorothy Wright Wallace reflected in 2022,

> For the Black community, we thought that it would be opening doors. We really, truly believed that. To show the pride, because we didn't have that goal before. It was like we were all coming out of our shells. And we had them on our shoulders. And to have that kind of pressure, they certainly accepted it, and took it, and ran with it. And we felt like we were somebody . . . Even though we weren't playing the game, we were playing the game, everybody was playing the game, and they made us feel we were part of the game.

Although born nine years after the 1934 Championship, Dorothy and her generation thought of those players "like movie stars": "They may not have had the money and the houses and everything else, but they were our heroes. And we felt pride. They gave us pride that we didn't quite have before. And it just elevated us. And it still does today, for me."

POST 1934:

1935 AND 1939

THE 1934 SEASON WAS JUST PART OF ONE YEAR IN the lives of the players, but it is a time they returned to consistently and repeatedly as the years passed, a time the community still revisits today with pride. 1934 didn't mark the end of the All-Stars: the team continued to play through the 1930s with a roster including many of the same players, alongside some new names. Undoubtedly the outbreak of war in Europe was a factor leading up to the team disbanding in 1939, though that proved to be a very difficult season for the All-Stars for many other reasons. Though Harding, Chase, Ladd, Terrell, and Jenkins still appeared together in the *Chatham Daily News* box scores for other teams—such as the mostly Black Taylor ACs and the predominantly white Chatham Arcades and Shermans—after the war and into the 1950s, they never played as the All-Stars again.

The focus of this book is 1934, rather than the team's full existence between 1933 and 1939. But it is still worth briefly exploring a couple of incidents in the life of the team that sheds some light on

what the 1934 Chatham Coloured All-Stars experienced and overcame. The first happened the following season, in June 1935, and the
second occurred in the autumn of the All-Stars' final season in 1939.
In both cases, the voices of the All-Stars and their fans appear in the
pages of the *Chatham Daily News*, shaping their own stories, challenging outside interpretations, and demanding their perspectives
be heard and respected.

The 1934 OBAA championship took the Chatham Coloured
All-Stars and Black baseball in Canada into uncharted terrain. But
it is important to remember that breaking a barrier is not the same
as dismantling a system. While the 1934 season showed the players,
the East End, and the city of Chatham that racial barriers could be
broken, subsequent seasons showed how deeply entrenched racist
practices and attitudes were and how many obstacles still remained.

1935

Through their existence, the Chatham Coloured All-Stars developed
a reputation for being a tough team and one that was sometimes
called out for playing too roughly. As Blake Harding told those
attending the eighty-fifth anniversary celebration of the 1934 championship, "The Chatham Coloured All-Stars weren't angels, but they
worked hard." But if they were occasionally rough, if they, as Blake
said, "gave what they got," what were they responding to? A key series of events in June 1935 might begin to offer some answers.

In a column from June 22 of that year, Calder deals with the
All-Stars' reputation for being problematically rough, using a recent
game against Strathroy as an illustration:

> Numerous and expected have been the complaints made to
> this department concerning repeated roughness of Chatham
> Coloured All-Stars in games this year, more particularly in
> Thursday's engagement with Strathroy. There will be no line
> drawn here between pleasing and distasteful tactics on the
> field, but the Stars should know that their supporters do not
> appreciate certain features of their play.

Your reporter is no believer in docile baseball. The game was meant for men who can give and take; body contact is not unpleasant in any sport.

Yet it does seem that Chatham's representatives in the intermediate A section of the Ontario Baseball Amateur Association are creating an unfavourable impression when they knock opponents to the ground with stunning force three times in a single game.

The Stars may argue that base runners should slide or that it is impossible to tag the incoming runner without using a good deal of force but their excess roughness Thursday was so evident as to cause comment throughout the entire crowd. Some have said that Chatham likes sports without a kick. The impression is naturally wrong. What Chatham likes is sports with a clean kick. . . . This is no arraignment of the Stars. They provide colourful and highly pleasing entertainment. The fans have responded to their efforts by turning out as they turn out for no other Chatham team. But the Stars are sadly disillusioned if they think they are showing the proper kind of aggressiveness in battering down rivals on the base-lines.

The team could quite easily taint the circuit by inviting flying spikes from rival clubs or even starting fights on the field. Baseball can provide a clean kick too.

If we read nothing but this column, preserved in the sports pages of the *Chatham Daily News*, the All-Stars emerge as a perhaps too-rough team, occasionally overstepping the limits of acceptable on-field play. Indeed, this was my initial impression until the late stages of research for this book. I happened upon a small clipping in Julia Chase's scrapbook, one that I'd skimmed over dozens of times. Upon closer examination, I realized it was a letter to the editor of the *Chatham Daily News*, with the heading "Voice of the People. Stars are Sportsmen." The author makes an impassioned defense of the team's character, while offering a rationale for why the team sometimes played the way they played:

Dear Sir: In the issue of June 22nd under the column headed "Analyzing Sport," I find a probable well-intentioned rebuke or reprimand re the sporting conduct of our Chatham Stars which I must challenge.

Conceded, that the game in question may have bordered on the rough side, it is indeed surprising how soon and easy it is for some of us to forget. It would probably tax too much the memory of the author to ask him to remember the pink tea reception we were accorded by the same team in their home town.

Other than making cripples of no less than three (3) of the Chatham Stars by the friendly spike route (of course these were conveniently accidental); subjecting them to a tirade of embarrassing badinage that would nauseate a leper, headlining in their (Strathroy) paper a description of the game pregnant with such democratic sentences as "Dark Days for the Darkies," "The Boys from Dixie," and other complimentary remarks about the hue of our flesh and the attire of our wives and girlfriends everything else might be construed as friendly and conducive to fostering a feeling of camaraderie between the two teams.

Of course we do not want the Chatham public to think for a moment that the game in question was a grudge-one, but I wonder just how much of the supernature they expect in the line of human reaction even from a coloured team.

We do appreciate the support of the past given by our grand townspeople, we do cherish the kindnesses and receptions tendered us in victory, but we implore you to attempt to see the game as it is going on this summer from an unbiased sporting angle and if our baseball means anything to sport and the community we ask only for Canadian sporting justice from a Canadian sporting town.

In conclusion we are, after all, just so many more human, British subjects desirous of reciprocating in a world of give and take. We are conscientiously desirous of uplifting sports

in Chatham. For the old Maple City—and for democracy—
be with us.
—A coloured fan.

This letter is the only print response I've discovered that offers a
Black citizen's eyewitness account of an All-Stars game and how the
players were often treated.

The Coloured Fan's clues led me to that month's *Strathroy Age
Dispatch*, where headlines like "Dark Days for the Darkies" and "The
Boys from Dixie" and comments about the colour of the All-Stars'
skin and the appearances of their wives and girlfriends are preserved in microfilm. The June 20, 1935, Strathroy paper, for example,
shows an All-Stars–Strathroy game from the home town supporters'
perspective:

> At the conclusion of the game some irate Chatham fan or
> player assaulted D. Fortner, the base umpire following the
> decision at third base when the visiting player was called
> out to end the game. That is very poor sportsmanship
> and the writer of this column sincerely hopes that
> Strathronians at home and abroad—fans and players
> alike—will always take umpire's decisions as they are given
> on the playing field. Strathroy sporting public has a clean
> sheet in this respect.

The Coloured Fan's letter and these stories from Strathroy made me
return to Calder's column of June 22 and consider it from a new
perspective.

The Coloured Fan's letter also seems to have had a similar effect
on Calder. A couple of weeks later, on July 6, 1935, an unattributed
article called "Value of a Smile" appears, written in a voice that
sounds very much like Calder's. This is the only contemporaneous
article I've found in the *Chatham Daily News* that acknowledges
the disrespect the All-Stars were subjected to as a result of their
race. It reads:

A soft answer turneth away wrath. Most people, at some time or other, have heard that—but now the members of the All-Stars baseball team of Chatham know it to be absolutely true.

This clever aggregation of coloured athletes, who carried off a provincial championship last year, and who are now running second in their group, have been having a somewhat difficult experience with the Strathroy team and their supporters, not as far as the games are concerned, for the Stars have shown they are the superior team, but they have been compelled to put up with stinging insults, largely because of their racial characteristics. At first, they resented it, naturally, and in a couple of games they are said to have given their opponents what they were asking for, which certainly did not tend to reduce the feelings of animosity and unpleasantness.

Then came this week's game in Strathroy.

Captain Don Washington got his men together before the contest, for final instructions, and he just had one thing to tell them. No matter what the team or the crowd may say or do, he advised them, take it smiling—and play ball. Then the boys went out to win—and they did.

Jeering remarks from the spectators were met with a good-natured grin. When the umpire gave an unsatisfactory decision, it was greeted with a game smile. When opposing players attempted to get their goat, they handed back banter with a laugh. When Washington got on first base he laughingly told the opposing pitcher he would steal two bases—and he did. The crowd soon began to cheer for the Stars and to give them a "good hand" when they deserved it, and when "Flat" Chase hit the longest ball ever recorded on the Strathroy diamond the enthusiasm was unbounded.

There was a tense atmosphere in the Strathroy ball park before the game started. It could almost be felt. There was an uncomfortable suspicion that the game would end in fisticuffs. But the Chatham Stars just smiled and took everything in good spirit—and they won the crowd as well as the game.

Captain Washington has upon many occasions proved he is a clever player. The other day he also proved he is somewhat of a philosopher and diplomat. He knows the value of a smile.

What Calder describes here—Washington's advice to not engage but to continue to play the game with respect—is akin to what Hall of Famer Monte Irvin said about being subject to racism on the ball field:

An incident would crop up here and there. They would call you a name or something. But being black we got used to that and we didn't let that deter us. Sometimes through adversity I think it made us better players because we could try harder. They would make us mad. And rather than fight or anything like that we would want to play so as to beat the opposition. We developed that kind of mentality. I think it was that kind of mentality that took us through.

We'll never know for certain whether Washington's two stolen bases or Chase's record-breaking home run were motivated by the jeers of the crowd that day. But we do know that, as Calder writes, the team "went out to win—and they did."

Undoubtedly there were times when the team's resolve to be better and more professional than their opponents crumbled and they could no longer "take it smiling" and just play ball. After reading the Coloured Fan's letter, I recalled Blake Harding's comment that "when it got nasty, [the All-Stars] were just as nasty and aggressive and tough as anybody else out there. And if you wanted to play to hurt one of them, they gave what they got." In other words, the All-Stars were not "giving" without provocation. Blake's statement doesn't attempt to excuse the All-Stars' behaviour, but it reminds us that the All-Stars were acting on and reacting to what they encountered both on and off the field.

The Star Sports

WINDSOR, WEDNESDAY, SEPTEMBER 4, 1935

Chatham's Colorful Contenders for O.B.A.A. Honors

PROUD POSSESSORS of the Intermediate B championship of the province, Chatham Colored All-Stars are the only colored club ever to participate in Ontario Amateur Baseball Association competition. They won the title for the first time last year and this season are making a strong bid to retain it. Regarded as an outstanding drawing card in O.B.A.A. ranks, the club comprises, left to right, back row: Flat Chase, Don Washington (captain); Goy Ladd, Willie Shagonosh, Wilf (Boomer) Harding and Les Hyatt (manager); front row: Stan Robbins, Len Harding, Fen Jenkins, Jack Robinson (bat-boy), Don Tabron and King Terrell. Percy Parker and Louis Pryor, coaches, are missing from the picture.

1935 Chatham Coloured All-Stars. Windsor Star, September 4, 1935. Courtesy of the University of Windsor, Archives and Special Collections.

Voice of the People

While inviting contributions to this department—the People's Forum—The Daily News wishes it understood that the views herein contained are not necessarily the views of this paper. Letters submitted for publication should be as short as possible.

STARS ARE SPORTSMEN

Chatham, Ont., June 25, '35.

To the Editor, The News:—

Dear Sir:—In the issue of June 22nd under column headed "Analyzing Sport" I find a probable well intentioned rebuke or reprimand re the sporting conduct of our Chatham Stars which I must challenge.

Conceded, that the game in question may have bordered on the rough side, it is indeed surprising how soon and easy it is for some of us to forget. It would probably tax too much the memory of the author to ask him to remember the pink tea reception we were accorded by the same team in their home town.

Other than making cripples of no less than three (3) of the Chatham Stars by the friendly spike route (of course these were conviently accidental); subjecting them to a tirade of embarassing bandinage that would nauseate a leper, headlining in their (Strathroy) paper a description of the game pregnant with such democratic sentences as "Dark Days for the Darkies," "The Boys from Dixie," and other complimentary remarks about the hue of our flesh and the attire of our wives and girl friends every thing else might be construed as friendly and conducive to fostering a feeling of comaradie between the two teams.

Of course we do not want the Chatham public to think for a moment that the game in question was a grudge-one, but I wonder just how much of the supernature they expect in the line of human re-action even from a colored team.

We do appreciate the support of the past given by our grand towns-people we do cherish the kindnesses and receptions tendered us in victory but we implore you to attempt to see the game as it is going on this summer from an unbiased sporting angle and if our baseball means anything to sport and the community we ask only for Canadian sporting justice from a Canadian sporting town.

In conclusion we are, after all, just so many more human. British subjects desirous of reciprocating in a world of give and take. We are conscientiously desirous of uplifting sports in Chatham. For the old Maple City—and for democracy— be with us.—A colored fan.

This letter submitted to the "Voice of the People" section of the Chatham Daily News was published June 26, 1935 in response to an earlier critique of the All-Stars' allegedly rough play. Courtesy of the Chase family.

Ken Milburn, Andy Harding, and Boomer Harding in military attire.
Courtesy of the University of Windsor, Archives and Special Collections.

Fergie Jenkins, Sr, Andy Harding, and Ross Talbot in Crystals and CYO uniforms. Courtesy of the University of Windsor, Archives and Special Collections.

PANTHERS AFTER SECOND WCBA CHAMPIONSHIP

Seeking their second straight WCBA baseball crown are these Kent Panthers of Chatham. Seated are B. Harding, C. Hurst, K. Calvert, B. Wright, D. Toward, L. Foster, and E. Chase. Standing, M. Cross, R. Reaume, A. Scott, C. Cooper, B. Selby, H. Chase, D. Baldwin, B. Gibson and A. Wright.
(Staff)

The 1958 Kent Panthers sees Boomer Harding on the same team as Earl Chase's sons, Earl Jr and Horace. Courtesy of the University of Windsor, Archives and Special Collections.

Sagasta Harding and Don Tabron, the two remaining players, represent the 1934 Chatham Coloured All-Stars at the Toronto Blue Jays' event honouring the team in 2002. Courtesy of University of Windsor, Archives and Special Collections.

1939

Four years later, in June 1939, the All-Stars were in last place in their four-team Industrial League, which had been formed three years earlier. Jack Calder had moved on to write about sports for the Canadian Press, and Art Cartier had taken over the All-Stars coverage. He summarizes their season to date: "Coloured All Stars, the team that many figured would make something of a runaway of the Industrial Baseball League at the start of the season reached the opposite extreme when they bowed to Kent Bridge, 9–1, last night at Stirling Park. The Stars haven't won a game this month." As the season wraps up, they barely scrape by to secure a place in the Industrial League playoffs. Whereas the 1934 season was one of excitement and hope, the 1939 season appears to have been one of deep frustration.

One of the particular challenges seems to have been the fielding of a full team, let alone a strong one. In Cartier's words, "they are plenty tough" when they have a strong lineup, but "under any other condition, they are never more than an even choice to win." In 1939, the box scores for the All-Stars list at least twenty-six players on their roster, suggesting that fielding a consistent team was more challenging than it had been in previous years. It is almost certain that economics played a key role in these difficulties. The players were five years older than they'd been in 1934, many now had young children and other responsibilities. Most of the "imported" players from the team's early days had moved on to jobs and careers elsewhere. One story notes that a game started an hour and a half late because the team couldn't find enough players, and another describes how a "little fourteen-year-old schoolboy stole the show in Saturday's doubleheader at Athletic Park. He was Albert Scott who was shoved into a uniform when the Colored All Stars found themselves short-handed a few minutes before scheduled starting time." A small number of familiar players form the core of the 1939 team. Flat Chase is their only consistent pitcher, and Cartier describes the Harding brothers and King Terrell as "among the district's most enthusiastic baseballers." This story also notes the team has players who "have difficulty getting off work for every game" and others who "want to be coaxed before getting into a ball uniform." Here, Cartier articulates a reality about amateur baseball in general, but it was a particularly acute reality for working-class players of colour in the 1930s: "It has been a little hard for some of the Stars to get off work to play ball on Saturdays than it is for some of the other players. This contributes to the fact that they have won only one Saturday game all season."

Not surprisingly, the fan interest ebbed and flowed with the team's ups and downs. As Cartier writes, "The Stars failed to win a game during the entire month of June and their showing yesterday came just when many of their supporters had begun to lose interest." As early as July, Cartier's prognostications for the 1939 season are mixed: "The many who feared that the Stars would not finish their Industrial sked or engage Tilbury in an O.B.A. playdown due to lack of players and interest are pleased to learn that they are wrong. In winning three of their last four Industrial starts the Stars have kept alive a playoff hope that was very dim only a couple of weeks ago." In addition to the All-Stars' record and inability to field a team, there are a few other hints about increased tensions that surround the team both on and off the field.

Simmering racial tensions at All-Stars games are not new, but in 1939 they appear in the Chatham news coverage in more detail. Stories, such as this one from August 8, 1939, expose racial tensions between the All-Stars and Kent Bridge, both on the field and among the fans in the stands. A game at Athletic Park on August 5, which Cartier describes as a "wild free-for-all," again revolves around close plays and accusations of overly aggressive fielding. In the ninth inning of a game that already had "plenty of close decisions," Kent Bridge went into the final half-inning trailing 4–3. The first batter to face Chase was pitcher Bus Read, who was on first after being hit by a pitch. The next batter, Pickard, grounded out but sent Read to second. Pole, the next at-bat, was also hit by a pitch. With runners on first and second base, Stephens singled to centre and Read scored the tying run. Ladd fumbled the ball, and the runners advanced an extra base on his error. "Then," writes Cartier, "came the play that was the fuse to the dynamite that followed":

Johnny Hughes hit to the box and Pole was trapped
between third and home. Pole jockeyed up and down the
base line, while the ball changed hands half a dozen times;
then with a desperate lunge managed to get by pitcher Flat
Chase and cross the plate.

Chase and his mates protested that Pole ran far off the
baseline in order to avoid being tagged. Plate umpire Ted
Flynn shook his head. Then he asked base umpire Fred
Peardon. Peardon also shook his head.

Tempers rose and, as Cartier describes, "menacing gestures came
from several quarters, wild words were tossed with apparent abandon." Chase "made a move at a Kent Bridge coach" and then other
Kent Bridge players stepped in. The umpires, Cartier writes, "parted
the main gladiators while players poured onto the field from the
dugouts as well as several spectators." The tensions on the field
spilled into the stands: "One of the spectators got into an argument
with a colored youth. The two clinched and rolled to the ground.
Some seconds elapsed before that part was over, its termination
being hastened by the appearance of a colored lady who directed
the youth off the field." Chase was ejected, and the game resumed
twenty minutes later. Cartier describes the last moments of the
game in this way: "Gouy Ladd went to the mound for the Stars,
the players returned to their places, the fans who dared to interfere
returned to the bleachers and the game was completed without a
murmur." The game might have been completed without a murmur,
but it soon caused considerable controversy in both the Industrial
League and the local newspaper.

On the front page of the August 8 sports section of the *Chatham
Daily News*, a story runs with the headline, "Managers Discuss Wild
Ball Game." This article includes three statements about the game.
Ed Wanless, president of the Industrial League and sponsor of the
Wanless Trophy, says: "The league executive will meet tonight in
the Wanless Store at eight o'clock to have the whole affair straight-
ened out. The umpires will be called to give their explanations. The

principals in the argument will tell their story. The managers of each of the four [Industrial League] teams will give their opinion. Then the executive only will go to conference and decide what is to be done." Bert Williams, manager of Kent Bridge, states that he will be unable to be present at the game but notes that

> the Kent Bridge boys had a meeting on Saturday night and they decided that they would play no more games with the All Stars, even if it meant their chance to win the Industrial title. Kent Bridge players and fans regret very much what happened and it is our claim that there was something intentional when our pitcher and catcher were both hit by pitched balls that ninth inning.

Though it's impossible at this distance to know whether or not Chase intentionally hit the Kent Bridge players, if he did, it would have been an unusual game strategy with the team up by only one run in the bottom of the ninth. It also seems uncharacteristic for Chase and the All-Stars, whose competitiveness would have prioritized walking away with a victory over bruising a couple of their opponents. It is obvious from Williams's statement that he believed the Stars were responsible for what happened, a claim that further builds the case that the All-Stars were too rough and tumble for the league. Len Harding's statement as manager of the All-Stars seems intended to counteract Williams's accusation: "We will play the same kind of ball against Kent Bridge as they play against us. All we ask is a fair deal and we hope we get it at the meeting Tuesday. We'll have our answers ready at that time." Harding's statement echoes Blake Harding's explanation of the All-Stars giving as good as they got.

The officials' decision is printed under this headline from the August 9 sports page: "No More Rowdyism, Edict of Industrial League Heads":

> The Chatham Industrial baseball league executive will not countenance any rowdyism in future games of the league.

Players who disregard this ruling will find themselves out in the cold, so far as the league is concerned, for the balance of the season. The officials of the league "cracked down" on the rough stuff at a meeting held in the office of Ed Wanless, president, last evening. The warning was given [to] the representatives of the teams after the fight at last Saturday's Kent Bridge–All Stars game had been investigated. "It was a disgraceful affair and this sort of thing will not be tolerated," declared President Wanless. "If you fellows want to kill baseball in this city, there is no better way to do it. Any incidents of this kind in the future will result in the suspension of those taking part and we don't mean maybe. We don't care who it is, he will get what he deserves, suspension for the balance of the season."

I have not located a direct response from the All-Stars to this Industrial League statement on the Kent Bridge game, but another story published in the *Chatham Daily News* on August 16, 1939, describes the depths of their frustrations with the league, and the unfair treatment they believed they were receiving.

On August 12, 1939, the Chatham Coloured All-Stars played another Industrial League team, the Libbys, and won 2–0. The game summary published August 14 begins "The All-Stars defeated Libbys 2–0 and the Steel finished on the long end of a 7–4 score against Kent Bridge. As a result the Stars are now perched in second place in the league standing with the Kent Bridge boys on the third rung of the ladder." Libbys occupy last place in the league. The article goes on to say that the All-Stars–Libbys game was "played under protest of the latter club. The game scheduled to get underway at 1:45 o'clock did not get underway until nearly three o'clock and only seven innings were played. Libbys based their protest on the late start of the game." The All-Stars played well, and they, like the *Chatham Daily News*, assumed they had won. On August 16, Art Cartier reports that Libbys protests have overturned the All-Stars' win: "Last Saturday's [August 9, 1939,] game between Stars and Libbys was awarded to the latter team on the recommendation of plate umpire Fred Peardon." The game appears to have been delayed several times, allegedly due to the All-Stars' inability to field a full team at game time and due to misunderstandings about whether it would be an official Industrial League game, which would count in the standings, or an exhibition game, which would not.

> Umpire Peardon's statement to the league was that he decided to award the game to the Canners after giving the Stars more than half an hour extra time. This announcement found the Stars unwilling to play as an exhibition game. The official then ordered a seven-inning [league] game played, recognizing a protest by the Libby management. Stars won, 2–0. "I figured it would be best for fans and the league to have some sort of a first game," Peardon explained. And the majority of the executive agreed.

The league president, Wanless, did not put the decision to a board vote, stating that "it was entirely an umpire's decision and required no special ballot." The executive then invited both teams to have a doubleheader on the following Saturday. The overturning of the game meant the All-Stars sunk back to third place in the League. If Libby won both games, they would then move to third place, pushing the All-Stars to fourth. Len Harding's response on behalf of the All-Stars was this: "If we are going to lose that game we won Saturday, we are content to drop out and let Libbys and Kent Bridge start their playoff." Libbys and Kent Bridge went on to the semi-finals later that week.

After withdrawing from the Industrial League, Len Harding's letter to the *Chatham Daily News* sports editor appears in the paper on August 18, 1939, explaining their perspective on the game in question and elucidating some of the confusions in the previous days' coverage:

> The management of the All Stars feel that baseball fans of the city should be informed of the circumstances which resulted in the decision of the team to withdraw from the City League.

On August 12th, a game was scheduled between Libbys and All Stars. The August 11th edition of The News stated that the game would be the second of a double-header.

We claim that this fact was not considered at the executive meeting which sanctioned the forfeiting of the game to Libbys.

At 1:45 it was raining and the game was not called. At 2:05 the Stars management states that there was no umpire present, and that the grounds had not been prepared for the game after the rain.

At 2:20 Umpire Peardon announced that the game was being forfeited to Libbys and that an exhibition game would be played. The Star management refused to play an exhibition game.

Umpire Peardon then informed both the Stars and Libbys management that a seven inning game would be played under protest. He assured the Star management that the game would not be forfeited. According to regulations a protest game cannot be given to either team, but if the protest is sustained, can either be re-played or thrown out.

A forfeited game must be called by the umpire. When Umpire Peardon called the game, the Stars were ready to play. Previous to 2:20 Umpire Peardon had never said, "play-ball," and Libbys team had not taken the field.

In this letter, Harding not only takes issue with what transpired at the game, but also with how the league handled the issue and whose perspectives were heard: "At the executive meeting Umpire Peardon admitted that he assured the Star management that they were play-ing under protest, and that the game had not been forfeited. Only the statement of the umpire was accepted by the executive." Speaking on behalf of the team, Harding writes, "The Stars management are not withdrawing from the Industrial League merely because the game was taken away from them, but because they object to an admitted, unfair misrepresentation by Umpire Peardon. The management feel that the executive were partial towards the Libby team in upholding the misrepresented decision of Umpire Peardon. This incident has been the culmination of a series of unfavorable decisions and incidents towards the Star ball team." Harding's final comment takes the issue far beyond just one game, and possibly beyond the 1939 season. His earlier demand for "a fair deal" has, yet again, not been met. Harding's use of the word "culmination" suggests the team has hit a point of no return. By August 1939, the days of meeting unfairness "with a smile" are gone.

While they were navigating the Industrial League controversy, the All-Stars were concurrently planning a series with Tilbury: "Chatham Coloured All-Stars and Tilbury Motors, Kent County's only two contenders in OBA Intermediary A Competition, will open their long awaited three out of five series at Tilbury on Sunday, the Stars management announced today [August 17]." In practical terms, leaving the Industrial League could be read as a largely symbolic act since the All-Stars are still able to participate in the OBA playdowns. Nevertheless, their departure signals the team is drawing boundaries about what is acceptable and what is not acceptable. Disrespect, their gesture says, will not be tolerated.

In the post-season, they seem to have recaptured some of their earlier magic, perhaps motivated by what they endured in August. After beating Tilbury in a five-game series to win the Western Counties Baseball Association Intermediate "A" championship, the All-Stars go on to play the Leamington Barons. On September 13, 1939, in a write-up about the first game of Leamington series, we learn that "the Stars have been playing smart baseball lately and deserve encouragement in their efforts to go places along the OBA Championship trail." The All-Stars beat Leamington in two straight games, but find themselves in the papers yet again for accusations of rough play:

> An argument in the seventh inning resulted in the
> banishment of three players, Ross and Benny Talbot of
> Chatham and Garton of Leamington. Garton is alleged
> to have said something that Ross Talbot didn't like and
> the Star player walked over to the coaching line and

clipped Garton lightly on the chin. Players rushed in from both sides and in the general mix-up that always follows such affairs, Benny Talbot, a Star coach, aimed one at catcher Roach. Umpires Peardon and McPherson cleaned up things and a good ten minutes elapsed before play was resumed.

This incident sparks another editorial about fighting, aggressive play, and the future of baseball. Cartier writes: "Any time you want to kill amateur sport and kill it fast, just have the occasional outburst of temper on the part of players." In ways reminiscent of Calder in June 1935, Cartier continues: "There is absolutely no excuse for such feeling on the field of sport. Even intentional rough play is not expected in baseball. The Leamington player, if guilty, deserved a sock on the jaw for what he said to the Chatham boy. But the fist-swinging act should have been delayed until after the game . . . And the fighting, if it must come, could still get under way after the customers had gone home." Interestingly, Cartier does not challenge that fists should have flown; he just believes they should have flown only after the game was over.

After winning the series against Leamington, the All-Stars play and beat the defending OBA Intermediate A Champions, the Aylmer Steam Laundrymen, in two close games to win the OBA semifinals. They then move on to the finals to play the Meaford Knights in the last days of September, 1939.

Cartier's "Sport Talk" column often ends with a section called "Hunch Department," where he offers his predictions about various sporting matchups. At the beginning of the All-Stars–Meaford series, he predicts "the series looks like Chatham's whether it ends in two straight or goes the limit." All signs seem to point to a recurrence of the All-Stars' 1934 championship. Indeed, the series box scores look similar to the 1934 lineup. The core of Len Harding, King Terrell, Flat Chase, Boomer Harding, Ross Talbot, and Gouy Ladd are all present alongside Ferguson Jenkins, Andy Harding, Dutch Scott, Willie Shognosh, and a player with the last name of Johnson. Aside from the lineup, there are other remarkable similarities between the

1934 OBAA and the 1939 OBA finals. In 1939, the Stars win the first game 13–1, lose the second game 9–1, and then, as was the case in 1934, there was a controversy surrounding the third game.

The series was beset by rain delays and rain outs, which resulted in a fair bit of rescheduling. With the series tied at one game apiece, there was the same back-and-forth between Chatham and Meaford that we saw in 1934 about when and where the third and final game would be played. The OBA determined the third game would be played in Hanover, roughly eighty kilometres from Meaford and 250 kilometres from Chatham. The All-Stars' opposition to Hanover was rooted in the fact that, while they had suggested that the game be played at a place halfway between Chatham and Meaford, the OBA made the decision "strictly without the consent of the Chatham management." Nor was this decision what Chatham had in mind: Meaford would have travelled a distance three times shorter than the All-Stars would. Compounding matters of the distances are the distinct financial disadvantages this decision causes for the All-Stars. Cartier writes: "Meaford claims that a large crowd from their district will attend this game and a gate around four hundred dollars is predicted. However, Meaford will not guarantee the Chatham team their expenses of $158.00 to make the trip. OBA regulations allow a team one dollar a mile for traveling at this stage of the race." There is of course a distinction between allowed and guaranteed expenses, but, given that their expenses will be greater than Meaford's, the All-Stars are understandably cautious.

In addition to not having their expenses guaranteed, Cartier notes, Archie Stirling "did a bit of figuring" and "came up with the information that the All Stars have travelled over 1,600 miles for O.B.A. playdowns this season outside of their own Kent group and that the only outside competition which Meaford engaged in was one trip to Chatham." In short, "the Chatham team is being asked to make its third Northern trip in contrast to one made by Meaford. The Chatham boys have lost considerable time from work on account of this series for trips to Meaford and [distance] necessitates leaving the night before. It has cost the boys plenty so far as OBA allowances do not completely take care of traveling when a game is postponed."

We can imagine the All-Stars' debates about how to proceed under these unfair conditions. On the one hand, they were one game away from potentially winning another OBA championship. On the other, to play that third and final game, they would have to accept unequal treatment and the financial disadvantages incurred by travelling to Hanover.

The Chatham team decides to leave the decision as to whether they play the final game to their fans. Cartier writes, "while feeling that under existing circumstances it would be most unfair to make the trip to Hanover," the All-Stars are "content to let the decision rest with the Chatham fans. Fan opinion and fan opinion alone will decide whether they make the trip tomorrow. Readers of the *Daily News* are invited to call the News sports desk at 1465 or Happy Parker's Barber Shop at 1247 and express their opinions. The final decision will be made around eight o'clock this evening."

The next day, Len Harding issued a statement, printed in the *Chatham Daily News*, explaining that the team had decided to follow fan opinion and refuse to go to Hanover. Harding's statement is long and detailed, but the most salient lines are these: "All we ask is a fair break and everyone knows that we would gladly travel as far as the other fellows, perhaps a little farther. But Hanover, only sixty miles from Meaford, is out of the question."

The paper also includes some of the fan feedback that came into the sports desk, revealing how fans, presumably both white and Black, unanimously agreed that while the All-Stars would win, there was something more important at stake. "I think Chatham would be plenty soft if they made the trip under present conditions," said one fan. Another said, "The O.B.A. is a big organization, but I don't think it is too big to have this bluff called." On the surface, this controversy was about money. However, underlying all of these comments—from Len Harding's to Art Cartier's to the anonymous fans'—is an acknowledgement that all of the arrangements showed a distinct lack of respect for the Chatham team. It was clear that the All-Stars, infamously competitive as they were, had quite simply had enough. It was also clear that the Chatham community was overwhelmingly supportive of the All-Stars' decision, even if it robbed them of another OBA championship.

On October 23, Cartier reports that "at noon today neither the OBA convenor Archie Stirling nor the management of the Chatham Coloured All-Stars had received any word from the OBA regarding their decision not to play the third and deciding game of the Intermediate 'A' final with Meaford Knights at Hanover last Saturday." Citing Chatham's failure to show up in Hanover as a concession, Meaford believes they are the champions but, as Cartier writes, "official word to this effect in this part of the province" had not yet been received. "Meanwhile," Cartier adds, "the All-Stars are not packing away their uniforms for the winter. Just in case." On October 25, 1939, Cartier's column leads with the reprint of a Canadian Press story out of Meaford that claims the Knights were awarded the OBA title because the All-Stars refused to play in Hanover. The vice-president of the OBA, J.C. McDonald, also alerted the Meaford team that Chatham might be suspended by the association for their actions. The OBA continued their silence for several days, and the *Chatham Daily News* is full of considerable back-and-forth between the teams and the regional media.

On October 31, 1939, Cartier's column includes a statement from OBA declaring that neither team had been awarded the championship and that the matter will be decided upon by an OBA subcommittee. The OBA secretary, adds Cartier, suggested "that due to the lateness of the season it was improbable that the final game could be played." On November 3, 1939, Cartier reports that the All-Stars offered to play the third and final game in at a "neutral point halfway with each team looking after its own expenses," but Meaford declined. Finally, on November 6, the OBA subcommittee decides that "no OBA Intermediate A champion will be declared for 1939."

After this announcement, the *Chatham Daily News* was filled with calls to abandon the OBA for something more local and respectful of this region. At the same time, the *Owen Sound Sun Times* was filled with outrage in response to what they perceived as the unfairness of the OBA in not awarding Meaford the championship. Fans and commentators drew parallels between the 1934 and 1939 series. In the Chatham paper, Cartier directs readers' attention to a letter to the editor of the *Owen Sound Sun Times*, where a fan,

J.J. Shaw, accuses Chatham of orchestrating the deciding game in Guelph in 1934:

> The third [game] was a tie called on account of darkness. Penetang wanted the game played the following week but Chatham, knowing that Penetang had only one pitcher, insisted that they play the following day in Guelph or they would claim the game by default. The game was played, and Chatham won. Had Penetang refused to play, the game would have been awarded to Chatham. Now why Meaford was not awarded the championship when Chatham refused to play in Hanover is beyond my comprehension. Just what has Chatham got that gives them the preference with the OBA executive. This sort of shuffling will ruin baseball in this part of the country where it has been playing for the love of the game and no favours asked. Yours for clean sport, J. J. Shaw.

Cartier moves on from this letter to recount a different perspective about what happened in 1934. "Since the Northerners are asking for it, here is what happened in that Penetang series." He then summarizes much of what is already received opinion, while insisting that calling the third game for darkness "is remembered as one of the darkest spots on the OBA record." Shortly thereafter, a new column appears in the *Chatham Daily News* sports pages under the heading "Roustabouts by A. Roustabouter." This writer, who may or may not have been Cartier, revisits J.J. Shaw's letter from the week before to re-examine the game called for darkness. "Let us recall the circumstances," the author begins.

> The teams entered the eleventh inning with the count 1–1. Chatham put a run across in the first of the frame. With [one man] out in the last of the eleventh, the game was called on account of darkness and the score reverted to the tenth inning. It was a few minutes after five o'clock and while it was a cloudy day, there was sufficient time to have

continued the game until the third man had retired. In fact, a week before in Chatham, a game was not finished until 6:30 o'clock.

The writer then goes on to include several details that did not appear in the accounts published in the 1934 papers. According to the Roustabouter, several Chathamites were present at the game, including then-alderman W.J. Easton and team supporters Pete Gilbert and Archie Stirling: "The Chatham men complained about the decision of umpires in calling the game [for darkness]." Reportedly, Snyder said, "The OBA appoints the umpires and cannot overrule them," and Stirling allegedly shot back with, "The OBA can appoint umpires who know when it is dark." Later in the column, the Roustabouter revisits the questionable call of darkness under a subheading that says, "Local Men Unable to Explain Decision." Apparently when Stirling, Gilbert, and Easton returned home to Chatham, "they were at a loss to explain the umpires' action in calling the game on account of darkness." As Penetanguishene's chances of winning were "about nil, the game was called. They claimed it was still light enough to play."

It is uncertain whether or not Jack Calder knew of these concerns at the time. If he did, he chose not to include them. In all likelihood, the All-Stars winning the championship made the "called for darkness" debate unnecessary. But it is obvious that the team supporters in 1939 saw what happened in 1934 as evidence of a longer narrative of disrespect. As the Roustabouter says, the All-Stars "had, in the 1934 and the 1939 series, a just cause for which to fight and they won. If you are fighting for what's right you win out in the long run, [this] is true in baseball as well as in anything else."

In 1934, the All-Stars were a team that wanted to bring home a championship, at, in Cartier's words, "any cost." In 1939, when they were a single win away from another OBA championship, they decided that accepting an unfair offer for a chance at that victory was too great a cost, so they walked away. To do otherwise would have been to accept the ongoing disrespect and unfair treatment the team had endured. Their counter-offer on November 3—to play at a "neutral point halfway with each team looking after its own expenses"—conveys the quintessence of this team: they were competitive, they wanted to win. But they would not tolerate disrespect or unfair treatment.

★ ★ ★

The second game of the 1939 OBA championship series was the last game these men played as the Chatham Coloured All-Stars. Players would, of course, be on teams together in the remaining decades of their playing lives but never again under the name of the All-Stars. In a 1946 article, Doug Scurr cites the beginning of the war as the cause of the team's disbanding: "the armed forces sapped their unit too greatly." But Andy Harding didn't enlist until 1941 and Boomer joined up in 1943. Little was recorded about why the team folded, but a more likely cause of their demise than the breakout of war was their struggles to field a consistent team and whatever emotional costs or inter-personal fallout occurred over the 1939 season. Players' growing families and shifting priorities likely also played a role in the decision to disband the team.

The end of the All-Stars was certainly not the end of their playing careers. During the war, Boomer played both baseball and hockey in different capacities with the military. Players who stayed in Chatham—Gouy Ladd, King Terrell, and Flat Chase, to name a few—continued to play baseball for local teams. In 1944, Chase played for the London Majors and helped them win the Canadian Sandlot Championship. Various All-Stars played for local mixed-race teams, such as the Chatham Arcades, the Chatham Shermans, the Chatham Crystals, and the Chatham Hadleys. In 1958, the mixed-race Kent Panthers won a Western Counties Baseball Association Championship with familiar names like Boomer Harding on the roster alongside those of the next generation, including Flat Chase's sons Earl Jr and Horace.

Perhaps the post–All-Stars team that excited the Chatham fans the most were the Taylor ACs. In his June 12, 1946, article "Chatham Coloured Stars Return Under New Name," Scurr writes about the new Taylor ACs team as if the All-Stars have "returned to the diamond wars": "Some of the old timers were noticeably absent, but many were back in uniform, even though they rode the bench to give younger players a chance to prove what they had. 'Flat' Chase started the game on the sidelines as did Harding and 'King' Terrell . . . 'Flat' went to the mound and showed he still has plenty of speed despite his age, which incidentally, he keeps a closely guarded secret." There is an obvious wistfulness for the All-Stars in Scurr's look at the Taylor ACs. They did not, as he hoped, become a "worthy successor for the 'Stars' of old," but he was right in his prediction that the All-Stars would be "talked about in Chatham and Western Ontario for years to come."

CONCLUSION

THE 1934 SEASON SHOWED THE ALL-STARS AND THE East End of Chatham that, given the chance, Black men could compete as equals on a level playing field with white men, breaking social, economic, and cultural barriers wherever possible. The underlying sentiment in the oral histories with the players, their families, and East End residents echoes what Negro National League and MLB player Monte Irvin expressed about the importance of Negro leagues baseball in the US: "More than anything else, our games gave black Americans hope all across the country." For many within the Black community, these games indicated the possibility that, as Irvin said, "If these ball players can succeed under these very difficult conditions, then maybe we can too." For the East End, Chatham winning the first OBAA championship was about something much, much bigger than personal glory or civic and community pride. Having first earned respect on the field made it easier to demand it outside the ballpark.

Though long overlooked and forgotten outside of their East End home, in recent years considerably more attention has been paid to the All-Stars, and not just on milestone anniversaries. More stories and short films appear each year, particularly in and around Black History Month. More often than not, the story is about how the team overcame adversity in 1934 and won the OBAA championship. Very little has been said about their radically different trip to the OBAA championship in 1939, and what that journey indicated.

While 1934 showed that barriers could be broken, June of 1935 and the fall of 1939 were reminders that many of those barriers still needed to be fully dismantled. The Chatham Coloured All-Stars walking away from the 1939 OBA final game is just as important to the telling of this team's barrier-breaking story as was their winning the 1934 championship. But, as Irene Moore Davis says about the challenges of writing about Black Canadians, "The ugly realities of

"The Chatham Coloured All-Stars: A Story in Four Panels"
by Scott Chantler (2017).

history can feel easier to skip over than confront. As a storyteller, however, I know that I must tell the story from its beginning, no matter how painful or seemingly complicated. Otherwise, we cannot appreciate the end."

There is discomfort in looking too closely at the 1939 series because it disrupts what we want to take away from the All-Stars' experiences five years earlier. The stories of 1935 and 1939 remind us that while sports had the power to open doors, change can still be slow. To tell the story of the Chatham Coloured All-Stars by focusing exclusively on the 1934 season or by pointing to the recognition long overdue in their induction into the Canadian Sports Hall of Fame in 2022 is to preserve only part of the story.

As important as the 1934 OBAA championship was to those players, it was only one part of their lives. The men on this winning roster were farmers, labourers, drivers, military personnel, police officers, civil servants, city workers, tradesmen, hotel workers, chefs, business owners, and entrepreneurs. We see these men taking on careers different from those listed beside their fathers' names in the 1921 census. Boomer Harding was the first Black postman in Chatham as well as the first Black person to skate at the Olympia, the Detroit Red Wings' arena. Andy Harding became the first Black police officer in Chatham. King Terrell spent the rest of his working life at the William Pitt Hotel, while Cliff Olbey moved to Windsor and worked at the Prince Edward Hotel. Gouy Ladd drove a truck and supervised the sanitation department for Chatham. Ross Talbot became a successful poultry farmer outside of Chatham, and Stanton Robbins spent the rest of his life in North Buxton. Wellington Shognosh returned to Walpole Island and became involved in local politics. Don Washington reportedly ran a tavern in Detroit. Don Tabron played baseball throughout Detroit and for a time with several Negro Leagues teams. But he also became one of the first Black apprentice electricians at Ford's River Rouge factory, eventually opening up Tabron Electric, a family business that ran for fifty years. Sagasta Harding moved to Romulus, Michigan, and worked for the Ford Motor Company for twenty-eight years. It was Tabron and Sagasta Harding, as the final two living members of that 1934

team, who represented the All-Stars at the Toronto Blue Jays' celebration of the team in 2001. Hyle Robbins also moved to Detroit
and became an electrician. Ferguson Jenkins Sr was a chef and a
chauffeur, but he was also frequently captured on film, alongside his
wife, Delores, following the progress of their son's MLB career.

The aspect that is most frequently overlooked in the telling of
the 1934 season is that the Chatham Coloured All-Stars were also
brothers, sons, fathers, husbands, uncles, and members of their communities. Talk to any of the descendants and it's abundantly clear
that the impact of these men's lives was strongest on those who loved
them. The earliest and most robust records of the men and this team
are newspaper clippings saved in scrapbooks by those who loved
them and saw their lives and accomplishments as worth preserving
and sharing across generations.

The centrality of love in the All-Stars story was first evident
when I spent an afternoon with Douglas Talbot at his dining-room
table just outside Detroit. He generously shared with me photographs, stories, and documents about his much-loved uncle Ross
Talbot. I left his house understanding that while I was researching
a baseball story, I was also learning about the men and women who
shaped and inspired the lives of the following generations. I could
feel the love Mr Talbot had for his uncle and knew that this deep
affection and respect was something that would never come across
in the newspaper clippings, box scores, or other documentation
gathered in brittle scrapbooks. But it was nevertheless the heart of
the story of the 1934 Chatham Coloured All-Stars.

Flat Chase was, of course, a legendary baseball player, but he
also had a tremendous impact on the lives of his sons, who lost him
at young ages. Horace Chase reflects,

> I'll be honest with you, I didn't have much time with him. I
> lost him when I was going on 17 and I was still playing ball.
> I wasn't working, I was going to school. I didn't have a lot
> of, like I couldn't go play golf with him, and I couldn't go
> to a ball game with him. Like I went to his ball game, but
> I couldn't go see Detroit Tigers play in Detroit, and there

was nothing in Toronto. I didn't get there because there wasn't enough money around to do things like that . . . I just sometimes wish I had more time to get to know him better, but when you lose them at, I'm 17 and he's 41, you haven't got much time . . . And that's why I try to spend more time with my family here, grandchildren and great-grandchildren. So, I say, "Grandpa's always around."

Love and loss are obvious in Donald Tabron's recollections about the impact of his father's life on his own and that of his children. At the time of our *Breaking the Colour Barrier* interview, Donald's own sons were aged ten and seven. He talked about making sure they knew the story of their grandfather: "My youngest son, I named after my father, Donald William Tabron, II . . . I talk about my dad often to my son because he is his namesake." Donald adds,

My [youngest] son could probably give you a decent amount of this oral tradition because I've sat him down and we've had these conversations. I've shown him the newspaper clippings and different things, different pictures, so even though they never got a chance to meet, he knows all about him . . . But my oldest, he can tell you all about his grandfather, even though they never had the pleasure of meeting each other. But he can tell you "my granddad played the Negro leagues, he ran a business, he was a good athlete" and so forth. As my son matures, I'll expose him to more and more things about his grandfather and his namesake."

Tellingly, when Blake Harding spoke on behalf of the All-Stars' families at the Canadian Sports Hall of Fame induction ceremony, his stoicism faltered only once. There was a hitch in his voice when he said, "I heard an audio tape of my father and he's been passed away thirty-some years ago." Documenting that love, respect, and admiration for the men who played on the 1934 team is, to me, as important as recording the All-Stars' winning percentages, batting averages, and provincial championships.

Julia Black Chase, Flat Chase's wife, assembled a rich scrapbook documenting Flat's baseball career. Courtesy of Horace Chase.

Blake and Pat Harding at the University of Windsor, March 2018.

Blake Harding representing the families at the Order of Sport induction ceremony, October 2022.

Blake Harding, Donald Tabron Jr, and Fergie Jenkins Jr at the Order of Sport induction ceremony, October 2022. Earl Chase Jr (not pictured) was also in attendance.

But as we've seen, few today would know the history of the Chatham Coloured All-Stars without the women—mothers, wives, sisters, and daughters-in-law—who collected and preserved newspaper clippings, made and shared scrapbooks, and gathered oral histories from the community. These women's efforts not only form the foundations of this book but made possible the preservation and documentation of the Chatham Coloured All-Stars' legacy.

Earl Chase Jr told the *Breaking the Colour Barrier* project that his family's scrapbook started with Julia Black Chase: "My mother started the scrapbook in '33 or '34 when Dad and they were playing ball. I've got the scrapbook back there and she kept the write ups from the paper and stuff like that, of the team and what was going on . . . My mother kept all of it." The scrapbook is, in many ways, exactly what one would imagine it to be: brittle photographs and yellowed newspaper articles cellotaped onto large black pages.

The Harding family scrapbooks came from Sarah Holmes Harding's original clippings. As Pat describes, "Boomer's mom started doing the clippings. She would clip everything that she could find about any of her sons." When asked why Boomer's mother might have collected and saved all this material, Pat explained, "She loved her children—all of her children—and their achievements. It was a very achievement-oriented family." Pat made clear to me that Sarah Holmes Harding's collecting, preserving, and documenting her children's athletic and educational achievements is also an embodiment of the respect that was so essential to this team and the community that supported them.

Similar impulses appear to have been at the core of Myrtle Tabron's collection of clippings about her brother's baseball career. As Donald Tabron Jr describes, when his father went to Chatham he mailed the newspaper clippings back to his sister after every game "just to let her know that he was doing well, he was okay. He didn't know that she was putting together those clippings in a big scrapbook and saving them. Once he finished playing baseball, he came back and she had this scrapbook full of newspaper clippings . . . And he kept them throughout the years, and then at a point kind of passed them down to my mother and myself, for safekeeping."

From an early age, Donald Tabron seemed concerned with preserving this fragile legacy of his father. Donald was a young boy when he first became interested in his father's scrapbooks. As his father aged, Donald felt the need to preserve them even more urgently. But, he recalls,

> I didn't really know how to go about that at [age] 10 or 12. But, the best idea that I could come up with was, to stay up all night and—the [clippings] that had his name on—I actually put transparent tape over to try to keep them so they wouldn't rip, or they wouldn't deteriorate. Because I, at least, knew paper deteriorates. I don't know if I was doing the right thing or not. But all of the clippings for the most part that have his name or box scores, I put tape over all of those and put them into a framed picture just to try to keep [them safe].

The Chases are equally dedicated to preserving their mother's scrapbook. Early in the *Breaking the Colour Barrier* research, Horace Chase loaned us his photocopy of the scrapbook—for an hour—so that we could make a copy. He stopped by the copy shop soon after we arrived to supervise. His older brother, Earl, has the original scrapbook, and it took several years for me to summon the courage to ask if I might digitize it. In his *Breaking the Colour Barrier* interview, Earl made frequent mention of the fragility of the scrapbook and the need to preserve it. He said of the pages, "they are starting to disintegrate" and follows up noting "I want to save the book, so I have to protect these, and get some vinyl wrap for the pages." When I went to Chatham to digitize the scrapbook in 2020, I noticed Earl had acquired archival-grade plastic sleeves to protect the pages and an acid-free binder to keep the pages together. The Chases saw that digitization was another way of preserving the original and sharing it with others, particularly the younger generations who were expressing interest in seeing it. Both brothers came to the Chatham-Kent Black Historical Society to oversee my scanning, and they seemed relieved to have another version of the scrapbook that could be shared with other family members.

The natural disintegration of these fragile documents was only one of the dangers these historical records encountered in their lifetime. Pat Harding reminds us of other possible sources of peril. She describes how Sarah Holmes Harding passed the clippings on to Boomer, who kept them in his shed. When he died, Blake's mother, Joy, put them in boxes but wasn't at all certain about what to do with them. Eventually, Blake and Pat took them and, as Pat says, the boxes then "sat in our house for a while." Had Blake and Pat not taken these boxes, it's unclear what Boomer Harding's print legacy would have been. After a time, Pat and Blake had the idea of putting Boomer up for induction into the Chatham Sports Hall of Fame. As part of the nomination package, Pat compiled three scrapbooks to document Boomer's lifetime of sports achievement.

In creating these scrapbooks, Pat did something the other descendants did not do: she not only kept the original documents, but she used them to do additional research and curated them to tell the story of Boomer's lifetime contributions to sports in Chatham. She said,

> It took me a long time because I had to go through all the newspapers. Because sometimes they weren't cut, sometimes they were the whole newspaper and I would go through all that. And then I started reading these stories and didn't have the endings, so I had to go to the library and to the museum and different places to get other material that would close that story off. And it took about five years to put it together.

In the end, Pat created three thick binders of meticulously researched and documented material, of which this story is only part. Pat's "leave no stone unturned" scrapbooks are informed by the belief—reiterated throughout our oral histories—that Black athletes had to be at least twice as good, if not more, to be considered for recognition alongside their white peers. All of this work paid off, and Boomer Harding was inducted into the Chatham Sports Hall of Fame in 2003.

Throughout the three binders, it's clear that Pat understood that she was not simply cutting articles out of the newspaper and putting them in albums: She was writing history and authoring a version of the past. She took her responsibilities extremely seriously. Pat reflects, "I could see when I put the scrapbooks together a very important story [emerged]." She recalls how Boomer had once given her some books on Black history. And as she read them, he told her, "You can't believe everything you read." Boomer's advice shaped how Pat curated her scrapbooks: "When I was doing this, I was making sure that I got as much information that was true. I never put anything in that I could not find three sources for at some point somewhere, whether I could photocopy them or not. Because, in his name, I wanted it to be the truth." Unlike family scrapbooks made for a smaller, private audience, Pat created these scrapbooks as public documents to be read by the wider community and shared with future generations. Her motivation, as she says, was one of admiration:

> I loved and respected my father-in-law very much and I
> wanted to do it for him. But then, when I started putting
> it together, my heart just fell in love with the Coloured
> All-Stars. I read about the struggles that they had and
> the prejudice that they had to overcome to simply play
> ball. And I just felt it was a terrific story. I thought that
> all the people that played on that team were heroes. And I
> wanted something beyond just the Hall of Fame, for people
> to know it, to know that story, and I wanted it together.
> And after the induction I was hoping to be able to get it
> published or, you know, something to keep it. And so I just
> had to wait until the time was right. And then you [at the
> University of Windsor] took over and my dream came true.

For Pat, it wasn't enough to preserve this story. Wanting to make it alive and shareable to all ages in a range of formats, she approached the University of Windsor to help her create a website that could share Boomer's story. That request led to the *Breaking the Colour Barrier: Wilfred "Boomer" Harding and the Chatham Coloured All-Stars* project, which includes a website, digital archive, oral histories with family members, school curriculum, travelling displays, a set of baseball cards, a cartoon, a mini comic, and, now, this book.

As I've worked on this book, I've kept firmly in mind Pat Harding's belief that these scrapbooks have the potential to change how people think about history. When you see this documentation, she says, "it becomes real. A lot of people in Chatham, and a number of other communities, do not believe there was ever any prejudice in this community. They absolutely do not believe it. This is all documented so that it is hard to refute." Knowing history, Pat believes, is vital for the community's future: "If you forget your history, you don't have a whole lot. You just go back and make mistakes, over and over again."

In October 2022, I sit in the auditorium on Front Street in Toronto watching the Chatham Coloured All-Stars being inducted into the Canadian Sports Hall of Fame. Eighty-eight years to the month after they won the OBAA championship, they continue to change hearts and minds. As applause fills the room and images from Pat Harding's scrapbooks float across the screen, I am reminded of something Pat often tells me about the digitization of her scrapbooks: "People are going to know about this history. And they won't forget."

ACKNOWLEDGEMENTS

THIS IS A BOOK THAT IS INDEBTED TO THE MEN WHO went out on a not-even playing field and made history. It is equally indebted to the women who clipped articles out of newspapers and put them into scrapbooks to preserve the history of their families and their community.

It is also a book deeply indebted to the generosity and trust of those who shared their family stories with me and let me into their lives. I have attempted to proceed in ways that I hope reflect my gratitude for the opportunity I've been given to help preserve and share the story of the 1934 Chatham Coloured All-Stars. Above all, I hope this book embodies my deep respect and affection for those I've met along the way, in person and in print.

I am deeply grateful for the generosity and trust of Mr Horace Chase, Mr Earl and Mrs Shyla Chase, Mr Ferguson Jenkins, Mr Douglas Talbot, and Mr Donald Tabron, who shared their stories with me and answered all of my questions with warmth and reflective candor. I am equally grateful that Mr Blake and Mrs Pat Harding gave their trust to the University of Windsor team to help preserve and share this story. Since then, they have supported me unwaveringly in this work, while also pushing me to ask the difficult questions. Whenever I got stuck, they reminded me to ask, "What would Boomer do?" and then the answers were clear. I feel particularly blessed to have had their love and guidance in my life.

The origins of this book come from The *Breaking the Colour Barrier* project, which was a partnership between the University of Windsor, the Chatham Sports Hall of Fame and the Harding Family, with the support of the Chatham-Kent Black Historical Society. The *Breaking the Colour Barrier* project was generously supported by an Ontario Trillium Foundation grant. Additional funding and support for this project and this book came from the University of Windsor's

ACKNOWLEDGEMENTS

Leddy Library; Department of History; Faculty of Arts, Humanities and Social Sciences; and the Humanities Research Group.

None of this could have been possible without the crucial support of Chatham Sports Hall of Fame, especially Don Bruner and Mike Murphy for their enthusiasm, support, and trust. I am also indebted to the assistance and support of the Chatham-Kent Black Historical Society. I am particularly grateful to Samantha Meredith for her never-ending enthusiasm and ability to answer the obscurest of questions cheerfully and ably. Many thanks and my deepest admiration to Mrs Dorothy Wright Wallace for her trust, support, warmth, and willingness to support this project and my work on this book.

I would also like to acknowledge the contributions of the original *Breaking the Colour Barrier* team members: Dave Johnston and Miriam Wright from the University of Windsor, and the fantastic team of student researchers.

Thank you to those who shared their memories with us for that project: Horace Chase, Earl Chase Jr, Shyla Chase, Fran Dungey, Blake Harding, Pat Harding, Tracey Harding, Fergie Jenkins Jr, Andrea Levisy, Pauline Parker Miller, Jennifer Miss, Cleata Morris, John Olbey, Gary Pryor, Donald Tabron, Douglas Talbot, Kevin Wallace, Dorothy Wright Wallace, and Pauline Williams.

For the foundational primary source materials, I am indebted to Sarah Holmes Harding, Julia Black Chase, and Myrtle Tabron, and to the Chase family, Fran Dungey, and Tracey Harding for loans of family scrapbooks. I am also grateful for those who had the foresight and skill to conduct, preserve, and share invaluable interviews: Dan Kelly, Wanda Milburn, Vivian Chavis, the Multicultural History Society of Ontario, and LeSean Harris. Thank you to those who write for, preserve, and share newspapers: Jack Calder, Mark Malone, Art Rhyno, INK's OurDigitalWorld. For research help: the Chatham-Kent Black Historical Museum, the Chatham-Kent Public Library, and Vanessa Jenner at the Strathroy Public Library.

Research assistants made significant contributions to the early project as well as to this book. Thank you to Lauren Miceli, who single-handedly scanned, described, and organized every item in the Harding family scrapbooks and did some of the earliest research on this project. To Ron Leary and Linda Bunn for reading years of microfilm and finding many useful leads. To Colin Martin for his superb fact-checking, quote-checking, footnoting, editing, and finding needles in haystacks. Thanks, too, to Lauren Lopez, Nicole Corbo, and Devon Fraser for their contributions.

I am also grateful for the opportunity to work with the excellent people at Biblioasis. Thank you to Rachel Ironstone for her stellar edits, Michel Vrana for his beautiful design work, Sharon Pfaff for her early enthusiasm and Madeleine Maillet for her energetic publicity campaign. Thanks also to Vanessa Stauffer for her brilliance, vision, and inspiration. Many thanks to Dan Wells—the perfect editor for this book—for his sage advice, high expectations, baseball knowledge, and careful, thoughtful edits.

Along the way, many people have answered questions, sent me information, shared resources, and generously offered their advice, encouragement, and friendship: Alec Affleck, Selinda Berg, Patricia Calder, the Canadian Baseball History Conference, Scott Chantler, Dayna Cornwall, Scott Crawford, Joan Dalton, Irene Moore Davis, Gwen Ebbett, Griff Evans, Doug Fox, Sarah Glassford, Gary Gillette, Kerry Harding-Couture, Susan Holbrook, Leslie Howsam, Bill Humber, Carolyn Ives, Elaine Mah, Chip Martin, Paul Martin, Jerome Martin, Cathy Maskell, Siobhan McMenemy, Suzanne McMurphy, Jennifer Mumford, Andrew North, Elena North, Karen Pillon, Nina Reid-Maroney, Christian Trudeau, Natasha Wiebe, @WBU_Owls, and Julia Zarankin.

Finally, thank you and much love to Dale Jacobs. He talked about the Cubs the first day we met and bought me my first Tigers cap. He has answered all my baseball questions, big and small, and listened patiently to every thought I've ever had about the Chatham Coloured All-Stars. I am endlessly grateful for having him on this and every journey and for reminding me of why well-told stories matter.

ABOUT THE AUTHOR

HEIDI LM JACOBS' PREVIOUS BOOKS INCLUDE THE novel *Molly of the Mall: Literary Lass and Purveyor of Fine Footwear* (NeWest Press, 2019), which won the Stephen Leacock Medal for Humour in 2020, and *100 Miles of Baseball: Fifty Games, One Summer* (with Dale Jacobs, Biblioasis, 2021). She is a librarian at the University of Windsor and one of the researchers behind the award-winning Breaking the Colour Barrier: Wilfred "Boomer" Harding & the Chatham Coloured All-Stars project.

NOTES

A NOTE ON *BREAKING THE COLOUR BARRIER*

The *Breaking the Colour Barrier* project was a partnership between the University of Windsor, the Chatham Sports Hall of Fame, the Harding Family, and the Chatham-Kent Black Historical Society. It was generously supported by an Ontario Trillium Grant. Additional funding has come from the University of Windsor, its History Department, Leddy Library, Faculty of Arts, Humanities, and Social Sciences, and the Humanities Research Group. Additional funding for this work has come from the Social Sciences and Humanities Research Council of Canada. Scott Chantler designed the baseball cards, created the four-panel cartoon and the mini comic, and Stacie Teasdale designed the travelling exhibits and other visuals for the project.

INTRODUCTION

17   **a significant oral history project** . . . These interviews are part of the Multicultural History Society of Ontario's Oral Testimony series, one of the largest collections of its kind in North America. Interviews were mostly done in the 1970s and 1980s.

17   **Andrew and Sarah Harding had eight children** . . . The children of Andrew "Bill" (1886–1947) and Sarah Holmes Harding (1883–1951) are Florence (1903–1909), Georgina (1905–1973), Beulah Cuzzens (1907–2003), Carl (1911–1985), Leonard "Len" (1912–1942), Wilfred "Boomer" (1915–1991), Andrew (1919–2000), and Wanda Milburn (1924–1995).

17   **"an old grant from the federal** . . . Blake Harding, "Interview with Blake and Pat Harding: Interview One," interview by Miriam Wright, *Breaking the Colour Barrier: Wilfred "Boomer" Harding & the Chatham Coloured All-Stars (1932–1939)*, University of Windsor, May 25, 2016.

18   **"while there was a high degree** . . . Irene Moore Davis, personal correspondence, April 16, 2021.

18   the Holmeses "had a doctor in the family . . . Blake Harding, Wright interview one.

18   "We became Black children . . . Beulah Cuzzens, "Interview with Beulah Cuzzens by Vivian Robbins Chavis," transcript and recording, Multicultural History Society of Ontario, September 9, 1980.

18   The 1921 census gives us a . . . *Sixth Census of Canada*, 1921.

18   "was the one that gave them . . . Pat Harding, "Interview with Blake and Pat Harding: Interview Two," interview by Miriam Wright, *Breaking the Colour Barrier: Wilfred "Boomer" Harding & the Chatham Coloured All-Stars (1932–1939)*, University of Windsor, May 25, 2016.

18   "my dad recalls stories of . . . Blake Harding, Wright interview one.

18   "The boys were all encouraged . . . Pat Harding, Wright interview two.

23   "he taught them what work was . . . Ibid.

23   When I went to high school in the '30s . . . Wanda Milburn, "Interview with Wanda Milburn, Ken Milburn, and Vivian Chavis by Wilson Brooks," transcript and recording, Multicultural History Society of Ontario, September 28, 1980.

24   Wilfred "Boomer" Harding, who excelled in . . . In his high school years at Chatham Vocational High School, Boomer won numerous Western Ontario Secondary School Athletic Association (WOSSAA) titles for pole vaulting, hockey, basketball, and soccer. In the October 6, 1933 *Chatham Daily News*, a headline in the sports pages reads "Wilfred Harding is Senior Champ of Secondary Schools." In a regional track and field event, Harding gained fifteen points, four points ahead of the next competitor, in running broad jump, pole vault, and running high jump events.

24   all the barriers he helped break . . . Boomer married Joy Handsor in April 1940, and together they had one son, Blake, who married Pat. Boomer worked at the Chatham post office as a letter carrier from 1940 and retired in 1975 after thirty-five years of service. As a veteran of WWII, he was a member of Branch 628 of the Royal Canadian Legion. In his later years, he was part of national teams competing in darts, where he placed among the top senior players in the country. He also officiated for various sports in the Chatham community, such as softball, baseball, hockey, and soccer. He was a member of the Campbell African Methodist Episcopal Church and a proud and devoted grandfather to two grandchildren, Kerry and Andrew. Boomer died September 14, 1991, at seventy-six years of age.

24   Harding family lore says he was . . . The story is that Boomer is named after a character named "Booming Nut." Comics scholar Gene Kannenberg has suggested that "Booming Nut" is likely a misheard version of "Boob McNutt," a syndicated comic strip by Rube Goldberg that ran between 1918 and 1934.

Boomer would have been about three years old when the strip began, making this a likely possibility for the source of his nickname.

25 **Notably, he was the first Black player** ... Willie O'Ree is credited with being the "Jackie Robinson of hockey," by breaking the National Hockey League's colour barrier in 1958. Manny McIntyre was another barrier-breaking baseball and hockey player. He was part of the "Black Ace"—with Ossie and Herb Carnegie, the first all-Black line in professional hockey—and the first Black Canadian to play professional baseball when he played in the Border League for the Sherbrooke Canadians.

25 **"They claimed on public skating night** ... Boomer Harding, "Interview with Boomer Harding by Wanda Harding Milburn and Vivian Robbins Chavez," transcript and recording, Multicultural History Society of Ontario, August 27, 1980.

25 **Boomer was "one of several and they were** ... Blake Harding, Wright interview two.

25 **But on hockey teams, Blake says, Boomer** ... Ibid.

26 **his father "found that he could** ... Ibid.

26 **"It was always important for him** ... Ibid.

26 **an anecdote from his father's time as a postal worker** ... Blake Harding, interview with LeSean Harris, July 30, 2022.

26 **sports were much more than just** ... Blake Harding, Wright interview two.

26 **"He was very quiet, but** ... Ibid.

27 **Robinson, Blake says, "was picked** ... Ibid.

27 **"Dad, Uncle Ken [Milburn], and Uncle Andy** ... Ibid.

27 **If you talked to any of the real** ... Ibid.

28 **Next winter, if all goes well** ... Jack Calder, "Analyzing Sport," *Chatham Daily News*, June 1, 1934.

28 **"My Uncle Carl, he was** ... Blake Harding, Wright interview one.

29 **my father was a white mulatto** ... Jennifer Miss, "Interview with Jennifer Miss," interview by Alastair Staffen, *Breaking the Colour Barrier: Wilfred "Boomer" Harding & the Chatham Coloured All-Stars (1932–1939)*, University of Windsor, October 5, 2016.

29 **Carl "was a very good hockey player** ... Boomer Harding, Milburn and Robbins Chavis interview.

29 **Carl would "ride with my dad** ... Wanda Harding Milburn, "Interview with Wanda Harding Milburn by Wilson Brooks," transcript and recording, Multicultural History Society of Ontario, September 28, 1980.

29 **Carl could get better jobs** ... Beulah Cuzzens, Robbins Chavis interview.

29 **"I think he missed opportunities** ... Jennifer Miss, Staffen interview.

30 **Because of the colour differences** ... Ibid.

30 "I think it is important that people . . . Ibid.

30 "There were challenges . . . Ibid.

MAY 1934

32 of the three hundred or so people . . . Ferguson Jenkins Jr in conversation with LeSean Harris, July 30, 2022.

33 In addition to a baseball diamond . . . Details from this description of Stirling Park comes from Dorothy Wright Wallace as well as from photographs in the Chatham Kent Museum's collection of photographs of Stirling Park from the 1920s.

33 "Leo Belanger's back yard is . . . "Casual Comment on Sport," *Chatham Daily News*, June 30, 1933.

33 The 1934 Shepherd's city . . . *Shepherd's City of Chatham (Ontario) Miscellaneous, Business, Citizen and Street Directory for the Year 1934–1935* (Chatham, ON: Shepherd Printing Co, 1934).

33 The All-Stars and the Duns were part . . . The Chatham City League appears to have been in operation since at least as early as 1919. In the spring of 1934, the Chatham City League was reclassified in the OBAA and became listed as "Intermediate B."

36 "swings, teeters, traveling rings . . . Bob Widdis, "Notes from speech honouring Archie Stirling," n.d. Chatham-Kent Black Historical Society.

36 The fellows didn't know whether . . . Doug Scurr, "Chatham Coloured Stars Return Under New Name," *Chatham Daily News*, June 12, 1946. Stirling's comment about the team "sent all over the [nearby] country" has been misinterpreted as them playing across Canada. I have no record of them playing anywhere but Ontario.

36 "They drew terrific crowds . . . Art Cartier, "The First Coloured All Star Team Ontario Title 1934," from *Politics and Other Games and Notes*, Vol. 2 (London: London Free Press, 1966).

37 "a group of friends who . . . Blake Harding, Harris interview, July 30, 2022.

37 From what I can remember it was . . . Kingsley Terrell, "Interview with Kingsley Terrell by Wanda Milburn," transcript and recording, Multicultural History Society of Ontario August 6, 1980.

37 "This evening at Stirling Park . . . Jack Calder, "Analyzing Sport: Boosting Baseball," *Chatham Daily News*, May 17, 1934.

38 "Stars Win Opening Game of . . . Jack Calder, "Stars Win Opening Game of City Baseball League: 1934 Inaugural Indicates Real Battle for Honours," *Chatham Daily News*, May 18, 1934.

38 The All-Stars, '33 champions of . . . Ibid.

39   Through Calder's 1934 columns ... Because I have been unable to locate offi-
     cial City League or OBAA records for statistics, rosters, box scores, or other
     details of the All-Stars' seasons, I have used all the published game announce-
     ments, box scores, and game recaps to document the All-Stars' season and the
     player statistics. The statistics and standings found here may differ from those
     printed in the *Chatham Daily News* because theirs only include City League
     games and not exhibition games. Furthermore, my calculations of statistics
     are slightly different from those I have published elsewhere because additional
     games and box scores have since come to light. The extant record of the sea-
     son leaves a few gaps, particularly in terms of the exhibition games. There are
     a few instances where I found a win referenced but not a recorded score, or I
     found a game announced but no score or outcome is mentioned. All statis-
     tics cited in this book should be understood to be based on the information
     available at the time of writing. Any errors in calculation are mine.

39   "If you haven't been to Stirling ... Jack Calder, "Analyzing Sport," *Chatham
     Daily News*, May 23, 1934.

39   Washington and Tabron came to play ... For the sake of consistency, I have
     changed all players' names to the proper spellings throughout the book, cor-
     recting errors that serve as a reminder of the limitations of optical character
     recognition (OCR) in historical newspaper work of this kind and of the
     dangers of relying on digital search functions as a research tool.

40   This was and remains the traditional ... Chatham-Kent borders the
     Lunaapeew at Delaware Nation, which is part of the McKee Purchase Treaty,
     and the unceded territory of the Bkejwanong Walpole Island First Nation.
     While a lesser-explored area in this book, it is essential to remember that the
     story of this region begins with the colonization of Indigenous lands. The
     cities, towns, settlements, and communities mentioned within this book are
     all founded on these lands.

42   records reveal a Black man ... Natasha L. Henry, *Emancipation Day:
     Celebrating Freedom in Canada*, (Toronto: Dundurn Press, 2010), 73.

42   "the Fugitive Slave Law of 1850 ... Carmen Poole, *Conspicuous Peripheries:
     Black Identity, Memory, and Community in Chatham, ON, 1860–1980* (PhD
     dissertation, Ontario Institute for Studies in Education, University of
     Toronto, 2015), 28.

42   came to Upper Canada "armed ... Irene Moore Davis, *Our Own Two Hands:
     A History of Black Lives in Windsor From the 1700s Forward* (Windsor, ON:
     North, Star Cultural Community Centre, 2019), 9–10.

42   shows that slave-keeping was prevalent ... Afua Cooper, *The Hanging
     of Angélique: The Untold Story of Canadian Slavery and the Burning of Old
     Montréal* (Athens: University of Georgia Press, 2007), 74.

42 In the early 1830s, destinations . . . Moore Davis, *Our Own Two Hands*, 16.

43 the vast majority of those seeking freedom . . . See Karolyn Smardz Frost and Veta Tucker Smith, *A Fluid Frontier: Slavery, Resistance, and the Underground Railroad in the Detroit River Borderland* (Wayne State University Press, 2016), 12, and Moore Davis, *Our Own Two Hands*.

43 "dissuaded from making the journey . . . Moore Davis, *Our Own Two Hands*, 19.

44 "prior to the nineteenth century . . . Quoted in Moore Davis, *Our Own Two Hands*, 10.

44 examples of enslaved people crossing . . . Moore Davis, *Our Own Two Hands*, 10.

44 "Although Canada may have . . . Smardz Frost and Tucker Smith, *Fluid Frontier*, 15.

44 "the grand difference betwixt Yankee and . . . Samuel Ringgold Ward, *Autobiography of a Fugitive Negro: His Anti-Slavery Labours in the United States, Canada, & England* (John Snow, 1855), 146–147.

44 "a deeply racist and discriminatory . . . Smardz Frost and Tucker Smith, *Fluid Frontier*, 3.

44 Black settlements were established in . . . Daniel G. Hill also notes that prior to the middle part of the nineteenth century, there were also Black settlements around what are now London, Brantford, St. Catharines, Niagara Falls, Hamilton, Toronto, Oro, Collingwood, and Owen Sound. For further discussions of these areas, see Daniel G. Hill, *The Freedom-Seekers: Blacks in Early Canada* (Toronto, ON: Stoddart, 1981).

46 the Black population of Chatham shrunk . . . Poole, *Conspicuous Peripheries*, 178.

46 and in 1931 to 1.48 percent . . . The 1931 Canadian census lists the population of Chatham as 14,569 and the Black population as 214. *Seventh Census of Canada*, 1931, Volume II.

46 including the Intercounty League's London Majors . . . Founded in 1925, the London Majors are still in existence though they have undergone several name changes in their nearly hundred-year existence.

46 "he didn't hold a bat like . . . Kingsley Terrell, Milburn interview.

47 a "good, fast runner" . . . Kingsley Terrell, Milburn interview.

47 "a classy southpaw" . . . "Harding's Nine," *Chatham Daily News*, n.d. 1946.

47 "an arm about as strong . . . Kingsley Terrell, Milburn interview.

48 describe the Detroit River as . . . Smardz Frost and Tucker Smith, *Fluid Frontier*, 11.

48 The Detroit Tigers had a great . . . Archie Stirling, "A Brief History of Baseball" in Chatham's Victoria Day Baseball Games Official Program, May 22, c1960, *Breaking the Colour Barrier: Wilfred "Boomer" Harding &*

the Chatham Coloured All-Stars (1932–1939), http://cdigs.uwindsor.ca/
BreakingColourBarrier/items/show/957, 8–9.

49 **Dutchy Scott was one among others** . . . According to Samantha Meredith of
the Chatham-Kent Black Historical Society, her research suggests there may
have been other possible white players playing with the All-Stars, including Albert Mason, Harry Murphy, Jack Scott, William Land, and Marvin
Wrightman.

50 **"the lives of blacks in Chatham** . . . Poole, *Conspicuous Peripheries*, 181.

50 **"an area of the city sown in** . . . Ibid.

51 **"There was no TV in those** . . . Ernie Miller, "Boomer Harding—One Great
Guy," *London Free Press*, September 7, 1978.

52 **"We either played baseball or** . . . Bill Reddick, "From the Bullpen: Chatham
Colored All-Stars," *Chatham Daily News*, October 4, 1984.

52 **"There was no place else to go** . . . Ibid.

52 **describes Stirling Park as "our** . . . Dorothy Wright Wallace, interview with
LeSean Harris, August 5, 2022.

52 **"It was, she says, "the centerpoint** . . . Ibid.

52 **Orville Wright** . . . Orville Wright (1907–1985) was a charter member of the
J.G. Taylor Community Centre. Along with his wife, Evelyn, he was active
in making the centre a vital place for the community. In a document relating
to Wright's winning of the 1963 "Service to Mankind" award, the Taylor
Centre is described as being "strictly non-denominational" and "anyone and
everyone is welcomed." According to this document, "Negro, White, Indian
and Oriental children" called him Uncle Orville. In addition to supporting
children's and youth programs, the Taylor Centre also organized sports teams
such as the Taylor Athletic Club and the Taylorettes Junior Softball Club.
Several All-Stars would play for the Taylor ACs. Taylor Park in Chatham
currently has a pool named Orville Wright.

52 **"We had fun in those days** . . . "Chatham's First Champs Played the Game
for Fun," *London Free Press*, October 20, 1967.

52 **we lived at the ball park."** . . . Reddick, "From the Bullpen,"

52 **"You'd choose up sides** . . . John Olbey, "Interview with John Olbey," inter-
view by Deirdre McCorkindale, *Breaking the Colour Barrier: Wilfred "Boomer"
Harding & the Chatham Coloured All-Stars (1932–1939)*, University of Windsor,
July 6, 2016.

52 **He remembered everyone sharing** . . . Ibid.

53 **"It was good because there** . . . Ibid.

53 **"The greatest ball players seldom** . . . The Eatons fall–winter catalogue from
1935 shows a mid-priced pair of hockey skates for children for $3.75 and a
hockey stick for $0.75, plus all the pads, guards, and other equipment each

player would need, indicating outfitting a single child for hockey would cost at least $10. The Eatons catalogue from spring–summer 1934 shows a children's baseball glove for $1.00, a bat for $0.25, and a ball for $0.85. All of these items could be shared between teammates, making baseball significantly more accessible and affordable.

53   **That's why softball has made** . . . Calder, "Analyzing Sport: Boosting Baseball."

53   **often a hat was passed** . . . Advertisement for OBAA Baseball, *Chatham Daily News*, May 24, 1934. Advertisement for All-Stars and Walpole Island game, *Chatham Daily News*, May 24, 1934. Advertisement for Kent Bridge Tournament, August 13, 1934. Prices converted through the Bank of Canada's online Inflation Calculator.

54   **unlike in daily life, "when it got nasty** . . . Blake Harding, Wright interview one.

54   **baseball culture "was almost dead** . . . Blake Harding, Harris interview, July 30, 2022.

55   **Going into the last of the seventh** . . . "Stars Win Two Straight in City Baseball League," *Chatham Daily News*, May 22, 1934.

55   **"Every member of the winning** . . . "Walpole Island Team Drops Game to Chatham Stars," *Chatham Daily News*, June 1, 1934.

55   **Chase began proceedings in** . . . Ibid.

56   **"working on the mound for** . . . Ibid.

56   **"They used to crowd Stirling** . . . Horace Chase, "Interview with Horace Chase," interview by Genevieve Chevalier, *Breaking the Colour Barrier: Wilfred "Boomer" Harding & the Chatham Coloured All-Stars (1932–1939)*, University of Windsor, July 17, 2016.

57   **they could do something together** . . . John Olbey, McCorkindale interview.

57   **hearts and minds were nonetheless changed** . . . Blake Harding, Wright interview one.

58   **a five-and-a-half inning 9–3 blowout** . . . "Braggs Lose to Stars in City League Game," *Chatham Daily News*, May 31, 1934.

JUNE 1934

59   **five of the top ten batters** . . . "City Baseball League Statistics," *Chatham Daily News*, June 5, 1934.

60   **Their roster is printed in** . . . "Reach Ball Was Maltreated. Local Colored Giants and Buxton Boys Were Responsible," *Chatham Daily Planet*, June 15, 1915.

60   **In August 1915, another article** . . . "Chatham Boys Won. The Giants of Chatham went to Buxton on Monday where they played the Invincibles. The

game resulted in a win for the local ball players, the score being 6 to 5. The following is the line-up of the victors: G. Williams c, H. Crosby p, J. Parker 1B, D. Williams 2B, P. Holden 3B, P. Parker ss, C. Currie in, J. Kersey LF, P Jenkins RF." "Chatham Boys Won," *Chatham Daily Planet*, August 25, 1915.

60 **In-depth genealogical research** ... The Chatham Giants appear to have still been playing in 1924 when they reportedly won eleven out of twelve games in the South Western Ontario League, and they are said to have played and defeated a team from Detroit 3–0 on Labour Day 1924 in North Buxton. "Chatham Giants: Chatham-Kent Sports Black History Month," *Chatham-Kent Sports Network*, February 20, 2013.

60 **one or both of the teams may have** ... Robert Douglas Day, *Impulse to Addiction: A Narrative History of Sport in Chatham, Ontario, 1790–1895*, (master's thesis, University of Western Ontario, 1977), 239.

60 **Day's research has also brought to light** ... *Chatham Tri-Weekly Planet*, July 11, 1888, and July 20, 1888. Quoted in Day, *Impulse to Addiction*, 270.

61 **Black baseball in this region** ... Black baseball, of course, was not something that existed only in Chatham or Southwestern Ontario. A full discussion of Black baseball in Canada, let alone the diverse history of baseball in Canada, is beyond the scope of this book, but there has been important work done in this area by a number of scholars. Colin D. Howell contributed early research on the rich tradition of Black baseball in the Maritimes dating back to the nineteenth century, and recent research by Roger P. Nason has built on that. William Humber's *Diamonds of the North: A Concise History of Baseball in Canada* documents that Black baseball has a rich history across Canada, from the all-Black Goodwills of London team who played the all-Black Rialtos of Detroit in 1869 to the unnamed Black player who played for the Moose Jaw Territorial Championship team in 1895 to the baseball team in Amber Valley, Alberta, a community established by the arrival of Black settlers from Oklahoma around 1909 to 1911. More recently, research has revealed parallel stories about Black baseball in Quebec, New York, and Vermont that resemble the fluidity of baseball between Chatham, Windsor, and Detroit. Christian Trudeau has written about an African-American team, les Panthères Noires—the Black Panthers—who were admitted into the Quebec Provincial League in 1936 and played until 1938 and Chappie Johnson's team, "The Chappies," who play inconsistently in Quebec between 1925 and 1935. In 1935, there are reports of the Chappies playing in a tournament in Granby, Quebec, featuring teams such as the Zulu Cannibal Giants, the Japanese All Stars, the Cleveland Clowns, and the House of David.

61 **and an unnamed team from Colchester** ... In addition to both historically Black settlements in the Chatham-Kent area, Colchester was a frequent

destination for African Americans seeking safety and emancipation and had a sizeable Black population, as did Harrow.

61   "The New Canaan AME ... "New Canaan," *Essex Free Press*, May 17, 1912.

61   "On June 28, a team of ... "Leamington," *Amherstburg Echo*, June 9, 1905.

61   "The coloured ball team from ... "New Canaan," *Essex Free Press*, July 30, 1909.

62   the region's only Black newspaper ... *The Dawn of Tomorrow* was a newspaper founded by James F. Jenkins in 1923 and was published in London, Ontario. It called itself "the national negro weekly, devoted to the interests of the darker races."

62   Coursey was a highly successful ... Coursey's name surfaces here and there in box scores in the Chatham area in the 1920s. A photograph of him appears on the front page of the May 2, 1925, edition of the *Dawn of Tomorrow* with the caption describing him as a "well-known coloured athlete." The caption goes on to say that Coursey has been made manager of the McCormick's OBA baseball team for the coming season, and that this is "the first time in the history of London that a coloured boy has managed a white O.B.A. team. As usual Coursey expects to bring home the bacon." Additional research shows he was not only a baseball player but a track athlete. The available box scores and game recaps show him pitching for teams in London, including the London Braves in 1926 and Hotel London team in 1933. He also appears to have been on the executive committee for the new City Baseball League in London in 1933. Little else is known about Coursey beyond the fact that he was a City of London employee. Not much is known about how a man of African descent became the manager of an organized white baseball team in the 1920s, but it is a compelling story, and it serves as a reminder that there are many more stories like those of the Chatham Coloured All-Stars that need to be told to fully understand not only sports in Canada but also the more complicated narrative about race in Canada.

62   the commentary and word choice ... "Reach Ball," *Chatham Daily Planet*, June 15, 1915.

62   commonly known as a Reach baseball ... According to Andrew North, "When Al Reach retired from playing, he formed a sporting goods company, as Al Spalding had done before him. One of Reach's biggest sellers was a new cork-centred ball, which debuted in about 1910. The Reach ball was the official ball of the American League for decades." Personal correspondence, Sept 2, 2021.

64   "the effect of securing a day ... Downey's article about the impact the Lord's Day Act had on Indigenous lacrosse games is particularly interesting in this context. See Allan Downey, "Playing the Creator's Game on God's Day: The

Controversy of Sunday Lacrosse Games in Haudenosaunee Communities, 1916–24," *Journal of Canadian Studies* 49, no. 3 (2015): 111–143.

64   "Taking their stand against Sunday . . . "Stop Game," *The Border Cities Star*, September 14, 1931.

65   It seems a pity that baseball . . . "Sunday baseball. Kingsville Reporter," *Leamington Post*, June 8, 1933.

65   "Kent Bridge and Stars to . . . Jack Calder, "Kent Bridge and Stars to Replay Game: Stars on Long End of the Score, but Game is Protested," *Chatham Daily News*, June 5, 1934.

65   "King Terrell was the hero . . . Ibid.

65   the boys might just as well . . . Ibid.

66   the on-field officials signalled . . . The box scores show a rotation of consistent umpires in the City League suggesting they are likely hired and paid and thus, in theory, free from community biases.

66   "It was a tough game for . . . Calder, "Kent Bridge and Stars to Replay Game."

66   "The two umpires who officiated . . . William Scurr, "Sport in Short," *Chatham Daily News*, June 28, 1934.

67   "was on the mound for the Stars . . . "Stars Defeat Kent Bridge in League Game," *Chatham Daily News*, June 16, 1934.

67   "the action of the City Baseball . . . William Scurr, "Sport in Short," *Chatham Daily News*, June 5, 1934.

67   not only documents that the loss was . . . "Duns Hand Stars First Defeat of Present Campaign," *Chatham Daily News*, June 8, 1934.

68   Calder "had to be careful . . . Daniel J. Kelly, "The Chatham Coloured All-Stars 1933–34," (1977), *Breaking the Colour Barrier: Wilfred "Boomer" Harding & the Chatham Coloured All-Stars (1932–1939)*, University of Windsor.

68   "A lot of people who attend . . . William Scurr, "Sport in Short," *Chatham Daily News*, June 8, 1934.

69   the stories, standings, and recaps . . . Sports pages, *The Windsor Star*, June 5, 1934.

70   "baseball was played here . . . Stirling, "A Brief History of Baseball," 1.

70   "These games drew large . . . Ibid, 5.

70   what is now Rotary Park and Fergie Jenkins Field . . . This field, now called Fergie Jenkins Field at Rotary Park, was known as Athletic Park. When it was built, it was often referred to as the "New Athletic Grounds" to distinguish it from the "Old Athletic Grounds" bounded by Queen, William, and Duluth Streets. In 2021, a commemorative stone was placed at Fergie Jenkins Field in honour of the 1934 Chatham Coloured All-Stars. It still stands today.

70   Stirling notes that Chatham raised . . . Stirling, "A Brief History of Baseball," 8.

70   In 2022 dollars, this is . . . According to the Bank of Canada's Inflation Calculator, $3,800 in 1921 is the equivalent of $62,225 in 2022, and $8,000 is the equivalent of $131,000.

70   this suspension "ruined baseball . . . Stirling, "A Brief History of Baseball," 6.

71   "baseball in Chatham has every . . . Jack Calder, "Analyzing Sport: Baseball Just Beginning Here," *Chatham Daily News*, August 2, 1934.

71   "Last night's defeat was . . . Scurr, "Sport in Short," June 8, 1934.

71   "the City Baseball League game . . . Jack Calder, "Analyzing Sport," *Chatham Daily News*, June 27, 1934.

71   "Tonight the Braggs will . . . Ibid.

76   Blake Harding remembers his father describing . . . Blake Harding, Wright interview one.

76   "Though pressed to do it, . . . Jack Calder, "Stars Continue Winning Ways in Baseball League," *Chatham Daily News*, June 21, 1934.

76   A sparkling pitching duel . . . Archie Stirling Jr attended Assumption College, now University of Windsor, which also had an active baseball culture. Players from the Detroit Tigers, such as Bill Rogell, for one, are known to have come over to coach the Assumption players. Occasionally, these MLB players made their way to Chatham for various events.

77   young Archie Stirling . . . Jack Calder, "Teams Deadlocked Last Night in City League Baseball," *Chatham Daily News*, June 29, 1934.

77   An attraction which promises . . . Jack Calder, "Analyzing Sport," *Chatham Daily News*, June 28, 1934.

78   Placed in the lower right-hand . . . "Talbot Hurls Loop Leaders to Victory: Stars Continue String of City League Successes Defeating Kent Bridge," *Chatham Daily News*, June 26, 1934.

78   "a freak show." . . . Blake Harding, Wright interview one.

78   "We had a good ball club and . . . Kingsley Terrell, "Interview with Kingsley Terrell by Wanda Harding Milburn," transcript and recording, Multicultural History Society of Ontario, August 5, 1980.

78   "Exhibition Baseball! Walpole . . . Game advertisement, *Chatham Daily News*, May 30, 1934.

78   "There was never a place . . . Kingsley Terrell, Harding Milburn interview.

79   "we caused a small riot . . . Bill Reddick, "Chatham Coloured All-Stars: Former Players Recall Good Times, Bad Times of 1934 OBA Championship Season," *Chatham Daily News*, October 4, 1984.

79   "One or two loudmouths would make . . . Ibid.

79   "As for heckling, . . . Ibid.

79 In the same interview Talbot recalls . . . Ibid.

79 "Messages were scribbled on . . . Ibid.

79 while he remembers some of these events . . . Ibid.

79 "And we beat them and then . . . Ferguson Jenkins Sr, "Interview with Ferguson Jenkins Sr by Vivian Robbins Chavis and Wanda Milburn," transcript and recording, Multicultural History Society of Ontario, October 3, 1980.

79 Blake Harding is one of the rare . . . Blake Harding, Harris interview, July 30, 2022.

80 two of the Harding sisters told . . . The "Chatham, Ont." section of the *Chicago Defender* often chronicles who went to the All-Stars away games and frequently women's names are mentioned, as is the case for some of the nearby playoff games in 1934. The November 3, 1934 issue of the *Chicago Defender* includes this description: "Among those who attended the London game to see the Stars override Welland 11–7 in the O.B.A.A. playdowns were Mr. and Mrs. MacPherson, Mrs. K. Terrell, Mrs. C. Olbey, Mrs. M. Lass, Mrs. Highgate, Mrs. J. Cluff, and the Misses Julia Black, Sadie Stonefish, Katheline Terrell, Hilda Parker."

80 "I taught down in Shrewsbury, . . . Beulah Harding Cuzzens, "Interview with Beulah Harding Cuzzens by Vivian Robbins Chavis," transcript and recording, Multicultural History Society of Ontario, September 23, 1980.

80 "We had to fight our way . . . Ibid.

80 Inez [Andy Harding's wife] and . . . Wanda Milburn, "Interview with Kingsley Terrell by Wanda Harding Milburn," transcript and recording, Multicultural History Society of Ontario, August 6, 1980.

81 the All-Stars "had a tough time . . . Pauline Parker Miller, "Interview with Pauline Parker Miller," interview by Miriam Wright, *Breaking the Colour Barrier: Wilfred "Boomer" Harding & the Chatham Coloured All-Stars (1932–1939)*, University of Windsor, September 5, 2017.

81 "I can remember being in . . . Beulah Harding Cuzzens, Robbins Chavis interview.

81 "change hearts and minds" . . . Blake Harding, Wright interview one.

JULY 1934

83 "near-hurricane storm" . . . "Near-Hurricane Sweeps Districts Along Great Lakes," *Chatham Daily News,* July 7, 1934.

83 "Flat Chase and Ross Talbot . . . William Scurr, "Sport in Short," *Chatham Daily News,* July 9, 1934.

84 "The Duns," he writes, "think . . . Ibid.

84　The headline summarizing the July 10 ... "Stars Gain Thirteenth Win: Five Inning Game Goes to Leaders as Duns Collapse: Chase Hurls Three Hit Ball and Stars Pound Four Pitchers," *Chatham Daily News*, July 11, 1934.

84　"The Stars were 'on' last night ... William Scurr, "Sport in Short," *Chatham Daily News*, July 11, 1934.

85　"What they lacked in fielding finish ... "Stars Romp to Victory Against Dresden: Six Runs in Second Frame Aid Chatham Nine's Cause. Terrell Turns in Masterful Job of Relief Pitching, Allowing No Hits in Last Three and One-Third Innings Here," *Chatham Daily News*, July 12, 1934.

85　With three runs in and ... Ibid.

85　Dutch Scott ... Dutch Scott played periodically with the All-Stars.

86　"Chase, a hurler from Windsor ... "Wanless Trophy Series to Get Under Way Saturday," *Chatham Daily News*, August 24, 1933.

86　Flat "grew up in the ... Earl Chase Jr, "Interview with Earl and Shyla Chase," interview by Alastair Staffen, *Breaking the Colour Barrier: Wilfred "Boomer" Harding & the Chatham Coloured All-Stars (1932–1939)*, University of Windsor, July 11, 2016.

87　According to Boomer, "Work was ... Boomer Harding, Milburn and Robbins Chavis interview.

87　"Chase was on the mound ... "Chatham Stars, Juniors in Wanless Trophy Finals," *Chatham Daily News*, October 2, 1933.

87　"It was simply a case of ... "Stars Win Wanless Trophy in Two Straight Games," *Chatham Daily News*, October 10, 1933.

88　"smoke-ball artist of ... "Stars Meet Blenheim Nine," *Chatham Daily News*, July 20, 1934.

88　"the speed ball demon," ... Jack Calder, "Chatham Stars Win First Game of Playdowns," *Chatham Daily News*, September 10, 1934.

88　"smoke-ball king of ... Jack Calder, "Stars Begin OBAA Playdowns Thursday," *Chatham Daily News*, September 5, 1934.

88　"mainstay of the All-Stars' pitching ... Ibid.

88　.470 for the 1934 season ... This number contradicts the batting average I have published elsewhere. I had earlier calculated Chase's average as .488, but I have since located additional box scores making .470 the most up-to-date number. There are still box scores for games that I have not been able to locate, so this number may still not be accurate. Even with this lowered number, however, Chase's batting average still puts him in the top percentile of hitters.

88　"if Flat Chase were as good ... Stirling, "A Brief History of Baseball," 9.

88　twenty-five before the Detroit Tigers would ... The Detroit Tigers were the second last team to sign a player of colour. The Boston Red Sox were last when they signed Pumpsie Green in July 1959. Ozzie Virgil was Dominican, so he was also the first Latino player for the Tigers.

89   "it looked like he had . . . Kingsley Terrell, interview by Wanda Harding Milburn, transcript and recording, Multicultural History Society of Ontario, August 5, 1980.

89   He was a power hitter. . . . Ibid.

90   There's no doubt about it . . . Kelly, "All-Stars 1933–34."

90   "Chase threw the ball so hard . . . Bill Reddick, "Chatham Colored All-Stars: Reliving the 1934 OBA Drive," *Chatham Daily News*, October 5, 1984.

90   "ask him for a curve and . . . Kingsley Terrell, Harding Milburn interview.

90   Donise was catching this night . . . Ibid.

90   "Flat Chase was probably the best pitcher, . . . Ferguson Jenkins Jr, "Interview with Ferguson Jenkins Jr," interview by Heidi Jacobs, *Breaking the Colour Barrier: Wilfred "Boomer" Harding & the Chatham Coloured All-Stars (1932–1939)*, University of Windsor, October 1, 2016.

90   He admired Flat Chase as . . . Donald Tabron Jr, "Interview with Donald Tabron Jr," interview by Miriam Wright, *Breaking the Colour Barrier: Wilfred "Boomer" Harding & the Chatham Coloured All-Stars (1932–1939)*, University of Windsor, November 21, 2019.

91   "Flat Chase, Chathamite, was not only . . . "Chatham into Title Round," *Windsor Daily Star*, October 5, 1939.

91   "still throw his blazing fast ball . . . Scurr, "Stars Return Under New Name."

91   "Flat is a story in . . . Boomer Harding, Milburn and Robbins Chavis interview.

91   Strathroy people will talk for . . . Jack Calder, *Chatham Daily News*, nd. Chase family scrapbook.

92   "Every park Chase played in, . . . Reddick, "Reliving the 1934 OBA Drive."

92   we'd all look to right field . . . Boomer Harding, Milburn and Robbins Chavis interview.

93   Boomer calls this home run "one . . . Ibid.

93   "I remember there was . . . Kingsley Terrell, Harding Milburn interview.

93   "If you were in Welland today . . . Ernie Miller, "Boomer Harding—One Great Guy," *London Free Press*, September 7, 1978.

93   "one time we went . . . Reddick, "Reliving the 1934 OBA Drive."

93   a newspaper column from 1944 . . . "Chase Playing Against Baers," Chase family scrapbook, c 1944.

93   "Flat hit [a baseball] in Chatham . . . "Chatham's First Champs," *London Free Press*.

93   My dad told me he even caught . . . Horace Chase, Chevalier interview.

94 **back in about 1928 or '30,** ... The tunnel opened in 1930—so if he got stuck in the tunnel, it would have to have been after 1930.

94 **"something of a rumba"** ... Jack Calder, "Analyzing Sport," *Chatham Daily News*, September 12, 1934.

94 **"with the same effect he employs** ... Jack Calder, "Analyzing Sport," *Chatham Daily News*, July 6, 1935.

94 **Flat was without a jacket** ... "Chase Playing Against Baers," Chase family scrapbook.

94 **[Team backer] Pete [Gilbert]** ... Pete Gilbert (1888–1960) was a competitive curler and the founder of Maple City Gas and Oil. He was frequently mentioned as a supporter and backer of the All-Stars.

95 **"Go play ball, go** ... Horace Chase, Chevalier interview.

95 **"I think that was his only thing,** ... Ibid.

95 **My dad was like a supervisor** ... Ibid.

95 **"We weren't what you'd call** ... Ibid.

95 **"If we had a game** ... Ibid.

95 **always talking to my brother,** ... Ibid.

96 **"got a job working for** ... Earl Chase Jr, Staffen interview.

96 **"When I played ball he'd** ... Horace Chase, Chevalier interview.

96 **his dad "didn't do a whole lot** ... Ibid.

97 **I think he mentioned one time** ... Ibid.

97 **Horace observes that his father "didn't** ... Ibid.

98 **we were so happy in '47** ... Ibid.

99 **"Oh yes, well you had to** ... Ferguson Jenkins Sr, Robbins Chavis and Milburn interview.

99 **"It was the greatest thing** ... Ibid.

99 **"My dad was a centre fielder** ... Ferguson Jenkins Jr, Jacobs interview.

99 **Boomer Harding describes Fergie as** ... Boomer Harding, Milburn and Robbins Chavis interview.

99 **Jenkins "was a left-hand batter** ... Ibid.

99 **"Say we were in the ninth inning,** ... Kingsley Terrell, Harding Milburn interview.

100 **"He could've been in the Major Leagues** ... Ibid.

100 **He recalls listening to his father** ... Ferguson Jenkins Jr, Jacobs interview.

101 **"As far as I'm concerned, Fergie** ... Dorothy Wright Wallace, "Interview with Ferguson Jenkins," interview by Heidi Jacobs, *Breaking the Colour Barrier: Wilfred "Boomer" Harding & the Chatham Coloured All-Stars (1932–1939)*, University of Windsor, November 18, 2016.

101 **"My dad, basically was** ... Ferguson Jenkins Jr, Jacobs interview.

101 **"He didn't push me into the sport,** ... Ibid.

101 **her father "was best friends with** . . . Tracey Harding, "Interview with Tracey Harding," interview by Salma Abumeeiz, *Breaking the Colour Barrier: Wilfred "Boomer" Harding & the Chatham Coloured All-Stars (1932–1939)*, University of Windsor, August 15, 2016.

101 **"He'd seen me as an individual,** . . . Ferguson Jenkins Jr, Jacobs interview.

102 **Fergie's seen Larry Doby bring him** . . . Ferguson Jenkins Sr, Robbins Chavis and Milburn interview.

103 **"The crowd cheered** . . . Ferguson Jenkins Jr, Harris interview.

103 **they both describe the impact of** . . . Ferguson Jenkins Sr, Robbins Chavis and Milburn interview.

103 **"He would tell me, 'Son,** . . . Jordan Bastian, "Fergie Won't Forget His Road to the Majors: Cubs Icon Idolized Jackie Robinson during Childhood," MLB, April 14, 2021, https://www.mlb.com/news/fergie-jenkins-remembers-rough-road-to-mlb.

104 **Five generations of Canadians** . . . Ibid.

104 **"we couldn't go to Miami Beach,** . . . Ferguson Jenkins Jr, Harris interview.

104 **"We stayed at a brothel,** . . . Ibid.

104 **My father played baseball from** . . . Ferguson Jenkins, "Ferguson Jenkins 1991 Hall of Fame Induction Speech," National Baseball Hall of Fame and Museum, recorded July 21, 1991.

105 **A trio of extra-base hits** . . . Jack Calder, "Stars Shut Out Blenheimites," *Chatham Daily News*, July 21, 1934.

106 **if their exhibition games are included,** . . . Since winning percentages in baseball do not include ties or cancelled games, I have calculated their winning percentage using only the wins (twenty-on) and losses (two) and have not included the tie or nullified score in the game total (twenty-three).

107 **King Terrell and Shognosh hooked up** . . . Jack Calder, "Two Circuit Wallops Help Stars to Score Victory over Braves," *Chatham Daily News*, July 19, 1934.

107 **As of July 23, 1934, statistics** . . . "City Baseball League Record," *Chatham Daily News*, July 23, 1934.

107 **Reporting on the league's pitchers' wins** . . . This is another case where the statistics from the 1934 season need a little explanation. When compiling statistics for the team and the players, I have included every game for which I found a record of them playing, including exhibition games.

107 **she asks if "the reason why you** . . . Kingsley Terrell, Harding Milburn interview.

107 **coverage suggests that the All-Stars** . . . Jack Calder, "Analyzing Sport," *Chatham Daily News*, July 23, 1934.

108 **It's a wonder Chatham Stars, leaders** . . . Jack Calder, "Analyzing Sport," *Chatham Daily News*, July 31, 1934.

108 there will be a meeting of the executive . . . William Scurr, "Sport in Short," *Chatham Daily News*, July 28, 1934.

109 "At a meeting of the City Baseball League . . . William Scurr, "Sport in Short," *Chatham Daily News*, July 31, 1934.

109 "The League is in financial straits . . . Calder, "Analyzing Sport," July 31, 1934.

AUGUST 1934

111 "The Stars should be tuckered . . . William Scurr, "Sport in Short," *Chatham Daily News*, August 1, 1934.

112 "Optimistic supporters are calling . . . Jack Calder, "Analyzing Sport," *Chatham Daily News*, August 2, 1934.

112 "After being held scoreless . . . "Stars Beat Third Place Team Again," *Chatham Daily News*, August 1, 1934.

112 "The Stars were not at full strength . . . William Scurr, "Sport in Short," *Chatham Daily News*, August 1, 1934.

113 Thus when, at about one . . . "Blenheim Wins Against Stars," *Chatham Daily News*, August 9, 1934.

113 "The Stars don't mind . . . William Scurr, "Sport in Short," *Chatham Daily News*, August 15, 1934.

113 "The Stars," he continued, "are . . . Ibid.

113 The August 13 advertisement in the *Chatham Daily News* . . . advertisement, *Chatham Daily News*, August 13, 1934.

114 "considered one of the best . . . "Good Program for Local Baseball Fans This Week: Exhibition Games and Two Play-Off Tilts, Scheduled," *Chatham Daily News*, July 31, 1933.

114 "the largest crowd to watch . . . Jack Calder, "Chatham Team Divides Doubleheader with Detroit: Big Crowd Sees Stars Win Evening Contest in Eighth," *Chatham Daily News*, August 2, 1934.

114 "Two fast affairs are assured . . . Jack Calder, "Chatham Stars Meet Taylor's Detroit Stars," *Chatham Daily News*, July 31, 1934.

114 Elsewhere on the page, Calder anticipates . . . Jack Calder, "Analyzing Sport," *Chatham Daily News*, July 31, 1934.

115 If the box scores and game recaps . . . Ibid.

115 it is the first overt mention . . . Occasionally, their race is noted in small ads, but it is rarely mentioned in the coverage itself. It is likely the Chatham writers assumed their local readers already know the race of the All-Stars and thus felt no need to mention it.

115 the Emancipation Day celebrations . . . In the Chatham-Kent and Windsor-Essex areas, these events were major community celebrations within the

regional Black communities, Windsor's being particularly well known. Emancipation Day celebrations waned in the late 1970s for a range of reasons but have come into public consciousness in Canada again due to the official designation in 2021 of August 1 as Emancipation Day.

115 **"the most anticipated days . . .** "The annual African-Canadian tradition of Emancipation Day celebrated August 1, 1834, when "An Act for the Abolition of Slavery throughout the British Colonies; for promoting the Industry of the manumitted slaves; and for compensating the Persons hitherto entitled to the Service of such Slaves" came into effect. Called the Slavery Abolition Act for short, it liberated over 800,000 enslaved Africans from most British colonies, such as Antigua, Bermuda, and Trinidad, but it also included a small number in Canada." Natasha L. Henry, *Talking About Freedom: Celebrating Emancipation Day in Canada* (Toronto: Dundurn Press, 2012), 21.

115 **nowhere was this truer than during . . .** The records of Emancipation Day baseball games are a particularly rich source of information regarding baseball in Ontario's Black communities. As historian Natasha Henry notes, "Informal groups and professional teams played baseball matches. Young boys, men, and young girls formed teams for the day, local community teams participated, and all-Black clubs made up of trained baseball players also played." Emancipation Day baseball games, Henry writes, also "provided for a somewhat racially integrated exchange. Blacks played against Whites, but there were no teams mixed with players of both races . . . It provided a venue where Blacks could laugh at Whites and shout out comments without any fear of racial reprisal." Henry, *Talking About Freedom*, 108–109.

115 **"on the spacious grounds of . . .** "Celebrate Ninety Second Anniversary of Freedom," *Chatham Daily News*, August 2, 1932.

115 **it was also an occasion to mark, . . .** Ibid.

116 **Coverage from 1932 provides . . .** Ibid.

116 **Regional historian O.K. Watson . . .** O.K. Watson (1869–1954) was a lawyer and local historian from Ridgetown and a past president of the Kent County Historical Society.

116 **"delivered an intensely interesting, . . .** "Abolition of Slavery: O.K. Watson Gives Interesting Statistics to Rotary Club," *Chatham Daily News*, August 3, 1933.

116 **Reverend Dr W. Constantine Perry . . .** William Constantine Perry (1885–1958) was born in Jamaica and came to Canada in 1914. He attended McMaster University and graduated from Toronto Bible College; Edward Waters College conferred a Doctor of Divinity Honoris on him. In his thirty-nine years in the ministry, he served churches in Amhurst, New

Glasgow, and Truro in Nova Scotia and Windsor, Oakville, Chatham, Amherstburg, and Toronto's Grant Church in Ontario.

116 **Campbell AME Church** ... This church, built in 1888, was established by former enslaved people in Chatham in 1834 and was part of the Connectional African Methodist Episcopal Church.

117 **Contributions of the negro race** ... Perry thought that "youth would be inspired by a study of the lives of such men as" Booker T. Washington, Paul Lawrence Dunbar, and Frederick Douglass. "Negro Race Extolled in Club Speech," *Chatham Daily News*, August 1, 1934. A story in the following day's paper also records how Perry "suggested that the history of the negro race should be taught more extensively in the schools." "Says Colored Churches Here Should Unite," *Chatham Daily News*, August 2, 1934.

117 **"the freeing of the negroes** ... "Colored Folk Are Enjoying Celebration: Emancipation Day Marked by Sports and Evening Dance," *Chatham Daily News*, August 1, 1934.

118 **Edmund Odette, liquor commissioner has** ... "Beer Service is Demanded: Colored Man Claims He Has Been Refused Drink in Chatham," *Chatham Daily News*, August 10, 1934.

118 **set up under the new act.** ... The new act mentioned is almost certainly the Liquor Control Act of 1934. As has been noted by historians, laws related to drinking provide a "window into the complex relationships between public drinking, socialization, and the construction of appropriate social behaviour." Dan Malleck, "The Same as a Private Home? Social Clubs, Public Drinking, and Liquor Control in Ontario, 1934–1944," *Canadian Historical Review* 93, no. 4 (2012): 558.

118 **refused service in a hotel in Chatham** ... The Chatham City Directory of the time lists eight hotels in Chatham, but it is not clear from the context at which hotel this occurred.

119 **illustrate how discussions of race exist** ... Likely, the involvement of a prominent person such as an editor of a London newspaper helped to raise the visibility of this incident. We see a very similar incident happening in Windsor in 1949 where Walter Perry, the well-known organizer of the highly visible Emancipation Day celebrations, was denied service in a hotel and his experiences were reported in at least two articles in the *Windsor Star*. See R.M. Harrison, "Now," *Windsor Star*, September 6, 1949.

120 **Flat Chase put a thrilling finish** ... Calder, "Chatham Team Divides Doubleheader with Detroit."

120 **"Maybe last night's game** ... Calder, "Analyzing Sport: Baseball Just Beginning Here."

NOTES

120 **We see a different kind of** . . . To date, my research into the Taylor's Stars of
Detroit has not led conclusively to any information about who precisely this
team was, whether the team was named after a person or Taylor, Michigan.
Research similarly has not yielded the first names of the players on their
roster. In all likelihood, this team was an informal pickup team made up of
available players rather than any formally organized or league-based team.

120 **"The Stars were a little off** . . . Jack Calder, "Analyzing Sport: Let's Hope This
Is the Beginning," *Chatham Daily News*, August 2, 1934.

120 **"When it is considered** . . . Ibid.

121 **it is "important to recognize** . . . "Defining Negro League Baseball," Center
for Negro League Baseball Research.

121 **"Most people here have** . . . Donald Tabron Jr, Wright interview.

122 **cross-border games as early as 1869,** . . . William Humber, *A Sporting Chance:
Achievements of African-Canadian Athletes* (Toronto: Natural Heritage Books,
2004), 43.

122 **John Preston "Pete" Hill** . . . John Preston "Pete" Hill (d. 1951) was inducted
into the Baseball Hall of Fame in 2006 for his pre–Negro leagues and Negro
leagues career.

122 **During the August long weekend** . . . "Winners Toy with Losers," *Border
City Star*, August 4, 1931.

122 **Windsor's Wigle Park** . . . Wigle Park is located in the McDougall Street
corridor in Windsor. According to Moore Davis: McDougall, Mercer,
Assumption, Pitt, and Goyeau streets form "what would become Windsor's
Black district. This would remain the heart of the Black neighbourhood for
generations, well into the middle of the 1900s." *Our Own Two Hands*, 39–40.

122 **Some other Black American teams** . . . I am extremely grateful for the efforts
of the indefatigable Linda Bunn, a local historical researcher, who scoured a
decade or more of Essex County newspapers for mentions of Black baseball
on our project's behalf.

123 **"Paced by Don Tabron,** . . . Jack Calder, "Don Tabron Leads Stars to Easy
Win," *Chatham Daily News*, August 7, 1934.

123 **I never saw Don Tabron play** . . . Jack Calder, "Analyzing Sport: Most
Improved City Leaguer," *Chatham Daily News*, August 8, 1934.

123 **"Flat said he knew a guy** . . . Reddick, "Reliving the 1934 OBA Drive."

124 **Some recruiters came from Chatham** . . . Donald Tabron Jr, Wright
interview.

124 **"If there was baseball** . . . Ibid.

124 **Jenkins and Chase "were two** . . . Ibid.

125 **after a tornado destroyed the town** . . . This is likely what is called the Tri-
State tornado outbreak of March 18, 1925, the deadliest tornado outbreaks in

US history. If this tornado was part of that outbreak, Tabron would have been at least ten years old when the family moved to Detroit.

125 **the Great Migration** ... The Great Migration is also called the Great Northward Migration or the Black Migration. It is sometimes divided into the First (1916–1940) and Second (1940–1970) Great Migrations.

125 **Between 1910 and 1930,** ... US Department of Commerce, Bureau of Census, *Negroes in the United States 1920–1932*, 55; quoted in Elizabeth Anne Martin, "Detroit and the Great Migration, 1916–1929," *Bentley Historical Library Bulletin* No. 40, University of Michigan, 1993.

125 **the Black Bottom residential area** ... The name "Black Bottom" comes from the dark topsoil in the Detroit River bottomlands. As with many historically Black neighbourhoods in North America, residents of Black Bottom and Paradise Valley were displaced to make way for freeways and other urban redevelopment plans.

125 **"The rise of black professional** ... Lawrence D. Hogan, *Shades of Glory: The Negro League and the Story of African-American Baseball* (Washington, DC: National Geographic Society, 2006), 127.

125 **"black baseball clubs played** ... Hogan, *Shades of Glory*, 128.

125 **The rise of neighbourhoods like** ... Ibid.

126 **Hamtramck, which was** ... Hamtramck Stadium (once Roesink Stadium) is, as of writing, one of five Negro leagues ballparks still in existence. Hall of Fame players who played here include Satchel Paige, Josh Gibson, Turkey Stearnes, Cool Papa Bell, and others. It is currently undergoing a large-scale restoration.

126 **Upon their arrival in Detroit,** ... Donald Tabron Jr, Wright interview.

126 **"Detroit was very, very** ... Ibid.

126 **"a photographic memory** ... Ibid.

126 **"always very concerned that** ... Ibid.

126 **"a teenager besting adult** ... Ibid.

127 **"It's a difficult thing,** ... Ibid.

127 **after he "went to Chatham** ... Ibid.

127 **"an environment where he** ... Ibid.

127 **"The environment that Chatham provided** ... Ibid.

127 **"That year was one of** ... Bill Reddick, "Chatham Colored All-Stars: Reliving the 1934 OBA Drive," "From the Bullpen" column, *Chatham Daily News*, Oct 5, 1984.

127 **"had friends as an adult** ... Donald Tabron Jr, Wright interview.

128 **"A powerful early-inning** ... Jack Calder, "City Baseball League Playoffs Start: Stars Take First Game of Series," *Chatham Daily News*, August 13, 1934.

128 "**the good right arm** . . . Jack Calder, "Braggs Bow to Tabron's Great Work," c. August 13, 1934.

128 "**There was little doubt in** . . . Jack Calder, "Stars Ready to go to Town," *Chatham Daily News*, August 20, 1934.

129 **King Terrell was the hero** . . . Jack Calder, "Kent Bridge and Stars to Replay Game," *Chatham Daily News*, June 5, 1934.

129 **In a story entitled "One of** . . . Jack Calder, "Analyzing Sport: One of the Stars' Most Reliable Men," *Chatham Daily News*, August 17, 1934.

129 **is one of the League's most** . . . Ibid.

130 "**the most dependable man** . . . Jack Calder, "Analyzing Sport," *Chatham Daily News*, October 15, 1934.

130 "**One baseball player in** . . . "Chatham, Ont.," *Chicago Defender*, August 1, 1936.

130 "**seen a lot of people play** . . . Dorothy Wright Wallace, "Interview with Dorothy Wright Wallace," *Breaking the Colour Barrier: Wilfred "Boomer" Harding & the Chatham Coloured All-Stars (1932–1939)*, University of Windsor, November 18, 2016.

130 "**the rarest of baseball species:** . . . On the rareness of the left-handed third baseman, Simon Sharkey-Gotlieb notes that in 2017 Anthony Rizzo became "only the seventh left-handed third baseman in baseball since 1913, joining Mario Valdez, Don Mattingly, Terry Francona, Mike Squires (who did it 14 times), Charlie Grimm, and Hall of Famer George Sisler. He's the first to do it since Valdez of the White Sox spent an inning at third on July 2, 1997. According to Ryan Spaeder of the *Sporting News*, Rizzo's cameo marked the first time a left-hander has played third for the Cubs since George Decker in 1895—when the Cubs franchise was known as the Chicago Colts." Simon Sharkey-Gotlieb, "Rizzo Becomes 1st Left-Handed Throwing Third Baseman Since 1997," *The Score*, 2017.

130 "**I caught a lot of his [throws** . . . Boomer Harding, Milburn and Robbins Chavis interview.

131 "**spoke highly of just about** . . . Wanda Milburn and Boomer Harding, "Interview with Boomer Harding by Wanda Harding Milburn and Vivian Robbins Chavis," August 27, 1980, transcript and recording, Multicultural History Society of Ontario.

131 "**Well, I ain't going to** . . . Kingsley Terrell, Harding Milburn interview.

131 **Terrell, along with Chase, was one** . . . Boomer Harding, Milburn and Robbins Chavis interview.

131 "**going and coming from a** . . . Ibid.

131 **Robbins was "a right fielder; he** . . . Kingsley Terrell, Harding Milburn interview.

131 Hyle Robbins "played in the ... Ibid.
132 Talbot "was a good ball player. ... Ibid.
132 Terrell says "Yeah, the ... Kingsley Terrell, Harding Milburn interview.
132 our mascot ... Robinson's role was likely what we now call a "batboy."
132 "run out of town" with ... Kingsley Terrell, Harding Milburn interview.
132 "If they did, they didn't ... Pauline Williams, "Interview With: Pauline Williams and Cleata Morris," *Breaking the Colour Barrier: Wilfred "Boomer" Harding & the Chatham Coloured All-Stars (1932–1939)*, University of Windsor, July 10, 2016.
132 William Pitt Hotel ... Carmen Poole describes how "The Garner Hotel was, in its time, considered to be an impressive edifice with over 80 rooms. The William Pitt Hotel replaced the Garner Hotel in 1930 after a massive fire burned the latter down in 1929. The William Pitt Hotel boasted 140 rooms and employed a 40-person workforce, dwarfing its predecessor as a local giant in the hospitality industry. It also provided much needed main street retail space for the growing number of storefronts popping up over the interwar period." Poole, *Conspicuous Peripheries*, 22.
134 brief mentions of Black hotel teams ... In 1933, for example, the *Chatham Daily News* describes a game between a London team, the Posties or Post Men, and the Chatham Coloured Stars; "Chatham Stars Win at London," *Chatham Daily News*, August 28, 1933. Another story features the headline "Chatham Boys Win in London: Coloured Nine Trim Bell Hops 7–5 in Six Inning Game" and describes how "The Chatham Canadian All-Star coloured team rode into town yesterday to hand the fast travelling Hotel London Nine, their first defeat of the season, when they went home with a 7–5 score tucked under the belt, hot diggity-dawg! The game was played at the Trafalgar diamond and over 5,000 supporters of the local coloured lads saw their favourites done bow to the Chatham Nine in [a] closely contested game"; "Chatham Boys Win in London: Coloured Nine Trim Bell Hops 7–5 in Six Inning Game," *Chatham Daily News*, July 14, 1933. Harry Coursey, discussed earlier, appears on the roster for the Hotel London team pitching and playing left field. More research needs to be done on these regional hotel teams.
134 "He helped me get ... Dorothy Wright Wallace, Wright Wallace interview.
134 "He kind of mentored Eddie ... Ibid.
134 "Baseball in Chatham has ... Calder, "Analyzing Sport: Baseball Just Beginning Here."
134 "If Sarnia and Blenheim fans ... Jack Calder, "Analyzing Sport: Let's Give Them a Rousing Sendoff," *Chatham Daily News*, August 10, 1934.
135 "Your presence added to ... Ibid.

135 **It shouldn't be necessary to** . . . Ibid.

135 **Blake McCoig** . . . McCoig played for Chatham in 1920 when Chatham won the Kent League. Archie Stirling mentions this series in his history of Chatham baseball.

135 **"it brought a unity to the city** . . . Blake Harding, Harris interview.

136 **"Ardent followers of** . . . Jack Calder, "Analyzing Sport: Stars Ready to Go to Town," *Chatham Daily News*, August 20, 1934.

136 **"Seventeen errors, the greatest** . . . Jack Calder, "Stars Warm Up for Playdowns," *Chatham Daily News*, August 31, 1934.

136 **three snappy baseball games** . . . "Three Ball Games at Walpole Fair," *Chatham Daily News*, August 28, 1934. No record of this Saturday game has been found. In the game recap, the All-Stars are said to have played the Moraviantown team, not the Walpole Island All-Stars ("Stars Beat Moraviantown," *Chatham Daily News*, August 29, 1934). These might be different names for the same team or a different team in the tournament. The Moraviantown team is almost certainly an Indigenous team from the Delaware Nation.

136 **baseball culture of this First Nations community** . . . According to research, Walpole Island baseball teams date back to at least 1876 and were active in formal baseball leagues since the turn of the century: "by 1905, they were a dominant force in Kent and Lambton Counties and played American teams from Algonac and Port Huron, Michigan." See Ian Kennedy, *On Account of Darkness: Shining Light on Race and Sport* (New Westminster, BC: Tidewater Press, 2022), 38.

136 **In 1935, for example, Calder calls him** . . . Jack Calder, "Stars Hurler Gets Better with Every New Mound Job," Chatham Daily News, July 12, 1935.

137 **"Willy and Fergie were** . . . Boomer Harding, Milburn and Robbins Chavis interview.

137 **we learn he struck out** . . . "Chatham Juniors Beat Walpole Lads in League Game," *Chatham Daily News*, June 13, 1932.

138 **he "pitched excellent ball"** . . . "Walpole Lads Won the League Game at Ridgetown," *Chatham Daily News*, June 18, 1932.

138 **to be a "bang up hurler"** . . . "Casual Comment on Current Sport," *Chatham Daily News*, July 20, 1932.

138 **runs the risk of ruining** . . . Ibid.

138 **"The Stars have met with** . . . Jack Calder, "Stars Clash with Rivals from County," *Chatham Daily News*, Aug 3, 1935.

138 **records their team's roster, providing** . . . The box scores list Altiman at centre field, Shognosh on first base, Sands in right field, Navarre at second base, Sampson as catcher, Soney at shortstop, Jones at third base, Pinnace at

left field, and Murphy as pitcher. Although the *Breaking the Colour Barrier* project was not able to locate Shognosh family members who could speak with us about baseball during the 1930s, I remain hopeful these stories are or will be preserved in some manner for future generations and that researchers will uncover more of this vital tradition.

SEPTEMBER 1934

141 "The elements more or less ... Jack Calder, "Analyzing Sport: Rain, Rain, Go Away," *Chatham Daily News*, September 7, 1934.

142 "The game marked the return ... Jack Calder, "Stars Win Thrilling Game from Detroit," *Chatham Daily News*, September 4, 1934.

142 The Stars have progressed ... Jack Calder, "O.B.A.A. Playoff Contest at Athletic Park Tomorrow," *Chatham Daily News*, September 12, 1934.

142 "Several members of the Sarnia ... Jack Calder, "Exhibition Game Taken by Red Sox," *Chatham Daily News*, September 14, 1934.

143 describes their fielding ... Ibid.

143 "Welland," Calder declares, caught ... Jack Calder, "Stars Lose First Game to Welland," *Chatham Daily News*, September 21, 1934.

143 Chase the pitching ace ... Ibid.

143 they lose the exhibition game ... When Sarnia defaults the game for having "outside" players on their roster, the teams decide to turn the now-meaningless playoff game into an exhibition game.

144 "those fans who have been ... Jack Calder, "Analyzing Sport: Welland Here on Thursday," *Chatham Daily News*, September 17, 1934.

144 "phrase-making and insightful ... Bill Dwyre, "Introduction" in *The Roger Kahn Reader: Six Decades of Sportswriting*, ed. Bill Dwyre (Lincoln: University of Nebraska Press, 2018), xxii.

144 a flair for memorable summation ... Ibid, xxi-xiv.

144 "magical and spell-binding, ... Ibid, xxi.

145 There are unsigned articles ... One recurring theme in 1933 and 1934 is a longing for and the possibilities of a return to a golden age of Chatham baseball. Calder writes about this in 1934 and there are hints of it in 1933.

145 Calder "announced he was leaving ... "Sports News," *Vancouver Sun*, October 16, 1936.

145 a story by Calder covering hockey ... See, for example, Calder's stories "Dazzling Monarchs Rout Redmen 7–0," *The Sault Daily Star*, April 19, 1937, and "Billy Taylor Favoured to Make Grade with the Leafs," *Chatham Daily News*, October 19, 1939.

145 **his writing shifts after he joins** . . . For a fuller overview of Calder's military life and his experiences as a prisoner of war, see Ralph Keefer, Grounded in Eire: *The Story of Two RAF Fliers Interned in Ireland during World War II* (McGill-Queen's University Press, 2001). A longer biography of Calder written by Calder's niece Patricia Calder is in progress.

145 **He later escaped** . . . See, for example, "Bombing the *Gneisenau* 'Some Fun' As Toronto Observer Describes It," *Globe and Mail*, August 13, 1941; stories in the *Toronto Star* (August 15, 1942; July 8, 1943; August 15, 1943); and "I Flew Into Trouble," *Maclean's*, August 15, 1942.

145 **"Colleagues remember him as** . . . Alan Harvey, "Canadian Sports Snapshots," *Edmonton Journal*, August 27, 1945.

145 **A Jack Calder Memorial Cup** . . . Ibid.

145 **The Western Ontario Sports Writers** . . . Patricia Calder, *A Canadian Flyer's World War II Scrapbook* (Colborne, ON: Elsinore Books, 2022), 69.

147 **his later writings,** . . . Calder was both subject and author of articles during the war, displaying keen observational powers and sharp insights as observer on various raids and with regards to the social and political climate in Ireland while in internment. He made newspaper history in Canada for being the first Canadian flier to have a bylined story when his piece about the German pocket battleship *Gneisenau* appeared on front pages across Canada and the US. See "Jack Calder Interned in Eire After Bomber Is Forced Down," *Globe and Mail*, Oct 27, 1941.

147 **"the cold in his arm."** . . . Jack Calder, "Analyzing Sport: It Took the Stars to Do It," *Chatham Daily News*, September 5, 1934.

148 **"Flat Chase was credited** . . . Jack Calder, "Analyzing Sport: Stars Seem to Have Something," *Chatham Daily News*, September 10, 1934.

148 **"the smoke-ball king** . . . Jack Calder, "Stars Begin O.B.A.A. Playdowns Thursday," *Chatham Daily News*, September 5, 1934.

148 **Only a fair-fielding,** . . . Calder, "Analyzing Sport: It Took the Stars to Do It."

148 **"he would be a one-man** . . . Calder, "Stars Begin O.B.A.A. Playdowns Thursday."

148 **"counted on to turn in** . . . Ibid.

149 **"Ladd, who may soon be** . . . Jack Calder, "Analyzing Sport: Stars That Shine," *Chatham Daily News*, September 27, 1934.

149 **"They've developed from a team** . . . Jack Calder, "Analyzing Sport," *Chatham Daily News*, September 25, 1934.

149 **"Washington finished the game** . . . Calder, "Stars Lose First Game to Welland."

149 "Washington came from Detroit, . . . Boomer Harding, "Interview with Boomer Harding by Dan Kelly," *Breaking the Colour Barrier: Wilfred "Boomer" Harding & the Chatham Coloured All-Stars (1932–1939)*, University of Windsor, c. 1977.

150 "a fine target and good . . . Calder, "Analyzing Sport: Stars Ready to Go to Town."

150 "Don Washington, catcher . . . Calder, "Stars Begin O.B.A.A. Playdowns Thursday."

150 "the Stars are a remarkably . . . Jack Calder, "Analyzing Sport: In a Foreign Field Today," *Chatham Daily News*, October 15, 1934.

150 "He handles the ball all . . . Leonard Koppett, *The Thinking Fan's Guide to Baseball* (Toronto, ON: Sports Media Publishing, 2004), 69.

150 "Chase was without his . . . Calder, "Analyzing Sport: Stars Ready to Go to Town."

150 This ball game was on . . . Kingsley Terrell, Harding Milburn interview.

151 "Donise practically run . . . Ibid.

151 "junk and slow stuff . . . "Chatham's First Champs," *London Free Press*.

152 "Chase was a great pitcher . . . Bill Reddick, "'34 Champs Denied Opportunity in Pro Ball," *Chatham Daily News*, October 10, 1984.

152 Donise Washington was a catcher, . . . Kingsley Terrell, Harding Milburn interview.

152 "And you heard all over, . . . Ibid.

152 "Don Washington, catcher . . . "Don Washington Leaves Chatham," *Windsor Daily Star*, April 10, 1937.

152 recruited by Strathroy, "the first . . . Cartier, *Politics and Other Games*, 68–70.

153 They were coming to see us. . . Boomer Harding, Kelly interview.

153 "I was the only negro . . . Bill Reddick, "From the Bullpen: Chatham Colored All-Stars," October 4, 1984, *Chatham Daily News*.

153 suggests that Washington returned . . . Boomer Harding, Milburn and Robbins Chavis interview.

153 "the solid heart . . . John Olbey, McCorkindale interview.

153 a "clever player" . . . Jack Calder, "Value of a Smile," *Chatham Daily News*, July 6, 1935.

154 "Welland Beaten in Playoffs: . . . "Welland Beaten in Playoffs: Stars Even Round with Clever Win," *Chatham Daily News*, September 24, 1934.

154 "Flat Chase, who was the first . . . Jack Calder, "City Team Progresses in O.B.A.A.," *Chatham Daily News*, September 27, 1934.

154 "Again it was big Flat . . . Ibid.

264

154 **Kolored King of Klout** . . . Calder's problematic choice of initials here is most likely a youthful and misguided attempt to create a catchy visual alliteration rather than something more nefarious.

155 **"Chatham Stars, coloured baseball team** . . . Calder, "Stars Begin O.B.A.A. Playdowns Thursday."

155 **"A word about the coloured** . . . "Bits about the Stars," quoted from the *Welland–Port Colborne Tribune* in *Chatham Daily News*, September 25, 1934.

156 **describes the common practice in the 1880s** . . . Lawrence D. Hogan, *Shades of Glory: The Negro League and the Story of African-American Baseball* (Washington, DC: National Geographic Society, 2006), 34.

156 **"Every man on a team would** . . . Sol White, quoted in Hogan, *Shades of Glory*, 34.

156 **also a "low burlesque" bantering** . . . Hogan, *Shades of Glory*, 34.

156 **"black teams more often than not** . . . Hogan, *Shades of Glory*, 35.

156 **"Making a fool of oneself** . . . Ibid.

156 **he is listed as working at** . . . *Shepherd's Directory for 1934–1935*, B-136.

157 **Kelly says, "They said he used to** . . . Kelly, "All-Stars 1933–34."

157 **Boomer responds, "Oh—'ain't that** . . . Ibid.

157 **Parker had "one of those original** . . . Kingsley Terrell, Harding Milburn interview.

157 **"Percy Parker gave Sarnia fans** . . . Calder, "Analyzing Sport: Stars Seem to Have Something."

157 **"the human foghorn".** . . Ibid.

157 **describes how Parker "turned to** . . . Ibid.

157 **"third base coaching box vaudevillian** . . . Jack Calder, "Analyzing Sport: Stars Will Draw Them," *Chatham Daily News*, September 12, 1934.

157 **it was "hard to forget [Parker's]** . . . Scurr, "Stars Return Under New Name."

157 **may have served a dual purpose** . . . Parker's antics on the field may also connect with a longer tradition within Black baseball that started in the 1880s with players like Arlie Latham (1860–1952), often called the original "clown prince" of baseball. In 1947, sportswriter Robert Smith wrote, "Arlie is the man who practically invented the characteristic chatter of the ball diamond, the endless lilting encouragement which an infield gives to the pitcher, the glad shouts and gestures of the coaching box, the raucous ribbing of opponents, the earnest advice offered to base runners." See Robert Smith, *Baseball: A Historical Narrative of the Game, the Men who Have Played It, and Its Place in American Life* (New York: Simon and Schuster, 1947), 109–10. Latham's antics may have brought about the rule that coaches must

stay within the outlined coaching boxes on the first and third base lines, a rule still standing today.

158 Ross Talbot "has just returned . . . Calder, "Stars Begin O.B.A.A. Playdowns Thursday." The *Chicago Defender* notes that Talbot had been in Montreal. Dorothy L. Binga, "Chatham, Ont.," *Chicago Defender*, September 22, 1934.

158 "it's doubtful if Don Tabron . . . It is more likely that Tabron went to Detroit, not Windsor. Calder might have said Windsor because, as Boomer Harding said, it was "kind of a sin" against OBAA regulations to have players from another country, "but from Windsor, that was just Canada." Jack Calder, "Analyzing Sport: Stars Come Through at Welland," *Chatham Daily News*, September 24, 1934.

158 "Messrs. Washington, Ladd and . . . "Chatham, Ont.," *Chicago Defender*, October 6, 1934.

158 they will "have some long travelling . . . Calder, "Analyzing Sport: Stars That Shine."

159 Tilt Arranged to Aid Stars. . . . "Tilt Arranged to Aid Stars," *Chatham Daily News*, September 27, 1934.

159 "didn't have the financial . . . Blake Harding, interview with LeSean Harris. July 31, 2022.

159 they would have to pass . . . Ibid.

159 "The Stars have had a . . . Calder, "Analyzing Sport: It Took the Stars to Do It."

160 It took the Stars to do it. . . . Ibid.

160 Not in half a dozen years . . . Calder is likely referring to two Chatham teams who won their divisions of the Kent County League in 1928 but did not progress very far in the OBAA playdowns. See Stirling, "A Brief History of Baseball."

160 There's scarcely any need . . . Calder, "Analyzing Sport: Stars Will Draw Them."

160 "Children in arms may stay . . . Ibid.

OCTOBER 1934

161 "Maybe I am going to . . . Jack Calder, "Analyzing Sport," *Chatham Daily News*, October 1, 1934.

162 "supporters of the Stars were . . . "Chatham Stars Will Go East," *Chatham Daily News*, October 1, 1934.

162 "No definite word was . . . Jack Calder, "Chathamites in Crucial Contest at Athletic Park," *Chatham Daily News*, October 2, 1934.

NOTES

162 "Milton vs Chatham All-Stars . . . Game advertisement, *Chatham Daily News*, October 2, 1934.

162 "A huge crowd is expected to . . . Calder, "Chathamites in Crucial Contest."

163 "consider the protest of . . . "Meaford VS Penetang," *Chatham Daily News*, October 2, 1934.

164 "With the count knotted . . . Jack Calder, "Chatham Stars Win First Fame of OBAA Semi-Finals," *Chatham Daily News*, October 5, 1934.

164 "if yesterday's affair is . . . Ibid.

164 "Stars Badly Beaten in . . . "Stars Badly Beaten in Semi-Final Game," *Chatham Daily News*, October 9, 1934.

164 "Another splendid season . . . Jack Calder, "Analyzing Sport," *Chatham Daily News*, October 11, 1934.

165 "Clearly outplaying their . . . "Chatham Team Comes from Behind to Defeat Milton," *Chatham Daily News*, October 12, 1934.

165 "Chase, big Chatham pitcher . . . Ibid.

165 "as [Chase] goes, so go . . . Jack Calder, "Analyzing Sport," *Chatham Daily News*, October 12, 1934.

165 "Now is the time to think . . . Ibid.

165 they were offered $200. . . . Boomer Harding, Kelly interview.

165 "Here," writes Calder, "was a chance . . . Jack Calder, "Analyzing Sport," *Chatham Daily News*, October 13, 1934.

166 "Chatham people asked . . . Ibid.

166 "There's considerable time . . . Ibid.

166 "Chatham's own constellation, . . . Calder, "Analyzing Sport," October 15, 1934.

168 "The Stars did it. . . . Jack Calder, "Analyzing Sport," *Chatham Daily News*, October 16, 1934.

168 "The Chatham Stars arrived . . . "Chatham Stars Home, Ready for Thursday Game," *Chatham Daily News*, October 16, 1934.

169 You know there were quite . . . Kelly, "All-Stars 1933–34."

169 When we went to play Penetang . . . Reddick, "All Stars: Former Players Recall Good Times, Bad Times."

170 "The first time we went . . . Kingsley Terrell, Harding Milburn interview.

170 It was cold in Penetang . . . Reddick, "All Stars: Former Players Recall Good Times, Bad Times."

170 "the fans down there . . . Kingsley Terrell, Harding Milburn interview.

171 incidents of kindness and generosity . . . Challenges as to whether or not the 1934 All-Stars were subjected to racial discrimination in Penetanguishene still show up in letters to editors and other venues today. These comments reveal

a deep and not uncommon incredulity—one that still exists across Canada, particularly amongst white populations—that racial discrimination could happen in their towns or communities.

171 "It was decided to invite . . . "Club to Honour Baseball Team: Rotarians to Make Presentations to Coloured Stars," *Chatham Daily News*, October 17, 1934.

172 The sports pages feature multiple stories . . . *Chatham Daily News*, October 17, 1934.

172 "According to tentative plans . . . "Parade Planned," *Chatham Daily News*, October 17, 1934.

172 "Their bats poised for . . . Jack Calder, "Chatham Stars Can Take City's First OBAA Crown," *Chatham Daily News*, October 17, 1934.

173 "Whether Flat Chase could smoke . . . Jack Calder, "Analyzing Sport," *Chatham Daily News*, October 18, 1934.

173 "Today's game brings to . . . Ibid.

173 "a wild, queer affair." . . . Jack Calder, "Penetang Evens Final Series with Stars," *Chatham Daily News*, October 19, 1934.

173 "The two teams warmed up . . . Jack Calder, "Analyzing Sport," *Chatham Daily News*, October 19, 1934.

173 "a daffy, errorful marathon . . . Calder, "Penetang Evens Final Series."

173 "the Stars had sufficient breaks . . . Ibid.

174 "a curly-headed boy . . . Ibid.

174 Marchildon "pitched with all the . . . Ibid.

174 "Chatham Team Beaten By 10–9 . . . Ibid.

174 "tempers flared and fists flew. . . Ibid.

174 "It was then that Talbot . . . Ibid.

175 "the melee was set off." . . . Ibid.

175 "someone neglected to fasten down . . . Ibid.

175 "a close decision at third . . . "Penetang Defeats Chatham 10–9 to Tie Up Intermediate 'B' Titular Series," *London Free Press*, October 19, 1934.

175 "Dispute Delays Title Contest: . . . "Dispute Delays Title Contest: Ninth Inning Decision of Base Umpire Causes Argument: Visitors Leave Field but Return to Win," *Border Cities Star*, October 19, 1934.

175 "Irate players and a few . . . "Dispute Delays Title Contest: Ninth Inning Decision of Base Umpire Causes Argument: Visitors Leave Field but Return to Win," *Border Cities Star*, October 19, 1934.

175 a questionable decision by [McFadden] . . . The *Border Cities Star* lists the official as base umpire Steve Collier, but all other papers name McFadden as the one who made these calls.

176 "Between the changes of . . . "Dispute Delays Title Contest," *Border Cities Star*.

176 The Chatham runner was safe ... Ibid.

176 "Chatham has a place ..." Calder, "Analyzing Sport," October 19, 1934.

176 "When the Stars take the ... Calder, "Analyzing Sport," October 19, 1934.

177 "Flat Chase says he'll pitch ... Calder, "Analyzing Sport," October 18, 1934.

177 "It is an understood fact ... Jack Calder, "Analyzing Sport," *Chatham Daily News*, October 23, 1934.

178 With Chatham Coloured Stars leading ... "Stars and Penetang Play to Eleven Inning 2–2 Tie," *Chatham Daily News*, October 23, 1934.

178 The third game of the series ... "Chatham in the Tie with Penetang," *Sarnia Observer*, October 23, 1934.

179 "drear October afternoon that ... Calder, "Penetang Evens Final Series."

180 Was it suddenly that much darker ... For more discussion of the darkness controversy, see two recent books: Ian Kennedy's *On Account of Darkness: Shining Light on Race and Sport* and D.M. Fox's *On Account of Darkness: The Summer Ontario Baseball Broke the Colour Barrier*.

180 "there was no way they ... Kelly, "All-Stars 1933–34."

180 "It's hard to believe, but ... Without the benefit of a 1934 OBAA rulebook, which I have been unable to locate at time of writing, it is difficult to ascertain the precise rules around darkness. We do know that other games were reverted in the OBAA in 1934, but it is unclear how often this happened.

180 I would just listen ... Blake Harding, Wright interview one.

181 "both teams readily agreed, ... "Meet Penetang Next," *London Advertiser*, October 12, 1934.

181 the Stars "went out on ... "'Flatfoot' Chase Gives Up Only 5 Hits in Comeback," *London Advertiser*, October 24, 1934.

181 Chatham Coloured All-Stars are the ... Canadian Press, "O.B.A.A. Title for Chatham," *Border Cities Star*, October 24, 1934.

181 Penetang [Foundry Rangers] ... Research shows the official name of the Penetanguishene team is the Spencer Foundry Rangers and they were sponsored by a business that made cast iron woodstoves. This team has erroneously been called the Shipbuilders, a name associated with Collingwood teams. Doug Fox, personal correspondence, January 19, 2023.

182 refers to Flat Chase as performing ... "Tuesday's Game at Guelph Results in Score of 13–7," *Chatham Daily News*, October 24, 1934.

182 "Pitching was the reason we won ... Bill Reddick, "Reliving the Winning 1934 OBA Title Drive," *Chatham Daily News*, October 5, 1984.

182 "the coloured representatives of Chatham ... "Chatham Coloured Team Take Fourth Game 13–7 To Win Ontario Title," n.d.

183 "At last an OBAA title ... Jack Calder, "Analyzing Sport," *Chatham Daily News*, October 24, 1934.

183   and arrangements are already . . . Ibid.

183   "That championship for which . . . Ibid.

183   in the out-of-town coverage, . . . The *Windsor Star* calls them "the coloured
      squad" and the *Globe* calls them "a negro nine." Amidst other references to
      the team's race, a *Canadian Champion* (Milton, Ontario, paper) story from
      October 18, 1934, refers to them as "the Blackbirds." Players, especially Chase,
      are also described by their race, with such phrasing as "his coloured rival,
      Chase" or "big Flatfoot Chase, coloured hurler."

183   the author . . . Earlier in 1934, this column had been written by Chatham
      resident Dorothy L. Binga (1911–2006) and her name was featured at the top.
      This November 3, 1934, column contains a note saying Dorothy was conva-
      lescing at the home of a friend in Ohio, leading me to surmise this column
      was written by someone else. Her father, Bethune Binga (1884–1984), was, in
      later months, listed as author of this column, so he could be the author of this
      entry. Bethune Binga was the son of Jesse Binga (1865–1950), who founded
      the first privately owned African-American bank in Chicago in 1908.

184   "Never before in the history . . . "Canada: Chatham, Ont.," *Chicago Defender*,
      National Edition, November 3, 1934.

184   "At the regular meeting of . . . Ibid.

184   "We, the Coloured People of . . . Orville Wright, "Notes from Speech
      Honouring Archie Stirling," n.d., Chatham-Kent Black Historical Society.

184   "Mr. Stirling, he was a . . . Dorothy Wright Wallace, Wright Wallace
      interview.

184   "When they won the series," . . . John Olbey, McCorkindale interview.

184   "We won the Championship and . . . Kingsley Terrell, Milburn interview.

185   "making so much racket. . . . Pauline Parker Miller, Wright interview.

185   "mentioned coming back to Chatham . . . Donald Tabron Jr, Wright
      interview.

185   "The Daily News posted bulletins . . . "The Champion Stars," *Chatham Daily
      News*, October 24, 1934.

185   "Chatham Stars Given Great Reception . . . "Crowds Acclaim Victorious
      Chatham Team: Chatham Stars Given Great Reception on Return to the
      City," *Chatham Daily News*, October 24, 1934.

185   "amidst scenes of wild enthusiasm, . . . Ibid.

186   Twinkle, twinkle Chatham Stars . . . Joe Emmett, "Putting the Chat in
      Chatham," *Chatham Daily News*, October 27, 1934.

186   Parker is reported as . . . "Crowds Acclaim Victorious Chatham Team,"
      Chatham Daily News.

187   "repaired to the coffee shop . . . "Crowds Acclaim Victorious Chatham
      Team," *Chatham Daily News*.

187 "suitable gifts as a token . . . "Crowds Acclaim Victorious Chatham Team,"
       Chatham Daily News.

187 At the Wednesday banquet . . . "Chatham, Ont.," *Chicago Defender*,
       November 17, 1934.

188 "Thanks for the banquet. . . . Cartier, "The First Colored All Star Team,"
       Politics and Other Games.

188 "I never wore mine once. . . . Boomer Harding, Dan Kelly interview.

189 Boomer further reflected, "Now some . . . Ibid.

189 "there was very little acceptance" of . . . Blake Harding, Wright interview one.

189 "It opened some eyes, . . . Blake Harding, Harris interview, July 31, 2022.

190 My Uncle Andy was . . . Blake Harding, Wright interview one.

190 "It opened doors, and it . . . Blake Harding, Harris interview, July 31, 2022.

190 "They didn't get the breaks, . . . Ibid.

190 "As long as they were Stars," . . . Pat Harding, Wright interview one.

191 For the Black community, we . . . Dorothy Wright Wallace, interview with
       LeSean Harris, August 5, 2022.

191 "They may not have had . . . Ibid.

POST 1934: 1935 AND 1939

194 "The Chatham Coloured All-Stars weren't angels . . . Blake Harding,
       "Chatham Coloured All-Stars 85th Anniversary Celebration," Chatham,
       Ontario, October 26, 2019.

194 Numerous and expected have been . . . Jack Calder, "Analyzing Sport,"
       Chatham Daily News, June 22, 1935.

196 Dear Sir: In the issue . . . "'Stars are Sportsmen,' Voice of the People," Letter
       to the Editor, *Chatham Daily News*, June 26, 1935.

196 remember the pink tea reception . . . Pink tea is a term of this period, gener-
       ally referring to something very polite or genteel.

197 a Black citizen's eyewitness account . . . In signing the letter with "a coloured
       fan" rather than their own name, the writer of this letter does two things.
       First, the writer infers they were aware of the risks in signing one's own
       name to a letter that makes pointed reference to racial discrimination within
       the community. Second, and perhaps more importantly, by not identifying
       themself, the writer could be anyone in the Black community. In this way, the
       letter could be—as the headline says—the Voice of the People.

197 At the conclusion of the game . . . "Baseball Crowd Sees Smart Game,"
       Strathroy Age Dispatch, June 20, 1935.

198 A soft answer turneth . . . Calder, "Value of a Smile."

199 An incident would crop up . . . Monte Irvin, quoted by Jules Tygiel in the foreword to Hogan, *Shades of Glory*, x.

199 "when it got nasty, . . . Blake Harding, Wright interview one.

205 four-team Industrial League, . . . As is still the case now, small baseball leagues come and go. There isn't much information about the formation of the Industrial League, but it appears to have replaced Chatham's City League in 1936. The All-Stars, Libbys, Ontario Steel, and Kent Bridge made up this four-team league.

205 Art Cartier had taken over . . . Art Cartier (1914–2012) was the sports editor for the *Chatham Daily News* from 1937 to 1940, and his "Sport Talk" column is my main source of information about the All-Stars' 1939 season.

205 "Coloured All Stars, the team . . . Art Cartier, "Sport Talk," *Chatham Daily News*, June 19, 1939.

205 "they are plenty tough" . . . Art Cartier, "Sport Talk," *Chatham Daily News*, June 12, 1939.

205 twenty-six players on their roster, . . . Many of the names on the 1939 All-Stars roster also appear on Chatham Red Sox, the junior team managed by Ross and Ben Talbot, who also, for a time, appear to be managing the All-Stars.

205 a "little fourteen-year-old schoolboy . . . Cartier, "Sport Talk," June 19, 1939.

205 "among the district's most . . . Cartier, "Sport Talk," June 12, 1939.

205 "have difficulty getting off work . . . Ibid.

206 "It has been a little hard . . . Art Cartier, "Stars Battle Kent Bridge," *Chatham Daily News*, July 11, 1939.

206 "The Stars failed to win . . . Art Cartier, "Stars Shatter Losing Streak with 9–4 Win," *Chatham Daily News*, July 4, 1939.

206 "The many who feared that . . . Art Cartier, "Sport Talk: Colored All-Stars Start to Shine," *Chatham Daily News*, July 14, 1939.

206 Stories, such as this one . . . Art Cartier, "Free-For-All Marred Second Game Saturday," *Chatham Daily News*, August 8, 1939.

206 a "wild free-for-all," . . . Ibid.

207 "Gouy Ladd went to the mound . . . Ibid.

207 "Managers Discuss Wild . . . "Managers Discuss Wild Ball Game," *Chatham Daily News*, August 8, 1939.

207 "The league executive will . . . Cartier, "Free-For-All Marred Second Game Saturday."

208 the Kent Bridge boys had . . . Ibid.

208 "We will play the same . . . Ibid.

208 The Chatham Industrial baseball league . . . "No More Rowdyism, Edict of Industrial League Heads," *Chatham Daily News*, August 9, 1939.

209 describes the depths of their frustrations . . . "Withdrawal by All-Stars," *Chatham Daily News*, August 16, 1939.

209 "The All-Stars defeated Libbys . . . "Steel, Stars Ball Winners in Industrial," *Chatham Daily News*, August 14, 1939.

209 "Last Saturday's [August 9, 1939,] game . . . Art Cartier, "Managers Discuss Wild Ball Game," *Chatham Daily News*, August 8, 1939.

210 Umpire Peardon's statement to . . . "Withdrawal by All-Stars," *Chatham Daily News*.

210 Canners . . . The team was likely also knowns as the Canners because they were sponsored by Libbys, a food processing plant.

210 "it was entirely an umpire's decision . . . "Withdrawal by All-Stars," *Chatham Daily News*.

210 "If we are going to lose . . . Ibid.

210 The management of the . . . Len Harding, "Colored All-Stars Outline Stand in Open Letter," *Chatham Daily News*, August 18, 1939.

211 "At the executive meeting . . . Ibid.

212 "Chatham Coloured All-Stars and . . . Art Cartier, "Sport Talk," *Chatham Daily News*, August 17, 1939.

212 OBA . . . In 1938, the Ontario Baseball Amateur Association (OBAA) changed its name to the Ontario Baseball Association (OBA). This organization is still in existence, but it is now known as Baseball Ontario.

212 "the Stars have been playing . . . "The Chatham All-Stars Meet Leamington Here," *Chatham Daily News*, September 13, 1939.

212 An argument in the seventh . . . "The Chatham All-Stars Eliminate Leamington," *Chatham Daily News*, September 15, 1939.

213 "Any time you want to kill . . . Art Cartier, "Sport Talk," *Chatham Daily News*, October 9, 1939.

213 "the series looks like Chatham's . . . Ibid.

214 "strictly without the consent . . . Art Cartier, "The Chatham All-Stars May Decide to Refuse to Play Deciding O.B.A. Final," *Chatham Daily News*, October 20, 1939.

214 "Meaford claims that a large . . . Ibid.

214 "did a bit of figuring" and . . . Art Cartier, "Sport Talk," *Chatham Daily News*, October 27, 1939.

214 "the Chatham team is being asked . . . Cartier, "All-Stars May Decide to Refuse to Play."

215 "while feeling that under . . . Ibid.

215 "All we ask is a fair break . . . Len Harding, "Statement" in "Chatham All Stars Decide Against Going to Hanover," *Chatham Daily News*, October 21, 1939.

216 "at noon today neither . . . Art Cartier, "Sport Talk," *Chatham Daily News*, October 23, 1939.

216 story out of Meaford that claims . . . Art Cartier, "Sport Talk," *Chatham Daily News*, October 25, 1939.

216 "that due to the lateness . . . Art Cartier, "Sport Talk," *Chatham Daily News*, October 31, 1939.

216 "neutral point halfway . . . Art Cartier, "Sports Talk," *Chatham Daily News*, November 3, 1939.

216 "no OBA Intermediate A champion . . . Art Cartier, "Sport Talk," *Chatham Daily News*, November 6, 1939.

217 The third [game] was a tie . . . J.J. Shaw in Art Cartier, "Sport Talk," *Chatham Daily News*, November 11, 1939.

217 "Since the Northerners are . . . Cartier, "Sport Talk," November 11, 1939.

217 "Roustabouts by A. Roustabouter." . . . The "Roustabouts" columns begin to appear on or around October 24, 1939.

217 The teams entered the eleventh . . . The Roustabouter makes two factual errors which have been corrected here. "Roustabouts by A. Roustabouter," *Chatham Daily News*, November 18, 1939.

218 "The Chatham men complained . . . "Roustabouts," November 18, 1939.

218 the All-Stars "had, in the 1934 . . . Ibid.

219 "the armed forces sapped . . . Scurr, "Stars Return Under New Name."

219 But Andy Harding didn't . . . According to Blake Harding, Andy Harding enlisted in 1941 and trained at Ipperwash. He was released in 1946 with the rank of Sergeant. Boomer Harding enlisted in January 1943 and underwent basic training in Chatham and specialized training in Vimy Barracks, CFB Kingston. He was part of the Signals Corps (motorcycle dispatch) and served in England and mainland Europe. He was released in March 1946 with the rank of Corporal.

219 During the war, Boomer played . . . While in Kingston, Boomer played baseball for various military teams. In Europe, he played on a hockey team that travelled to entertain the troops.

219 writes about the new Taylor ACs . . . Scurr, "Stars Return Under New Name."

CONCLUSION

221 "More than anything else, . . . Monte Irvin, quoted in Hogan, *Shades of Glory*, 288.

221 "The ugly realities of history . . . Moore Davis, *Our Own Two Hands*, 6.

224 I'll be honest with you, . . . Horace Chase, Chevalier interview.

225 "My youngest son, I named . . . Donald Tabron Jr, Wright interview.

225 My [youngest] son could ... Ibid.

227 "My mother started the scrapbook ... Earl Chase Jr, Staffen interview.

227 The scrapbook is, ... The Harding and Chase family scrapbooks are very much in keeping with what scholars have written about scrapbooks' roles as a means of memory preservation and of asserting authority over the telling of history. For the most part, scrapbooks have been seen as a primarily female and domestic undertaking related to holding families together by preserving nostalgic items. See, *The Scrapbook in American Life*, eds. Susan Tucker, Katherine Ott, and Patricia Buckler (Philadelphia, PA: Temple University Press, 2006).

227 "Boomer's mom started doing ... Pat Harding, Wright interview two.

227 "She loved her children— ... Ibid.

227 essential to this team and the community ... A later Harding family scrapbook, Wanda Harding Milburn's, contains family clippings and photographs alongside newspaper articles on a wide range of social and cultural issues. There are newspaper clippings related to the local community but also some related to the larger Black world, including articles about race and sport in North America such as Jackie Robinson breaking the MLB colour barrier and the successes of Venus and Serena Williams on the tennis court.

227 "just to let her know ... Donald Tabron Jr, Wright interview.

228 I didn't really know how ... Ibid.

228 "they are starting to disintegrate" ... Earl Chase Jr, Staffen interview.

229 the boxes then "sat in our house ... Pat Harding, Wright interview two.

229 It took me a long time ... Ibid.

229 Pat created three thick binders ... These three scrapbooks tell the stories of Boomer Harding: his earliest days of high school sports, his years with the Chatham Coloured All-Stars and other baseball teams, his years playing hockey, his career as Chatham's first Black mail carrier, his work coaching and officiating sports, and finally his retirement activities of competitive darts and horseshoes. Pat included any mention she found of the All-Stars and continues to collect this material.

230 "I could see when I put ... Pat Harding, Wright interview two.

230 I loved and respected my father-in-law ... Ibid.

231 That request led to the ... See the headnote to this section on page 237.

231 "it becomes real. ... Pat Harding, Wright interview two.

INDEX